From the Land Beyond Beyond

The Films of Willis O'Brien and Ray Harryhausen

JEFF ROVIN

A BERKLEY WINDHOVER BOOK
published by
BERKLEY PUBLISHING CORPORATION

Jet Literary Associates, Inc.
124 East 84th Street
Suite 4A
New York, N. Y. 10028

SBN 425-03506-9

BERKLEY WINDHOVER BOOKS are published by
Berkley Publishing Corporation
200 Madison Avenue
New York, N.Y. 10016

BERKLEY WINDHOVER BOOK ® TM 1062206

Printed in the United States of America

Berkley Windhover Edition, October, 1977

This book could not have been written without the assistance of Mrs. Darlyne O'Brien;
Geraldine Duclow of the Free Library of Philadelphia Theatre Collection; Stephen
Wathen, Mary Corliss and Carol K. Carey of the Museum of Modern Art; the British Film
Institute; the Clinton Studios of New Hartford, Connecticut; Paula Klaw of *Movie Star
News*; Ernie Farino and Sam Calvin of *FXRH*; Hammer Films; RKO; Columbia Pictures;
Warner Communications; MGM; United Artists; Allied Artists; and my editor Sy Rubin.
The author would particularly like to thank Mr. and Mrs. Ray Harryhausen, whose
cooperation, hospitality, and enthusiasm made this project a sheer joy. Finally, special
thanks go to Mr. Charles H. Schneer, a rather extraordinary motion picture producer!

Design and Layout Ernie Haim

From the Land Beyond Beyond

Contents

*For David Strempfer
and a Youth Filled With Harryhausen*

Introduction

In the closing days of 1976, Paramount Pictures released Dino de Laurentiis' $24 million remake of the 1933 motion picture classic *King Kong*. Despite some superficial changes, the story was the same as it had been in the earlier version: a giant ape is discovered on an East Indian island, he falls in love with the expedition's sole female member, is captured and brought to New York, breaks free, goes on a rampage, and is shot from atop a skyscraper. As far as the general public knew—on the say-so of extensive TV and newspaper coverage, not to mention a *Time* Magazine cover story—de Laurentiis' *King Kong*, in Panavision and color, was a spectacular improvement over the quaint and corny black and white picture. But as far as the bulk of film aficionados was concerned, the new *King Kong* was not only ineptly made, it was a sacrilege.

The 1933 *Kong Kong* is the legacy of special effects genius Willis O'Brien, a motion picture craftsman who popularized the uniquely modern art form known as *stop motion photography*. Simply put, stop motion photography is a process wherein a poseable model is moved a fraction of an inch, a single picture or *frame* of film is exposed, the model is repositioned, another frame is exposed, and so on. When the finished film is projected, the model appears to be alive. Built eighteen inches tall and combined with live actors through various methods of superimposition (see chapter 3), the original *King Kong* was animated by Willis O'Brien in just such a fashion. And the character he created was one that, in the effective communication of anger, pain, joy, curiosity, or simple bestiality, continues both to move and thrill motion picture audiences the world over. On the other hand,

showing a remarkable lack of inspiration and resource, de Laurentiis gave us alternating Kongs, using a lackluster, life-size robot Kong in a few brief scenes, but relying primarily on the frantic gesticulations of makeup man Rick Baker in a gorilla costume. Unfortunately, despite his exuberance, there was a sad limit to how much emoting Mr. Baker could do from behind a plastic monkey mask.

On the surface of things, this conflict of the Kongs may seem irrelevant to anyone but a film buff. However, consider the broader implications. Because of the huge sums of money riding on *King Kong*, de Laurentiis not only launched a massive publicity campaign, but made certain to have the original *King Kong* pulled from circulation. He simply didn't want any competition for his ludicrously bad film. Not that this was the first time such a precaution has been taken. Remakes of the Fredric March film *Dr. Jekyll and Mr. Hyde* (1932), and John Wayne's *Stagecoach* (1939), caused those classics to be withdrawn in 1941 and 1966, respectively, and they have not yet been returned to us. Thus, it is conceivable that we may not see the original *King Kong* for another twenty or thirty years; the thought that any work of art may be shunted aside when the dollar talks is frightening indeed. To say the least, the Kong situation is a sad microcosm of the state of our entire culture.

Still, there is hope. Now that *King Kong* 1976 has had his loud but hollow roar, it's time to strike a blow on behalf of artistry.

Long after the pages in de Laurentiis' 1977 ledgers have yellowed and decayed, his tongue-in-cheek ape film forgotten, the world will still sit in awe of the character wrought by O'Brien: the one, the only *King Kong*. The reason is simple. Stop motion photography allows an artist to create life. Shut in a studio for the entire working day, and over a period of several months to a year, the animator's sole, constant companion is a figurine to which he is slowly imparting a personality. Every motion, from achieving an eyeline to bending a finger, is meticulously nursed from the puppet; it is an intimate stretching of time which transforms the mass of metal and rubber to a literal extension of the animator, imbued with his own sense of style, grace, action, reaction, emotion, and idiosyncratic movement.

We are fortunate in that stop motion photography, unlike other art forms, is a product of the twentieth century, and we are able to reconstruct much of its history and development. Yet it is clearly not enough to tell the story of this creative medium from a purely technical perspective. Accordingly, we'll be examining it through the work of Willis O'Brien and his brilliant heir Ray Harryhausen—men who have raised what the latter calls "kinetic sculpture" from a screen gimmick to a screen art through such movies as *King Kong, Mighty Joe Young, Twenty Million Miles to Earth, The Three Worlds of Gulliver, Jason and the Argonauts*, and most recently *Sinbad and the Eye of the Tiger.*

However, the work at which we'll be looking is even more than art in technique and execution. In substance, it is truly the stuff of which dreams are made. If you're familiar with these films, this book will be a fond remembrance of wonders seen. But if you're new to stop motion photography, prepare yourself for a rich and exciting adventure. You will encounter mythologies both old and new and utterly impossible; allow yourself to be swept away by their color, fantasy, and innocence. They represent the kind of magic that frees the spirit from cynicism and makes you realize how, with a dash of imagination, all things are possible.

CHAPTER ONE

Painting with Light

Unlike motion pictures created primarily with live actors and comparatively unextraordinary plots, stop motion films rely heavily upon special effects to spin their magic. But before we look at the birth and history of three-dimensional animation, and such attendant technical processes as mattes, front-, rear-, and miniature-screen projection, it is best that we arm ourselves with a working knowledge of film, its science and its roots.

Our story, quite properly, begins in 1646, in a setting better suited to the alchemist Makovan from Ray Harryhausen's *The Three Worlds of Gulliver* than to a German clergyman. Nonetheless it was here that the seed for the moving picture was planted. Seated in a small, cold room, the darkness of night fallen on all but the candlelit surface of a simple wooden desk, Jesuit Father Athanasius Kircher busily scratches notes and illustrations in a handsomely bound portfolio. He works on his book *The Great Art of Light and Shadow* (*Ars Magna Kucis et Umbrae*) for which he has just diagramed a cylinder with a concave mirror at one end and a candle in the middle. There is an opaque image painted on the mirror; the light that falls on this surface is reflected, causing the shadow of the illustration to be cast through the cylinder's open end. Kircher has invented the world's first projector. And, while he diffidently refers to it as "my invention," it causes more widespread excitement than any apparatus since Johannes Gutenberg unveiled his printing press over two hundred years before.

What was the basic appeal of this toy later known as the *Magic Lantern*? At first, of course, it was simply a novelty, something to engage one's parlor guests. However, when similar devices were

A stroboskop.

built by such seventeenth-century scientists as Thomas Walgensteen, Francesco Eschinardi, and Joannes Zahn, the versatility of the invention became apparent. These men found that they could project series of full-color illustrations by rendering them on glass discs or strips and passing them between a candle for illumination and a lens to focus the rays. Even more enticing was the contribution made by a Dutch scientist, Christian Huygens, in 1710: he projected a slide showing a man in bed, and moments later, introduced a second slide which made a painted cockroach seem to jump into the sleeper's mouth. Although a limited entertainment, this was, technically speaking, the first projected moving picture! However, it was as far as the art of simulating or projecting movement would progress for the next century. Then came the application of a phenomenon known as *persistence of vision*—and motion came into its own.

Persistence of vision, as even the earliest of peoples had come to recognize, is the unique ability of the eye to retain an image for one tenth of a second after the stimulus has been removed. Applying this principle to another parlor toy in 1832, Vienna's Simon Ritter von Stampfer came up

1

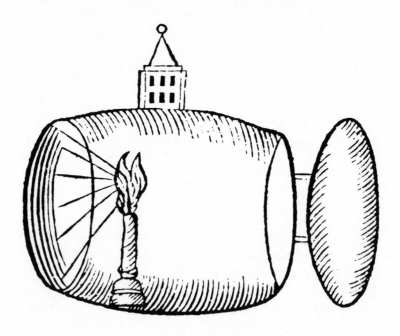

Kircher's own rendering of his Magic Lantern.

with the *Stroboskop*, a device which featured two parallel disks on one axis. There were successive drawings set about the perimeter of the disk farthest from the viewer, while on the second disk there was a thin slot corresponding to each illustration. That second disk was our first *shutter*: when the axis was turned, the shutter allowed the eye to see an image, blocked it, allowed the eye to see the next progressive image, blocked it, and so forth. Since the eye remembered each previous image during the interim period of darkness, it blended them together in a short, but fluid sequence. Of course, without the shutter to clearly define each picture, the illustrations would have spun by as an indistinct blur. In 1834, mathematician William George Homer simplified the two-plate unit calling it a *Zoetrope* and mounted the pictures along the inside base of a revolving drum. A slitted band sat like a halo atop the carousel and served as the shutter. Despite the ingenuity of these contrivances, they all had one serious shortcoming: the action was over within moments, and it could not be projected.

The next giant step toward the modern-day moving picture came nineteen years later, when the Austrian Baron Franz von Uchatius tinkered together a projector in which twelve drawings were

set in a circle behind twelve lenses, each of which was focused on the same spot. Surprisingly, Uchatius designed his machine so that the illustrations remained stationary while a kerosene lamp rotated inside the projector! Passing each picture, the light source flashed it on a wall. There was no need for a shutter, since the space between each picture served to block out the light. It was a clumsy device, but it worked; all that remained was to wed such a machine with photography.

The development of photography was concurrent with these experiments in movement and projection. Although chemists of the early seventeenth century knew that a mixture of silver nitrate and any carbon substance would become black when exposed to light, it was 200 years before scientists realized that a sheet of paper coated with silver salts could duplicate hazy images of anything to which it was exposed. The problem was the recorded images quickly went black. Chemicals were found to fix the pictures, and by 1837 Frenchman Louis Jacques Mande Daguerre was taking photographs—many of them still extant—on plates of polished metal. His contemporary, Englishman W.H. Fox Talbot, is credited with the all-important invention of the *negative*, an image in which light was recorded as dark and vice versa. These translucent pictures reproduced as positive on a receptive surface, and allowed multiple prints to be made from the single negative image.

Once the science of still photography had been mastered, it was only natural for cameramen to look toward the next horizon: the capturing of motion. It was in 1872 that Englishman Edward Muybridge made history by photographing a galloping horse as it tripped wires attached to nearly thirty successive cameras. However, since this was not the most convenient means of recording motion, two years later Parisian Jules Etienne Marey designed a shotgun with a lens at one end of the barrel and a film disc at the other. When he squeezed the trigger, the plate rotated, taking twelve pictures per second. By 1887, he was shooting moving objects with chemically treated strips of paper and a box camera, taking up to 120 exposures every second; by 1889, he was loading his camera with light-sensitive *celluloid*—a flexible and transparent substance made of gun cotton (nitrocellulose), camphor, and alcohol. Celluloid could be rolled inside a camera and thus used to record longer stretches of motion. That same year, English photographer William Friese-Greene further advanced the science by shooting motion pictures on *film*, which was photographic celluloid treated with fusel and banana oil (amyl acetate) and proved to be more pliant than any other medium. All the elements were now ready; the union of projection and these successively filmed images was about to be born.

Thomas Edison is commonly thought of as being the father of the motion picture, but this is obviously not the case. At best, he was a resourceful man who brought together engineers and various technical elements, creating the first public moving picture entertainment, the *Kinetoscope*. The Kinetoscope was a peep show in which forty feet of film unspooled between a light source and a shutter at a rate of forty frames-per-second; the patron looked on through a magnifying lens. The short films used in these machines were shot by W.K.L. Dickson at Edison's newly completed New Jersey studio, and the first Kinetoscope units were installed in New York City on April 14, 1894. The viewer paid a nickel to see the show. However, within two years, the voyeuristic novelty had worn off, and Kinetoscope revenue decreased sharply.

Edison's distributors urged him to look into a "screen machine" of the sort built by Auguste and Louis Lumiere in France. On December 28, 1895, the brothers Lumiere had premiered a film projector that ran sixteen frames of film per second past a stationary lens and light source; within a month, they were serving nearly 8,000 patrons per week from their *Cinematographe* salon. Apparently people felt more at ease watching moving pictures in a theatre-size group than alone in a stall. Not only had the Lumieres made moving pictures a social event, but they could accommodate more paying customers per performance. In addition, at sixteen frames-per-second, they were saving money by showing the same type of material as Edison's Kinetoscope, but with 60 percent less film. The "writing" was on the screen. Hearing of a similar projection device that was newly invented by Americans Thomas Armat and C.F. Jenkins, Edison's legal people bought the rights to market the unit as *Edison's Vitascope*. There were, of course, other such machines just becoming available the world over. But to Edison's credit, he went for the one with the steadiest, clearest projected image. Naturally Armat, who had bought out his partner's interests after a clash of personalities, was assured by Edison's staff that "while Mr. Edison has no desire to pose as the inventor of the machine, we can use Mr. Edison's name in such a manner as to keep within the actual truth, and yet get the benefit of his prestige. You understand that after...the business is fully established...we will make it our business to attach your name to the machine as the inventor. We are confident that you will eventually receive the credit which is due you." Needless to say, these proved to be the proverbial famous last words, since Armat was to end up as little more than an Edison projectionist. Posterity and business are seldom kind, and so it was Edison who made history, when on April 23, 1896, the Edison Vitascope opened at New York's Koster and Bial's Music Hall—the present-day site of Macy's. The projector presented its startled audience with views of crashing waves, dancing girls, pugilists, and scenes from the play *A Milk White Flag*. Public reaction was enthusiastic: the moving picture was here to stay. All that was needed now were—moving pictures!

Although most of the early films presented by

George Melies.

Vitascope, the Cinematographe, or Edison's sharp rival, the *Biograph* were simply one-minute travelogues or documentaries, the Lumieres had enjoyed considerable success with what is thought to have been the first fiction film: *Watering the Gardener* (1895). The entire picture was shot from one camera position and without a single break: a boy steps on a hose, the gardener peers into the spout to see what's stopped the flow, the lad steps away, and the gardener gets a faceful of water. Realizing that there was a market for similar narratives, the Lumieres, Edison, and the other new exhibitor-filmmakers included short dramatic interludes in their programs. However, these were all very simple works, such as *Biograph's* excerpt from *Rip Van Winkle* (1896) and Edison's famous May Irwin-John C. Rice *Kiss* (1896)—the controversial "first screen kiss," which was widely decried as immoral and gave rise to the first conflict over screen censorship. But the fiction film did not really enjoy a quality presentation until Frenchman Melies turned his imaginative eye to the medium.

Although he was the first genuine motion picture artist, it is more appropriate to our study that Melies was also the screen's first special-effects technician. Many of the 500 films he made between 1896 and 1914 involved fantasy or science fiction, and Melies developed whatever processes were necessary to make his works as convincing as possible. A professional magician and newspaper cartoonist, Melies was drawn to the medium in 1895 when he was among the first to see the Lumieres' moving pictures. Building a camera and projector of his own, he began presenting shows at the Theatre Robert-Houdin, a house he had purchased several years earlier as a showplace for magicians. Naturally enough, one of Melies' first screen presentations was a literal transcription of his stage magic act. However, audiences reacted to the film apathetically. The Lumieres were taking viewers all over the world: where was the wonder in a simple theatrical display? Humbled but undaunted, Melies made certain that his future productions had more visual appeal. Yet it was not until he had spent nearly two years producing short moving pictures that he even considered the possibilities of special effects on film. It was a discovery he made quite by accident. While Melies was busy photo-graphing a Paris street in 1896, his camera jammed. As he freed the tangle of film from its primitive feeder mechanism, he thought nothing of the incident and resumed his work. Several days later the film was developed, and as he watched it unreel, Melies was astounded to see a bus turn into a hearse. Not believing what he had seen, Melies rewound the film and watched it again: sure enough, he had not imagined the sudden and startling transformation. It was there. Thinking back, he recalled that the camera had stopped running just as the bus had entered the picture. By the time he had set things aright, the bus had driven on and the hearse had taken its place. Of course, the camera had not witnessed this intermediary action, so one vehicle had apparently been turned into the other. Deciding to repeat this trick under more controlled circumstances, Melies filmed a woman, stopped the camera, had his star walk off the set, and resumed filming. When this, his seventieth production was screened, the sixty-second lark did indeed live up to its title: *The Vanishing Lady.*

Thrilled with both the mechanical challenge of *The Vanishing Lady* and with public acceptance of his moving picture, Melies concentrated on fantasy as the medium for his film illusions, producing such efforts as *The Haunted Castle* (1896), *The Astronomer's Dream* (1898), *Cinderella* (1899), *Man with the Rubber Head* (1901), and his most famous work, the first science fiction film, *A Trip to the Moon* (1902). In these pictures, the filmmaker introduced longer, more involved narratives than had ever been created for the screen, as well as most of the special-effects techniques that were to become industry staples. These included the use of painted backdrops to suggest exotic lands; placing a tank of water between the camera and the actors to simulate underwater activity; slowing the camera speed so that more action would pass between frames and thus create fast-motion scenes; and reversing the process for slow motion; having a player featured twice in the same shot through *split-screen photography*—covering half the lens, shooting the performer, rewinding the film, flopping the mask, repositioning the actor, and exposing the previously hidden portions of film; creating transparent ghosts and goblins through *double exposure*—running the film twice through the camera, thus superimposing the two images; and so forth. It may very well be, as some film historians claim, that he also invented stop motion photography, although it is unlikely that we shall ever know. Though Melies' films were popular around the world—particularly in America, where *A Trip to the Moon* had been so much in demand that new negatives were shot and pirated prints struck from Melies' original film—the coming of World War I halted further progress. Melies' studio was commandeered by the French government as a research facility, film was difficult to come by (made of the same basic materials as explosives), and in order to survive, the moviemaker was forced to sell most of his films and equipment to junk dealers. Despite the fact that his imaginative and meticulously made moving pictures had contributed immeasurably to the geometric growth of the medium, no one came to Melies' aide. Fourteen years later, he was discovered selling newspapers on a Paris street corner. A collection was made and the industry bought him a kiosk, but Melies quit the stand in 1933 due to poor health and died five years later in a home for destitute actors.

Melies had proven that the screen could tell stories for up to ten or twenty minutes, and filmmakers the world over were quick to capitalize on the public demand for such entertainment. In the United States, most of these moving pictures were made in the Northeast, on Long Island, in New Jersey, and Connecticut, until, in 1910, moviemakers went west in search of more favorable weather. They found what they were looking for in the small California community of Hollywood: a warm climate with almost-continuous sunshine. It was also close enough to Mexico so that, when lawsuits arose over patents on motion picture equipment and components—so many inventors having been involved with the birth of the medium, infringements were inevitable—they could slip across the border and continue shooting until things simmered down.

During these post-Melies years, there were a great many advances in the medium. Apart from aesthetic sophistication, film stock itself improved, making it less grainy and more adaptable to different lighting conditions. There was new equipment: tracks on which to *dolly* the camera to or from the action, attachments—pioneered by Melies—with which to fade a scene in or out, powerful lights for shooting indoors, and so forth. There was the birth of the *star system*—the use of popular players to presell new films to the public—and there were filmmakers like the American D.W. Griffith, who perfected feature-length storytelling and the dramatic use of camera position in such classic films as *Birth of a Nation* (1915) and *Intolerance* (1916). It was Griffith who said of Melies: "I owe him everything." While all this was happening, Sergei Eisenstein in Russia was busily setting down the rules of film editing in his motion pictures *Potemkin* (1925) and the great Revolutionary epic *Ten Days That Shook the World* (1928). However well-made and moving these works were, only two filmmakers carried Melies' sense of fantasy into the post-World War I era. One was Walt Disney, who in 1923, began producing pleasant escapism in the form of animated cartoons. They were not the first such efforts: in 1905, French jeweler Emile Cohl had shot *Mr. Stop*, which is widely considered to have been the first cartoon, but Disney's works were easily the most popular animated pictures. The other was Willis O'Brien. Like Melies, O'Brien was a resourceful artist and engineer with an intuitive feeling for the new medium. Unfortunately like Melies, his story is one of neglect by his peers and great personal tragedy. Yet no matter what his problems or many disappointments, Willis O'Brien gave the movies all he had, and created a handful of film classics, one of which has since become a part of American folklore. Since we now know as much about movie history, science, and technique as was available to O'Brien, let's join him on a journey that began, one day, with a lump of clay....

CHAPTER TWO

O'Bie

With documentation of early film history being sketchy at best, it is difficult to say when the first stop motion film was made. Was it a lost Melies effort, or was it a work like *The Humpty Dumpty Circus*, made by Edison's production unit in 1897 with wooden, peg-jointed models of animals and acrobats performing in the titular carnival? We shall probably never know. Nor can we be certain that Willis O'Brien ever saw *The Humpty Dumpty Circus* or other animated shorts such as Edison's *Visit to the Spiritualist* (1897) or Edwin S. Porter's *The Teddy Bears* (1907). What *is* important is that, one afternoon in 1915, O'Brien conceived of substituting clay models for the drawings used in amimated cartoons. What followed is all the more remarkable when we consider that O'Brien's early life had hardly prepared him for the role of a filmmaker-artiste!

Willis Harold O'Brien was born on March 2, 1886, in Oakland, California. His mother was Minnie Gregg O'Brien; his father William ran a military academy and a hotel during Willis' childhood, and later served as Oakland's assistant district attorney. A well-to-do man, William unfortunately made some poor business investments in the early 1890s, thus forcing his family to adopt an alien, rather simple lifestyle. Young Willis was clever enough to realize that this change in station would be a terribly difficult period for his family. Because of this he resolved to give them one less mouth to feed, dropping out of school, running away from home, and accepting work on a cattle ranch. On occasional return visits to his parents, his brothers and sisters would chide him for his lack of formal education and for the crude cowboy vernacular he used. This criticism made him uncomfortable and even resentful, causing him to adopt the habit which he retained throughout his life: always saying as little as possible.

For the next four years, Willis was forced to face the humiliating fact that perhaps his departure from home had been hasty. He went from job to job with little success or satisfaction, his youth making him a ready target for exploitation. Once, he took a job on a chicken farm and was to receive fifteen dollars for a month's work; instead, Willis' boss gave him seven dollars and a book on raising chickens. He worked as a trapper in Oregon, sustaining himself primarily on oatmeal, his pelts ultimately to be stolen by a hunter to whom Willis had entrusted their sale. Among the teenager's other unrewarding jobs were bartending and serving as an attendant at various rodeos. In fact, his only satisfaction during this period came while working as a guide for scientists from the University of Southern California. They were searching the Crater Lake region for prehistoric artifacts, and talking with them about their work had captured O'Brien's imagination—an interest which would play a vital role in his career.

In 1903, without money or the prospects of employment, O'Brien swallowed his pride and returned to his parents' home. He went to work as a clerk in an architect's office; within a few months he had advanced himself to the position of draughtsman. But the job did not appeal to O'Brien and he left the company to become a sports cartoonist for the *San Francisco Daily News*. His forte was sketching boxers, but O'Brien found himself caught up in the activities themselves, and decided to become an athlete. Perhaps he was looking for the recognition he had been denied by critical parents and a long series of occupational disappointments. In any case, O'Brien's first stab at sports was to lose enough weight to become a jockey. He went on a crash diet but failed to make the grade, and elected to try his hand at boxing. For inspiration, he decorated his room with photographs of prize-fighters and began working out. He fought a total of nine small-time matches and won them all. Entering a tougher, more prestigious bout, the scrappy Irishman was smacked to the mat in round two and realized that he was not cut out for the ring. Bowing to pressure from his father, O'Brien then went to work for the Southern Pacific Railroad, holding positions as brakeman, and when the line expanded into the North, working as a surveyor. Unhappy with these jobs, the young man joined a San Francisco firm as a stonecutter, creating all manner of marble decorations.

At the shop, the disconsolate twenty-nine-year-old met a young cutter who, like himself, was interested in boxing. On one particularly slow afternoon, he and O'Brien decided to pass the time by molding boxers out of clay and putting them through their paces. One man would position his boxer to throw a punch; the other would mold a defensive stance. And it was in working thus that he first thought to film progressively positioned clay models as one would shoot successive illustrations in an animated cartoon. Drawing upon his fascination with prehistoric animals, O'Brien realized that they would make an ideal and unusual film subject, and made plans to shoot a very short motion picture. Sculpting a clay dinosaur and a caveman atop jointed wooden skeletons, he contacted a friend who was a newsreel cameraman and asked him to film the experimental short. Carrying the camera, models, and a miniature set consisting of rocks, sand, and twigs to the top of a bank building in San Francisco, O'Brien and his associate shot a variety of stop motion scenes. The film was developed, and while the action was jerky and the clay failed to hold its shape under O'Brien's touch, the illusion of life was astonishing. O'Brien was convinced that he had a marketable commodity in his clay puppet film. The question was what to do with it? O'Brien decided to bring his eighty-second-long test reel to San Francisco filmmaker-exhibitor Herman Wobber, hoping to convince him that the unique puppet process had commercial possibilities. Happily, the entrepreneur liked what he saw and advanced O'Brien $5,000 to expand upon and remake the simple film. What emerged was *The Dinosaur and the Missing Link*. Told entirely with stop motion models, the film is the tale of the wooing of the lovely Araminta Rockface by the dashing Duke and his nefarious rival Stonejaw Steve. Ms. Rockface agrees to wed the man who fetches her the finest meal. Grabbing their bows and arrows, the men go hunting. However, their fevered sharpshooting succeeds only in disturbing a monster bird, which attacks them. Elsewhere, a Neanderthal bully named Wild Willie pauses by a pond to drink and is slain by a brontosaur. Inevitably, another character, Mr. Theophilus Ivoryhead, happens by, and claiming to have overcome the vicious Missing Link, impresses Araminta with his heroism and wins her fair hand.

The quality evident in this short film shows that O'Brien did not simply pocket Wobber's money and hand him a halfhearted effort. For one thing, the animator took pains to refine his method of model making. Pliable clay would no longer suffice for skin, nor could a wooden skeleton endure the rigors of extended animation. O'Brien proceeded to craft the muscles and skin from rubber, which would not melt under the hot lights and constant use, and made his eight-inch-tall frames from metal, giving them screw joints which could be tightened to keep the limbs of the models sturdy. If an appendage had sagged during filming, there would have been no way to precisely reposition it and the entire scene would had to have been reshot. The sets, too, were constructed with greater care, O'Brien making certain that each detailed piece of scenery was glued firmly in place. If a leaf or pebble had jiggled during filming, it would have appeared to possess a life of its own on screen! Not surprisingly, the five-minute comedy took two months to shoot, and it was destined to bring O'Brien into the employ of our old friend Thomas Edison.

Wobber spent over a year trying to sell *The Dinosaur and the Missing Link* to a national distributor, but could find no takers. Then he heard that Edison's Forum Films was planning to market a movie series as an identifiable package, with four

The allosaur from Willis O'Brien's *The Ghost of Slumber Mountain*, pictured in an article from a 1919 trade journal.

A trachodon from *The Lost World*.

A styracosaur gores a young brontosaur in this specially posed publicity still from *The Lost World*.

One of O'Brien's static matte shots from *The Lost World*. Everything is miniature with the exception of the actors and their immediate surroundings.

or five short subjects under the aegis of Conquest Pictures. To balance the program, Edison wanted a one- or two-reel drama, a film of some educational value, a documentary, and a live-action or animated comedy. Wobber had *The Dinosaur and the Missing Link* screened for Edison, who was impressed with both the film and its creator. He included the comedy in the first Conquest offering, which was released on May 30, 1917, and opened to good notices. But most critics were partial to the stop motion entry. Typical was this review in *The Moving Picture World*: "*The Dinosaur and the Missing Link* is startling and amusing at the same time. The grotesque manikens are curiously human in their movements, and will excite the interest of the entire family." Indeed, the O'Brien segment proved so popular that it was retitled *The Dinosaur and the Baboon* and re-released as a separate short subject on August 11, 1917.

During the year that Wobber had spent peddling *The Dinosaur and the Missing Link*, O'Brien had gone ahead and shot a second stop motion film, *The Birth of a Flivver* (1916). Also five minutes long, this film concerned the efforts of two cavemen who, having invented the wheel, try to decide what to do with it. They build a cart and attempt to bridle an unsubmissive dinosaur; failing at this, the Cenozoic inventors discard the wheel as worthless. Edison bought the film and asked O'Brien to come East and head a small production unit in New York. Dubbed Manikin Productions, the group operated from the Edison Studios at 2826 Decatur Street in the Bronx. Accepting the position, "O'Bie," as his co-workers at the studio would soon be calling him, made the move late in 1916. His agreement called for a series of eight-minute-long films for which he would be paid $500 apiece and was expected to design and build the models, sets, props, and scenery, as well as do the lighting, animation, and cinematography. Still he was pleased to take the post for reasons other than creative and professional satisfaction. In San Francisco, O'Bie had been dating the seventeen-year-old Hazel Collette, whom he was engaged to wed. The problem as he soon realized was that he didn't *want* to marry Hazel, but couldn't summon up the courage to terminate their relationship. The New York offer gave him his out. And while

O'Brien never officially broke the engagement, he left California confident that time and distance would do the job for him. He was wrong. One of Hazel's aunts, fearing for her niece's honor, brought the girl East. Realizing that he was cornered, O'Bie agreed to marry Hazel.

O'Bie's first film in New York was *RFD 10,000 B.C.,* which was also shown as *RFD 2,000,000 B.C.* and *GFD 10,000 Years B.C.* The longest of his short subjects, running just over ten minutes, the film was shot with the same puppets that O'Bie had used in his first two pictures. The plot concerns a jealous prehistoric postman. Delivering mail via a dinosaur-driven cart, he learns that the girl of his dreams has received a tender stone valentine from another man. Replacing it with an insulting card, the letter carrier gloats over the havoc it causes, until the suitor learns of the substitution and literally tears the mailman limb-from-limb.

RFD 10,000 B.C. was released in mid-1917, and it was followed later that year by *Morpheus Mike, Prehistoric Poultry, Curious Pets of Our Ancestors, Mickey and his Goat, In the Villain's Power, The Sam Lloyd Picture Puzzle*, and a short-lived series called *Mickey's Naughty Nightmares*, also known as *Nippy's Nightmares*, in which O'Bie's stop motion models were combined with live actors using split screen and double exposure. Although the Conquest Pictures and especially the O'Brien shorts were well-received, Edison was forced to phase them out by the end of 1917. The Supreme Court had broken an Edison-supported monopoly known as the Motion Picture Patents Company, which had controlled the production and distribution of most moving pictures. In the wake of the Patents Company's demise, exhibitors went searching for profitable feature-length films rather than short subjects, and the Conquest program was an early casualty. Edison then shifted O'Bie to a series of weekly educational films, each segment of which was to feature the animator's popular prehistoric animals. This represented a new challenge for O'Bie. He had always constructed his beasts based on popular conceptions of their appearances, with little regard for anatomical accuracy. Collaborating with Dr. Brown of the American Museum of Natural History in New

York, O'Bie made certain that the designs for all future monsters would be scientifically correct. Unfortunately, financial troubles from their theatrical stranglehold forced the Edison Company to sell out to the Massachusetts film company of Lincoln and Parker. Realizing that he would no longer have the freedom that he had enjoyed under Edison, O'Bie left the company.

Spending several months both unemployed and generally dissatisfied with his lot, O'Bie was delighted, when early in 1918, he received a call from New Jersey-based producer Herbert M. Dawley. Dawley, who had been a major in the commissary department during the war, and a former art director of the Pierce Arrow Motor Company, was now a moviemaker. Like O'Bie, he was experimenting with stop motion photography. However, Dawley's concepts had taken a decidedly different course. Rather than work with miniature models, Dawley had constructed most of his animals life-size, padding their wooden skeletons with clay and covering them with painted cloth. Nor had he actually shot any film of these creations. He had simply taken still photographs and pasted them in a book. When the pages were flipped, the animals appeared to move. Interested in making a dinosaur film, but aware that his own work and methods were not of a professional caliber, Dawley offered the animator three months and $3000 to write, direct, and execute the special effects on a dinosaur film. O'Bie agreed, and the result was *The Ghost of Slumber Mountain*, the story of Uncle Jack (Dawley) who, pressed by a group of children, tells them a story. On a mountain-climbing expedition to the River of Peace, Jack, his dog, and their guide Joe, scale Slumber Mountain and reach Dream Valley. There, they find a cabin that was once the home of the wizened old hermit Mad Dick. Joe tells his companion that on a previous climb, he had actually *seen* the hermit, who was peeking through a strange telescope. Pitching camp, Jack can't shake the thought of the mysterious old man when suddenly, an ethereal voice lures him to the cabin. Breaking in, he finds the shed stocked with fossils and other prehistoric relics. He also spots the glass of which Joe had spoken. Touching it, Jack is greeted by the ghost of Mad Dick (allegedly played by O'Brien himself, through superimposition). The spirit leads Jack to a cliff and tells him to look through the telescope. Jack does and is astonished to see a brontosaur plodding through a ravine and into a lake (O'Brien simulated the water by animating gelatin). Turning the lenses elsewhere, Jack watches a giant, flightless bird known as the diatryma primping its feathers and then lunching on a snake. Next he witnesses a titanic struggle between two triceratops, with the surviving monster slaughtered by an allosaur. Just then, Mad Dick disappears and Jack finds himself confronted by the dinosaur. Although Jack shoots the meat eater, his bullets have no effect. Then, just as the monster is about to devour our hero, Joe and the dog wake him from his nightmare. Realizing that they have been had, the children playfully attack Uncle Jack, and our sixteen minute peek at a long-dead world is ended.

Originally, *The Ghost of Slumber Mountain* ran nearly forty-five minutes, but after previewing the film, Dawley decided that an audience would become bored with that much stop motion in a single sitting. So he clipped a great deal of the animation and planned to build other films around these scenes. However, regardless of the cuts, the World Superfeature film, released in June of 1919, was well-received. The public responded by returning Dawley a $100,000 profit on his meagre investment. As the trade bible *Exhibitor's Herald* advised, "Bill it big and you will surely get big results. It stood them out all evening in Winnetka, Illinois—high class patronage." And, while reviews were mixed, they all praised the special effects. The industry journal *Variety* summed up critical reaction to the film by saying, "the photography is excellent...the reconstruction and filming of the monsters is cleverly done...but the story, which hangs by the slenderest thread, is dull and tedious." Indeed, the picture's technical work garnered an unusual amount of press. Unfortunately, every article was twisted by Dawley so that he and *only* he would receive credit for the film. Characteristic was the coverage in the August 1919 edition of *Motion Picture Magazine*:

> Mr. Dawley, it is said, simply enlarged upon the old trick by which a knife, apparently without human aide, slices bread, by which chairs move about a room seemingly unaided, etc. By this

method, which requires infinite care and time, single animated pictures are taken of objects in sequence. That is, a knife is thrust into the loaf of bread, the hand is withdrawn from range of the camera, the object is photographed, the knife is moved slightly, the camera crank is turned, the knife is moved a fraction further, another picture is taken, and so on until the movement is completed. The final positive, upon being flashed upon the screen, gives the appearance of the knife in motion without human aide. Mr. Dawley wanted to film prehistoric mammoths in action, and he built huge models—of cloth, wire, and steel—of the dinosaurs and other monstrosities of the pre-stone ages. Placing these in front of the camera and slowly filming their movements—that is, by moving their head a bit and photographing, moving it again a bit more and again photographing—he attained the effect of prehistoric animals in action. Mr. Dawley was able to take something like twenty feet of film a day—that is, on days he worked hard and consistently. But the result! Astonishing, even to the fight to the death between huge creatures of the dim past.

Needless to say, O'Bie felt cheated by such articles, since any contribution which Dawley may have made to the animation was minimal. That the producer had little technical ability of his own is evidenced by the fact that every monster sequence in his next film, *Along the Moonbeam Trail* (1920), was either one of the edited shots or an out-take—a faulty scene—from *The Ghost of Slumber Mountain.*

As a result of all this, O'Bie severed his relationship with Herbert M. Dawley without any prospects for the future. The parting of ways would cause more than hurt feelings, but that lay several years in the future. For the time being, the animator had other problems. Hazel had just given birth to their first child, William, and Willis Jr. was on the way. And, while O'Bie loved his children, he felt trapped by the marriage and took out his resentment on his wife. The couple quarreled constantly about O'Bie's odd hours and drinking habits. It was truly a dark period, and it would have proven disastrous had the animator not become involved with Watterson R. Rothacker, one of the few gentlemen for whom he would work during his career.

In 1910, Rothacker, a former journalist and a canny businessman, had established the first organization in America devoted to the production of advertising films. Six years later, he formed the Industrial Moving Picture Company, a subsidiary which processed film, and like the Edison Company, launched experimental programs to develop untapped resources for the cinema, including the use of sound, aerial photography as a tool of warfare, and stop motion photography. It was in keeping with this program that Rothacker himself made the following press announcement in August 1919:

> For some time, Willis H. O'Brien, the man who produced the novelty effects in *The Ghost of Slumber Mountain*, has been in our employ, and is now engaged in producing a number of novelty pictures which we know to be very effective and attractive and far superior to anything Mr. O'Brien has previously done.

He went on to explain that he had followed O'Bie's career since the Conquest pictures, and had been much impressed by his work. Neither could Rothacker resist taking a shot at Herbert Dawley, who had recently snipped O'Bie's name from the credits of *The Ghost of Slumber Mountain:*

> When this picture was presented at the Strand (New York), Mr. O'Brien was given full credit for its production, but since then an attempt has been made to create the impression that the work was not done by him, which, of course, is contrary to the facts in the case. Mr. O'Brien is constantly improving his unique process which *we control.*

Three or four of the "novelty pictures" mentioned by Rothacker were actually completed, although their titles and subject matter are unknown. However, the O'Brien-Rothacker association is famous not for these shorts, but for a feature-length film that became a box office bonanza and a classic.

The Lost World, a Professor Challenger novel written by Sir Arthur Conan Doyle in 1912, is about the discovery of living dinosaurs on a time-forgotten plateau in South America. It was a natural vehicle for stop motion special effects. O'Bie told Rothacker that it was the most elaborate special-effects production in the history of motion pictures;

An Allosaur and brontosaur do battle in *The Lost World*.

A stegosaur from *The Lost World*.

coincidentally, the producer owned the motion picture rights to Doyle's novels. Rothacker recognized the clear commercial value of *The Lost World* as a film; he asked to see some stop-motion tests and drawings of the action. When O'Bie proved that he could indeed handle the project, Rothacker set the financial and preproduction wheels in motion.

One of Rothacker's first commitments was to spend over $1 million on the picture, money that would be lavished on sets, quality players, and special effects. The producer also agreed to shoot the film in Burbank, at the Brunton Studios of First National Pictures, where O'Bie set up shop and began working out technical details with Ralph Hammeras, one of the studio's key special-effects people. Only twenty-eight years old, Hammeras had come to Hollywood from Minneapolis seven years earlier to work as a film artist. Eventually, he branched off into special effects and free-lanced his skills from Brunton, where he eventually signed an exclusive contract with First National. Fortunately, Hammeras' forte was the *glass shot*, a process which was to be used extensively in *The Lost World*. A popular technique even today—it was widely used in such films as *Earthquake* (1974) and *Logan's Run* (1976)—the glass shot is a means of creating spectacle with relatively little money. No matter what the setting, be it jungle or metropolis, only a small portion of the life-size set is constructed, against which the actors will perform. On a large pane of glass, an artist carefully paints the surrounding landscape. This is placed between the camera and the players so that the detailed illustration begins where the actual set leaves off. The rest of the glass is left clear. As far as the camera's two-dimensional eye is concerned, the image is one continuous scene. Hammeras, as well as Fred Jackman, the head of special effects at the studio, were also of considerable assistance to O'Bie in designing and executing the film's many split-screen shots and *mattes*. One of the most complex processes employed in *The Lost World*, the *static matte* and *traveling matte* are both means of photographically dropping live actors into a miniature set, or dinosaurs into a life-size set.

Let's look first at the machinery of the less intricate static matte, which was used only when the element to be superimposed remained stationary for the entire scene, such as a shot of the explorers in our film hiding behind a boulder while a dinosaur is visible lumbering along the horizon. Obviously, the scene could not be shot through double exposure, which would have caused the monster to be visible *through* rather than *behind* the foreground elements. A small glass painting was rendered in solid black, forming a silhouette of the foreign element. The glass was then inserted into a *matte box*, a small, light-proof compartment which was fitted to the camera lens. When the models were animated, the matte prevented a portion of the film from being exposed. This reel was then rewound and the element to be added was photographed through a *counter matte*, a glass painting in which everything was black save for a clear area which precisely complemented the shape on the first matte. In this way, the boulder setting and the miniature were perfectly combined on a single piece of film. However, instances where the foreign element was to change shape or position from frame to frame, such as a shot of the players walking through foliage, encountering a dinosaur, and fleeing for their lives, called for the more complex process known as a traveling matte. First, the actors and their environment were filmed against a simple white backdrop. This produced two important matte elements: the negative, which surrounded the inverse image of the performers and the foliage with a solid black background where the white had been, and a positive, which was chemically burned in, printed so that the white background became transparent and the foreground elements turned black. Meanwhile, the monster was animated and photographed on a miniature jungle set. However, when the dinosaur film was developed, the positive was presented to an unexposed negative for printing *along with* the high contrast positive of the live players, the footage in which the foreground elements were opaque. This left a 'hole' on the negative print of the dinosaur footage into which the action on the first positive showing the actors and the foliage, could be neatly slipped on a second run through the printer. When developed, the positives had created a new or *second-generation* negative of the completed effect.

The Lost World was clearly an intricate

undertaking, and it goes without saying that, between animating the dinosaurs, helping director Harry O. Hoyt describe the monsters and their movements to the actors, and working with Hammeras on the special effects set-ups, O'Bie wanted to delegate the full-time job of building and caring for the film's fifty stop motion models to someone else. Rothacker then approved the hiring of the third member of the film's principal special-effects team, nineteen-year-old Marcel Delgado.

A Mexican by birth, Delgado first fell in love with sculpture in his home town of La Parita, where he used to sit and watch a local artisan carve religious icons. By the age of six, Delgado was busy sculpting figurines of his own, expanding this skill to include the building of intricate mechanical playthings. Unfortunately, with the coming of the Mexican Revolution in 1909, Marcel's father was forced to uproot his family of nine and move to Los Angeles, where life proved to be terribly difficult. None of the Delgados spoke English and they survived only by doing back-breaking labor for a succession of farmers. Marcel went to school, of course, but was forced by the death of his father in 1911 to leave the seventh grade and go to work.

It was a difficult time for the youngster. He spent several frustrating years in a series of unskilled positions before deciding to build a career for himself as an artist. Working as a grocery clerk for a weekly wage of eighteen dollars, he enrolled in evening courses at the Otis Art Institute. Although he couldn't afford the classes, Marcel made arrangements to tutor less advanced students in exchange for free tuition. For the first time in his life, Marcel had both a goal and the means to achieve it. That was when he met O'Bie, who had joined Otis to brush up his own artistic talents. O'Bie was much impressed with the prodigious Delgado and asked if he would like to leave his grocery job and come to work on *The Lost World* for seventy-five dollars a week. Delgado refused. He was afraid that working on the picture would cost him several years' delay in his dream to become a top artist. He was also wary of the industry with its much-publicized ups and downs—power struggles at the newborn studios, clashes in artistic temperament, financial debacles resulting from costly films, for example—and knew that the food store at least

assured him a steady if comparatively small income. But O'Bie was persistent. He repeated his offer on several different occasions, and each time the sculptor turned him down. Finally, O'Bie simply invited Delgado to the studio. He gave the young man a guided tour which concluded with a stop at a workshop filled with sketches and models of dinosaurs: Delgado later quoted O'Bie as saying, "It's yours if you want it," and the temptation proved too much for the sculptor. He agreed to do the picture. The staff was now complete. All that stood in the way of production was a lawsuit instituted by Herbert Dawley.

Addressing a banquet of the Society of American Magicians at the Hotel McAlpin in New York, Sir Arthur Conan Doyle had presented without explanation some wizardry of his own: O'Bie's test reel for *The Lost World*. The magicians and press were both stunned; in reporting the event, the *New York Times* speculated that Sir Arthur, a well-known devotee of psychic phenomena, had no doubt discovered a new world "in the ether" or else, "if fakes, they were masterpieces." Next day, the author explained to Society president Harry Houdini that these were simply preproduction clips from *The Lost World*. The *Times* carried his explanation, which happened to be the first that Dawley had heard of the project. Claiming patent violation, he initiated a $100,000 suit against Rothacker. And Dawley did indeed have a case: the wily producer had taken out patents on both O'Bie's techniques and on what he called the "articulated effigies," something that the animator had never thought to do on his own behalf. As Dawley explained it to the newspapers, O'Bie "learned the process by working in my office," and the animator's claims "that he did all the work and that the idea belongs to him" were sheer nonsense. Bristling as a result, but with his back against the wall, Rothacker organized a hurried gathering of the early O'Brien films, as well as documents and authenticated statements from people with whom O'Brien had worked. These proved beyond a doubt that O'Bie had been using stop motion long before he ever met Dawley. Still, the patents *did* belong to the producer. Only when confronted with the overwhelming evidence supporting O'Bie's claim to stop motion, as well as Rothacker's promise of a rousing legal battle, did Dawley agree to settle out of court.

It was 1923 before full-scale production began on *The Lost World*. By then, the players had been cast, the script finished. O'Bie had his new techniques down pat, and Hammeras and his crew had constructed most of the miniature sets. Delgado had completed his monster-building chores, having made considerable modifications in O'Brien's modeling methods. Basing his designs on the famous Charles R. Knight dinosaur paintings in the American Museum of Natural History, Delgado used sponge to flesh out his metallic skeletons, which he then covered with dental dam. Not only was the detail and skin texture of the sixteen- to twenty-inch-long monsters remarkably realistic, but inside each animal was a small rubber bladder which could be incrementally inflated or deflated between frames to simulate breathing. Nor was Delgado's job ended with the completion of the fifty dinosaurs. He had to be at the studio every day to repair torn or weakened models, often laboring through the night to have them ready by the start of the next day's shooting. As for the miniature sets, they were erected by Hammeras and his staff on an average of six feet long by three or four feet deep, and stood approximately three feet from the ground. Their height and size allowed O'Bie easy access to any corner of the set from cameraside, without cramping either the animator or the models or detracting from the detail of the props. As in O'Bie's earlier pictures, every set piece was carefully secured; leaves and grasses were either heavily lacquered or cut from tin to prevent them from moving between exposures.

With the exception of one scene, the animation in *The Lost World* was done solely by O'Bie. The exception was a dinosaur stampede. Staged on a set that was 75 × 150 feet, the sheer spectacle of the sequence made it necessary for O'Bie to work with a handful of assistants. However, every other foot of animation was created entirely by O'Bie from behind special partitions set up in the studio to assure his privacy. An interruption in the midst of animation might have caused O'Bie to forget in what direction a claw, jaw, or tail were moving, thus destroying the continuity of the shot. Another important consideration regarding the stop motion

work was fastening the dinosaurs to the set. As it was often necessary to position the models off-balance—when they were walking or fighting, for example—O'Bie had had to determine beforehand exactly where they would be moving. Drilling holes in the set, he disguised them with appropriate bits of sand or flora. When the holes were needed, O'Bie removed the plug, put a screw up into the set, and threaded it through a predrilled hole in the monster's foot. Scenes of dinosaurs flying or leaping were accomplished with thin strands of piano wire, suspended from an overhead brace and looped around the models. Careful lighting rendered these threads invisible in the finished film. But with all these meticulous preparations, the stop motion work was still at the mercy of that same lighting. It had to be constant from exposure to exposure to prevent a strobing effect in the finished film. Banks of steady Cooper Hewitt lights were used, suspended about two yards above the center of O'Bie's working area. Each miniature set was carried in and properly positioned when it was needed.

Working ten hours a day, O'Bie's daily output was 480 separate frames, thirty-five feet of film, which ran just over a half minute onscreen. At this rate, the stop motion photography took a total of fourteen months to complete.

Ironically, work on *The Lost World* was divided between Burbank and New York, as midway through production, First National moved East to the former Biograph Studio which, you will recall, was the seat of Edison's greatest competition when O'Bie was just breaking into the business. Newly renovated, the studio allowed movie executives to be near the powerful New York distributors. Filmmaking had become a big and ruthless business, and many producers felt uncomfortable being three thousand miles from the real industry battleground. However, by the midthirties, when improved communications and transportation reduced the importance of geography, most everyone had returned to southern California.

The Lost World was released on February 15, 1925, and created an avalanche of box-office revenue: receipts in just the premiere week at one New York theatre totaled $13,416. It also garnered unprecedented publicity for O'Bie and his special effects. However, before examining the film and a few of O'Bie's more impressive screen illusions, let's take a look at the tale that treated audiences to sights unlike any they had ever seen in their lives.

Professor George Edward Challenger (Wallace Beery) does not enjoy ridicule, but finds himself being railed by his London peers for suggesting that the late explorer Maple White had, in fact, discovered a plateau in Brazil that is inhabited by dinosaurs. Spurred by their scorn, the noted scientist organizes an expedition consisting of Maple's daughter Paula (Bessie Love); big-game hunter Sir John Roxton (Lewis Stone), who is in love with Paula; newspaperman Edward Malone (Lloyd Hughes), whose girl friend Gladys Hungerford (Alma Bennett) refuses to marry him until he does something noteworthy, and whose paper, *The Gazette*, wants him to report on the journey; Professor Summerlee (Arthur Hoyt); and aides Austin (Finch Smiles) and Zambo (Jules Cowles). No sooner is the expedition underway than Paula and Malone find themselves attracted to one another. However, while canoeing down the Amazon River, the couple's attention is forced from romance to survival when they spot a pterodactyl flying off with a fully grown alligator in its talons. Pushing on, they reach the base of the infamous plateau, and leaving Austin and Zambo behind, scale the sheer cliff. Felling a tree to cross a wide chasm, the explorers venture into a verdant jungle which lies athwart a smouldering volcano, watched, all the while, by a shaggy ape man (Bull Montana). After an encounter with an herbivorous brontosaur, who strands the intruders by nosing their tree bridge into the pit, the group presses on. They continue to witness amazing sights, including fights to the death between an allosaur and a trachodon, an allosaur and a triceratops, and an allosaur and a brontosaur; this last struggle ending with the long-necked brontosaur falling from a cliff into a lake, where it is trapped by rocks dislodged in its fall. Unfortunately, the expedition comes to an untimely end when the volcano erupts, coughing up smoke and lava and causing the monsters to run helter-skelter about the plateau, choking and falling into fissures. Trapped at the edge of a cliff, the adventurers would have met a similar fate had not Austin thought to send Paula's pet monkey up the mountainside with a rope ladder. With proper gallantry, Malone guards the rear while the others descend. It is a move which nearly costs him his life, as the ape man appears and begins to tug the ladder toward the ledge. Fortunately, sharpshooter Roxton is able to kill the brute and save Malone. Meanwhile, Challenger has found the brontosaur which fell from the cliff; it is alive and, convinced that no one will believe his story without living proof, he has the dinosaur caged and shipped to London. Unluckily, there is an accident in the British harbor which causes the crate to break and the monster to go free. Roaming the city streets more scared than aggressive, the animal levels buildings and crushes people until its weight proves too much for London Bridge and the span collapses beneath its weight. The creature is tossed into the water and, making for the open sea, heads for home. Meanwhile on the dock, Malone meets Gladys and learns that she could not wait for him to return and has married clerk Percy Bumberry. The reporter is now free to wed Paula. Their mutual love breaks Roxton's heart, but the nobleman maintains his dignity, wishes them well and, like Professor Challenger, moves on to other adventures.

Reviewing *The Lost World*, *Variety* echoed popular opinion of the film: "The photography, in itself, is a work that must have taken a tremendous amount of energy and patience to achieve. But no matter what the cost, either in labor or money, the results fully justify the means." Even the tough-to-please *New York Times* was impressed:

> *The Lost World* is an effort likely to provoke a great deal of discussion, as the movements of the dummies appear to be wonderfully natural. Some of the scenes are as awesome as anything that has ever been shown. There are several battles between different species of monsters, which are most effectively staged. In the initial scenes, these monsters were shown without any double exposure (*sic*) effects, and therefore their supposed huge dimensions could not be contrasted with human beings. Later, in the double exposures, the effect is remarkable. Through wonderful photographic skill and infinite patience in the camera work, Sir Arthur Conan Doyle's *The Lost World* makes a memorable motion picture.

One of the qualities which distinguishes the work of Willis O'Brien and Ray Harryhausen from that of most other special-effects personnel is their painstaking attention to detail. The sincere craftsperson realizes that it is the subtle, subconsciously perceived touches that can make or break a scene. And the roots of this professionalism originate with *The Lost World*. We have already mentioned the instance of the dinosaurs' breathing, but O'Bie knew that animals also salivate, and applied a glossy shellac, frame-by-frame, to simulate spittle. And, unlike the villains in a William S. Hart or Douglas Fairbanks movie, O'Bie wanted his creatures to bleed. For this he used chocolate syrup (which photographs like blood in black and white), progressively applied to all wounded or slaughtered beasts. O'Bie's gelatin water was also employed, and of course, his lifelike animation of the animals, from wicked snarls to cruelly snapping tails, was a breathtaking improvement over the limited expressiveness of the dinosaurs in *The Ghost of Slumber Mountain*. On the Lost World itself, superb mattes melded the five explorers with O'Bie's dinosaurs, glass paintings provided lush panoramic detail as well as the roiling skies and dramatic lighting during the volcano sequence. As for the eruption, it was worked without stop motion, the volcano being the five-foot-tall facade of a mountain. With a powerful lamp blazing through the crater from beneath the cutaway table-top set, smoke was piped through the boarded back of the miniature. Together, the surging cloud and sharp lighting produced a striking vision of the earth in upheaval. But awesome though these island scenes may be, they pale by comparison to the stunning climax of the brontosaur running amok in London. Set in the evening, dramatically illuminated by streetlamps, the rampage includes some marvelous scenes in which the monster pokes its head through the wall of a club and devastates its staid members, who are in the midst of a chess championship, a shot of the brontosaur suffering a burn while sniffing a lamppost, and a startling composite in which the dinosaur marches down a misty London street while thousands of people run in every direction, trying to get out of the creature's way. There was no skimping on these sequences. All of the outdoor live-action shots were staged under highly con-

trolled studio conditions, to give O'Bie exactly the lighting and action that he needed to match his monster footage. A pair of London streets was reproduced at the studio, over 600 feet long, they were stocked with two-hundred prop cars and a half dozen buses, with 2,000 extras fleeing the brontosaur which O'Bie would later add via traveling matte. The exterior of the Royal Museum was also reconstructed for the streetlight sequence. The scene in the club was worked with miniature models as the dinosaur approached the building, and with a lifesize sculpted head which technicians jammed through the wall of the chess tournament set. A full-scale mockup of the brontosaur's tail was also used to slap at a crowd of pedestrians.

Ultimately, *The Lost World* became one of the top-grossing films of the year. And it should have marked a turning point in the career of Willis O'Brien. After so many unfulfilling jobs, O'Bie had become the finest special effects artist in the world. While there were other giants in the field, such as Jackman, Norman Dawn, A. Arnold Gillespie, and others, none of them did more than exhibit supreme technical skill and occasional drama in scenes involving their miniature models, composite effects, or special mechanical gimmicks such as explosions, breakaway props, and so forth. But O'Bie, like Walt Disney, had turned interludes of fascination into a magnificent art form. There was literally no limit to the wonder which could be spun by his stop motion camera. The movies had their ticket to unique, big box office attractions. Unfortunately like most artists, O'Bie was to find himself at the mercy of people who hadn't the vision of Watterson Rothacker.

With the New York studios of First National as their base of operations, O'Bie and Ralph Hammeras decided to collaborate on a project that was certain to have the same widespread appeal as *The Lost World*: they would take viewers to a fantastic sunken continent in a motion picture entitled *Atlantis*. Working with Earl Hudson, the production supervisor on *The Lost World*, they conceived of a setting in which the submerged land had evolved a civilization living in awesome, torchlit caverns forming underwater air pockets. A network of tunnels allowed the Atlanteans to venture into the sea and gather food from the ocean bottom; special pills allowed them to breathe

A triceratops squares off with a styracosaur in *The Lost World*.

without the use of cumbersome diving equipment. The only danger of such forays lay in attacks by huge sea serpents which prowled the murky depths. Other hunts were conducted in the frozen northern reaches of Atlantis, where white-furred mastodons and other mammals were slaughtered and their meat kept literally "on ice" to feed the Atlanteans in times of famine. The government envisioned by the filmmakers was a monarchy, whose king was the master of an elite army that raided other nations for slaves.

O'Bie and Hammeras put in over three grueling months of preproduction work on *Atlantis*, drawing sketches and working out a plot wherein a group of modern-day explorers finds the long-hidden kingdom. However, this came at a time when First National was just realizing that the move to New York had been a mistake. Expenses were high, the weather was fickle, and so by 1926, they were busy constructing a new studio in Burbank. Early in 1927, Hammeras was transferred to the West Coast, Delgado was dismissed, and O'Bie was forced to accept a skimpy retaining salary. Hoping that better times would soon be upon them, Delgado, the man who so very much wanted an artist's career, took a job as a handyman at the studio—his nationality made him the object of scorn and snide jokes from the other workers— while O'Bie managed to survive on his modest stipend plus a $10,000 bonus given him by

Watterson Rothacker for his contribution to the success of *The Lost World*. It was, to say the least, another trying period for the animator. His relationship with Hazel worsened, he was once again drinking heavily, and he lost a great deal of money at the racetrack. Creatively, O'Bie managed within a year to produce drawings and a treatment for only an ill-fated film version of Mary Shelley's 1816 novel, *Frankenstein*. A movie based on H.G. Wells' *Food of the Gods* was also briefly considered, but studio executives were partial to *Frankenstein*. O'Bie's instincts about the property were correct: three years later, it made an enormously popular vehicle for Boris Karloff. As in the Karloff film, O'Bie planned to have an actor portray the Frankenstein monster. However, he intended to animate the creature in many long shots, thus enabling him to work feats of strength that would have been impossible for a human performer. Given the go-ahead to begin preproduction work, O'Bie was returned to the Burbank studio in 1929. Three months later, the film was dropped without explanation. Then, First National was sold to Warner Brothers—the outfit that had recently introduced the motion picture public to *Vitaphone*, the first sound film process—and O'Bie knew that his days at the studio were over. There were now more executives on hand, and O'Bie had learned one thing about studio heads: unless a proposal of his was actively supported by a producer with imagination, projects like *Atlantis* and *Frankenstein* were invariably considered too expensive for "novelty" films. *The Lost World*? A fluke, they would tell him as they proceeded to grind out soppy romances and routine action films. Rather than abandon fantasy filmmaking or watch his properties become entangled in red tape, O'Bie decided to move to another studio. He reasoned that things could not possibly be worse at Radio-Keith-Orpheum. He realized, too, that the time had come to face up to another impasse, that of his failed marriage. When he joined RKO in 1930, O'Bie severed relations with his wife. The children remained with Hazel, although O'Bie visited them whenever he was able.

At RKO, O'Bie was immediately given an okay to return to the motif that had brought him his greatest success, that of explorers vs. dinosaurs.

Thus, with Harry Hoyt, O'Bie devised a tale in the vein of *The Lost World* entitled *Creation*. The story concerns the adventures of a submarine expedition whose members are shipwrecked on a volcanic South American island. Going ashore, the sailors and their passengers—refugees from a storm-tossed yacht—are astounded to find a herd of brontosaurs and two battling triceratops. Shortly thereafter, members of the party sent to survey the island are attacked by a giant horned mammal known as an arsinoitherium, which chases the men onto a log that spans a deep ravine. Compounding their predicament is an attack by pterodactyls; as the arsinoitherium shakes the men from their treacherous perch, the winged dinosaurs snatch the remaining sailors for supper. Only one man survives: Steve, who came from the yacht and is in love with our heroine, the wealthy and snobbish Elaine. Returning to base camp, the resourceful young man takes charge of the remaining casta-ways. Weeks pass and, while Elaine softens toward Steve, the group builds a small hut and weathers numerous assaults by a variety of monsters. Meanwhile, gathering up the damaged wireless equipment from the sunken submarine, Steve, Elaine, her servant Bennie, and her brother Billy go looking for material with which to repair the unit, while Elaine's aunt and father mind the camp. Crossing the island, the foursome stumbles upon the ruins of an ancient temple and find it stocked with a fortune in gems. They also discover a pteranodon, which flies off with Elaine. Steve rescues the girl and the reunited party is attacked by a stegosaur. Hiding in the temple, it is their bad fortune to run into a ferocious tyrannosaur. Fortunately, the two dinosaurs have at one another and our heroes are able to escape. Fixing the transmitter, Steve sends out an SOS just as the island's volcano erupts. Monsters flee certain death in the boiling seas and the burning jungle; between the panicked dinosaurs and the holocaust, the brave castaways appear doomed. Luckily, a pair of aircraft which had received Steve's call for help arrives and rescues the adventurers.

RKO heads were pleased with the scenario for *Creation* and told O'Bie and Hoyt to begin production. However, everyone involved with the picture received instructions to refer to it only as

Willis O'Brien in his later years, tinkering with an armature.
Courtesy of Darlyne O'Brien.   © RKO General, Inc.

Jamboree; studio executives did not want the press or rival filmmakers getting wind of what the people behind *The Lost World* were cooking up now. But intrigue or no intrigue, O'Bie was overjoyed that the picture had been sold. And the first thing he did upon hearing the good news was hire Marcel Delgado to build the monsters. Delgado, who had returned to Los Angeles with O'Bie, was subsequently fired from his job at First National and went to work building props and miniature models for the William Fox studios. It is an understatement to say that he was thrilled with the opportunity to get back into the more challenging prehistoric melange. Forming a special production unit within RKO, O'Bie also commissioned artists Mario Larrinaga, Byron L. Crabbe, and Ernest Smythe to render *storyboards*—sketches showing how each shot of the script would look in the completed film. This detailed presentation let the special-effects team, set directors, and other key personnel know exactly what they were expected to produce. Meanwhile, O'Bie began practicing his mattes and animation with equipment that was considerably more sophisticated than it had been in the early twenties. Now that all films were being produced with sound, even his stop motion techniques had to be slightly modified. The mechanics of an optical soundtrack—the transcription of audio to lines which are printed on the film itself and then translated back to sound by the projector—dictated that the film be run at twenty-four frames-per-second rather than at the silent speed of sixteen frames-per-second. Thus, O'Bie had to orient himself to creating thirty percent more movement for every second of film. The walking, flapping, and even blinking cycles of his monsters had to be done with smaller incremental movements to achieve the same fluidity as before. Coordinating these various efforts called for the production of a test reel, and the scene chosen for filming showed a character named Hallett (Ralf Harolde) murdering a baby triceratops and being chased by its enraged parent. The results were extraordinary. The special effects and editing compacted more drama into a single reel than most features achieve in five reels! However, the footage was both time-consuming and expensive. By mid-1931, actual production had not yet gotten underway, but *Creation* had already cost RKO more than $100,000. Considering that an average feature film could have been made for that sum of money, RKO executives were rightfully perturbed. Nor was *Creation* their only worry. There was a Great Depression going on, and poor business had put RKO on the brink of bankruptcy. As a result, there were a number of sudden shake-ups in the organization, the most prominent of which was the resignation of William Le Baron, the vice president in charge of production. Unable to streamline the company and make it pay, he went to Paramount Pictures and was replaced by David O. Selznick, the man who would produce *Gone With the Wind* in 1939. To serve as his strong right arm, Selznick brought in a tough producer from New York, Merian C. Cooper. Cooper's first job was to analyze scripts and productions to decide whether they should be revised, allowed to continue, or dropped.

With the change in executives, O'Bie no doubt had sensed what was in the offing: the overbudget *Creation*, which promised to run up a tab of several million dollars before its completion, was canceled. Everyone in the special-effects department was crushed, although no one could have been more disappointed than O'Bie. He had now spent a total of six years chasing shadows, and the quick death to his happy year-long association with *Creation* was particularly painful. But Cooper realized that the aborted film and its maker were unique, and had plans for them both.

Big plans.

Advertising art for the original
release of *King Kong.*

26

CHAPTER THREE

The Eighth Wonder of the World

The late Merian Coldwell Cooper was one of film history's boldest, most adventurous figures. A much-decorated war hero, his moviemaking career began in September of 1922, when he was hired to join schooner captain Edward A. Salisbury as he shot movies around the world. To record their journeys, Cooper brought along another combat veteran, crackerjack newsreel cameraman Ernest B. Schoedsack. Unfortunately, after a year at sea, Salisbury's *Wisdom II* was destroyed by fire, along with the filmmakers' footage. Thereupon, Cooper and Schoedsack went to Paris with the idea of producing their own motion pictures. In particular, they wanted to make a documentary about the harsh life of peoples in the Middle East. The result was *Grass* (1925), a film shot in Turkey, Persia, and Syria. Their second film, *Chang* (1927), was filmed in Thailand and told the story of peasants battling both local carnivores and a herd of wild elephants. *The Four Feathers* (1929), starring Fay Wray and Richard Arlen, was their third coproduction, created in association with David O. Selznick. One of the last silent films, *The Four Feathers* is the story of an Englishman's heroism in the face of an African uprising. As per Cooper-Schoedsack tradition, the actors were filmed in Hollywood, but the African scenes were shot on location. However, after this film, Schoedsack went on to make other movies, while Cooper returned to New York to supervise the investment of his motion picture earnings in one of his great passions, the building of the two-year-old commercial aviation industry. In fact, Cooper was one of the early directors of the Pan American airline. But Cooper quickly became bored with life in business, and longed to return to motion picture making. So when Selznick sum-

moned him to join RKO, Cooper was happy to accept.

As he made the trip West, Cooper resolved that above all he must look into the possibility of making a movie based upon two ideas with which he had long been fascinated. One was the vision of a fifty foot tall ape battling biplanes from atop the newly completed Empire State Building in New York. The other was that of a lost world populated with huge lizards like the ten foot long dragons recently discovered on the Indonesian island of Komodo. In a vague scenario, Cooper had a notion of shooting scenes of gorillas in Africa, transporting an ape to Komodo to battle one of the great lizards, making them appear abnormally large through some form of camera magic, then filming the gorilla atop a model of the Empire State Building. The producer felt that this project could represent what he referred to as "the ultimate in adventure," magnifying, through fiction, the thunderous spectacle of the earlier Cooper-Schoedsack works. However, as Cooper well knew, the trouble with his property would be the expense required to mount the requisite expedition. Thus, it was with no small enthusiasm that Cooper viewed the *Creation* reel at RKO. The producer realized that O'Bie could bring his incredible monster film to the screen without ever leaving Hollywood! Thus, in the midst of evaluating the work being done at the studio, he asked O'Bie to have four sketches drawn of the proposed action. Cooper presented these to Selznick and, in a memo dated December 19, 1931, suggested the filming of tests to see how lifelike O'Bie's stop motion techniques could make what he called "The Giant Terror Gorilla." Selznick gave Cooper full reign, and the

An O'Brien-Crabbe sketch of the King Kong-tyrannosaur
confrontation. © RKO General, Inc.

The O'Brien-Crabbe interpretation of King Kong razing
Manhattan.

A preproduction painting of King Kong crashing through the gates of the native village. © RKO General, Inc.

A scene from the *King Kong* test reel. This shot did not appear in the finished film. © RKO General, Inc.

An early concept of King Kong.　　© RKO General, Inc.

first, tentative steps toward the filming of *King Kong* had been taken.

Since there wasn't a story, O'Bie went looking for appropriately dynamic scenes to film: he found them, quite literally, under his nose. He would refilm two of the sequences devised for *Creation*, showing the sailors trapped on the log and the tyrannosaur battle. However, instead of the arsinoitherium and stegosaur, respectively, the star of these scenes would be the enormous ape. The producer agreed with O'Bie's selection, and had Delgado fashion a clay likeness of the gorilla. When a sufficiently ferocious animal had been devised, Delgado built the gorilla's skeleton or *armature* from an aluminum alloy, attaching rubber pieces to the limbs so that they would stretch and bulge like real muscles. The framework was then padded with cotton which Delgado sculpted to the desired shape. A coat of liquid latex gave Kong his skin, while rabbit fur was used to create the ape's shaggy exterior. Meanwhile, O'Brien and his team readied miniature jungle sets in which glass paintings—often several layers thick and spaced several feet apart to give the setting depth—provided the exotic

A Crabbe-O'Brien sketch of King Kong killing the pterodactyl... © RKO General, Inc.

...and how that same scene looked in the completed film. © RKO General, Inc.

expanses of flora. Then, using Delgado's monkey and the tyrannosaur from *Creation*, O'Bie animated the fight. As always, he did the stop motion work by himself, although an assistant was on hand to creep beneath the tabletop to help fasten the shifting models to the miniature set. To stage the live-action scenes, Cooper borrowed the jungle sets and two of the stars—Robert Armstrong and Fay Wray—from his low-budget thriller *The Most Dangerous Game* (1932), then in production at the studio. These full-scale sequences were important not only for the test reel; they included the first *rear-screen projection* shot ever undertaken by the studio. It was a bit of wizardry that would figure prominently in the making of the monkey epic. Pioneered in the 1910s by special effects innovator Norman O. Dawn, this process allowed actors to appear in foreign settings without ever leaving the studio, and in many cases eliminated the need for mattes by flawlessly merging the players with miniature sets. In essence, the prefilmed background footage is projected onto a large translucent screen. Due to the semilucid nature of this surface, the projected image is visible from *both* the front and rear of the screen. The miniature scene has thus been enlarged to lifesize. Next, the camera and performers are placed on the *opposite* side of the screen, so as not to block the projector's oncoming light. When viewed through the camera lens, the actors and rear-projected image appear to be one scene. Of course, the lighting on the foreground action must be carefully done to avoid creating glare on the screen, and both the camera and projector must be perfectly synchronized so that the shutter of one is open at the exact moment a frame of film is being exposed. Too, the projector must be rock-steady, since any jostling of the film would be highly magnified onscreen. However, beyond its comparative simplicity, the rear-screen process has an advantage over the matte in allowing the player to *see* the menace to which he or she is reacting. For the test reel, Ms. Wray has been fitted in the limb of a tall tree by Kong, who has gone off to shake the sailors from the log. The rear-screen sequence showed her waiting nervously for the ape's return when a tyrannosaur appears to sup on our heroine. The girl's screams alert Kong, and the ape does away with the monster.

The stop motion and special effects work were completed within a few months, and early in 1932 Cooper presented his test reel to the RKO executives. There was a great deal riding on their reaction. Not only was Cooper's pet project on the line, but if it failed to sell, O'Bie, Delgado, and many of their associates would be fired to cut down on studio overhead. Fortunately, the footage was an unqualified hit, and Cooper was told to make his ape film.

Calling the simian star aborning King Kong was the idea of Cooper and popular mystery writer Edgar Wallace. Wallace had been commissioned by the producer to develop the property into a screenplay, and the name that Wallace suggested was King Ape. Cooper liked the 'King' title, but didn't care for the cognomen 'Ape.' Dipping into his knowledge of primitive tongues, he selected the more regal and mysterious-sounding 'Kong,' which meant gorilla in the language of East Indian natives. As for the plot, Cooper had already decided to tell a story in the timeless and highly commercial vein of *Beauty and the Beast*, but was content to leave the details to Wallace. Unfortunately, with the author's untimely death from pneumonia on February 10, 1932, whatever unique approach Wallace may have taken to *King Kong* died with him. (For example, in his first draft of the story, Denham was a circus impresario.) Thereafter, the scripting chores fell to James Creelman, and when he was unable to condense his long stretches of dialogue, the job went to Ruth Rose. Ms. Rose not only reworked the script, but made the film a family affair: her husband, who was busy directing *The Most Dangerous Game*, had agreed to direct the ape film. And who *better* to guide this awesome undertaking than Ernest B. Schoedsack!

Known during its year-long shooting schedule under the successive titles *The Beast*, *The Eighth Wonder*, and finally *King Kong*, after its featured player, the film was actually a vicarious fantasy for both Cooper and Schoedsack. They 'live' the adventure through the main character, motion picture producer Carl Denham (Robert Armstrong). Denham is about to embark on a voyage to shoot the greatest animal action film of all time. However, the producer wants to give *this* picture a pretty face, something his previous films had been

Carl Denham prepares to hurl a gas bomb at the oncoming King Kong.   © RKO General, Inc.

King Kong tears down the elevated train. Note people and lights in windows of buildings: this is something the producers of the remake didn't bother to include when redoing the sequence. Color like this can often make or break a scene. © RKO General, Inc.

without. Unfortunately, none of the theatrical agents can get him an actress with enough backbone for the proposed trip to an uncharted region of the East Indies. So the night before the freighter *Venture* is to sail, Denham haunts the streets of Depression-ridden New York to find a girl for his film. There, he happens upon a lovely young miss being accosted by a vendor for trying to steal an apple. Struck by her beauty, Denham gives the fruitman a dollar and spirits the girl away. Buying her a cup of coffee, he learns that her name is Ann Darrow (Fay Wray) and that she will be only too

happy to star in his picture—no matter what the danger.

Setting sail under the command of Capt. Englehorn (Frank Reicher), the ship cruises east for several weeks until, far west of Sumatra, it arrives at the ominous Skull Island. There, it is rumored, the savages live in fear of an awesome god known as Kong. Going ashore with his cameras, crew, and Ann, Denham films a native ceremony in which a young girl is apparently being prepared for some form of sacrifice. However, the intruders are discovered and the ritual celebration stops. The

King Kong breaks his bonds in a Manhattan theatre.
Courtesy the British Film Institute.   © RKO General, Inc.

aboriginal chief (Noble Johnson) offers Denham six of his women for the golden haired Ann, whom he wants as the bride of Kong. Denham refuses, and the filmmakers return to the ship. That night, the islanders sail to the anchored *Venture* and kidnap the girl. Dragged beyond a great wall and bound between two pillars, Ann is terrified to hear a crunching of foliage followed by the appearance of a huge gorilla. The ape snatches her up and disappears into the jungle. Meanwhile, finding a native bracelet on the ship and surmising what has happened, the foreigners head for the island. They arrive just as Kong is leaving. Separating into two parties, one group remains in the village while its complement follows the awesome ape.

Led by Denham, the group tailing the gorilla has its problems. Attacked by a plated stegosaur, they slay the creature only to be threatened by a long-necked brontosaur. Several of the men are slaughtered by the serpentine beast. Shortly thereafter, the survivors find Kong who, placing Ann in a tree limb, traps the sailors on a log that spans a monster-infested gorge. Most of the men are spilled from the limb, although Denham and Ann's lover Jack Driscoll (Bruce Cabot) are spared Kong's fury by the timely arrival of a tyrannosaur. As Kong battles the monster, Denham agrees to return to the village for help while Driscoll stays with the gorilla. He follows the ape to his mountaintop lair, watching as the simian fights a plesiosaur and then a pteranodon, which has tried to carry Ann away. During this latter struggle, the *Venture's* first mate is able to reach the girl's side and sneaks her down a vine and into a river. Enraged with their escape, Kong sets off in pursuit. He dogs them to the native settlement, muscles through the gate of the great wall, and stomping through the huts of his subjects, finds Denham waiting on the beach with a knockout bomb. The filmmaker hurls the grenade and Kong goes down. But Denham is not content: he sees a fortune in King Kong and builds a raft to float the behemoth to New York. Exhibiting the gorilla in a Broadway theatre, Denham learns a valuable lesson about the best laid plans of mice and moguls. As photographers arrive to take opening night pictures of Ann, her fiancé Driscoll, and Kong, the ape thinks that the flashbulbs are intended to hurt his bride. He

begins to roar and, as Driscoll spirits Ann away, breaks his bonds. Tearing apart people and buildings in search of the girl, the gorilla finally finds her in an hotel room. Smacking Driscoll senseless, Kong grabs Ann and, after destroying an elevated train, carries her to the top of the highest point in the city, the Empire State Building. Keeping track of Kong's progress on a radio at police headquarters, Driscoll thinks to attack the ape with airplanes. The officers agree, and Kong finds himself beset by four strange, stinging pteranodons. Their guns pump volley after volley into the ape and, before too long, Kong realizes that he is doomed. Caressing Ann for a final time, his throat is ripped by a vicious salvo. Glancing toward the ground nearly a quarter mile below, the great ape releases his grip on the tower and falls to his death.

By February 25, 1933, the date of *King Kong's* world premiere, David O. Selznick had moved to MGM and Merian C. Cooper was in charge of RKO. And so, the film's colossal success at the box office was a double-edged triumph: it was a fine reflection on Cooper's regime, as well as justification for his long-time belief in the project. Artistically, the picture was a feather in the cap of Ernest B. Schoedsack. Produced for just over $500,000, *King Kong* looked considerably more expensive. Thoroughly entertaining, with a brilliant build-up to Kong's first appearance, and a subsequent pace that barrels the viewer headlong from thrill to thrill, we can devote several volumes to a complete study of the film. However, as we noted in our Introduction, *King Kong* is, above all, the creative legacy of Willis H. O'Brien.

O'Bie had his disagreements with Cooper, quitting the film on several occasions over the question of Kong's character and design. But when O'Bie was alone with his model, the personal and professional clashes fled and he put his heart into Kong. As his second wife, Darlyne, recently explained, "O'Bie's personality shone through in everything he made King Kong do. I could see his sense of humor in everything Kong did. I am absolutely certain no one will be able to put into a picture what O'Bie did." What did O'Bie do to make King Kong one of the great tragic figures in film history? The story, of course, gave him the material

THE PICTURE THAT STAGGERS THE IMAGINATION

The *beaten copper* cover of the *King Kong* press book, which was included as
a supplement in the industry publication *The Hollywood Reporter*.

The poster for a *King Kong* reissue.   © RKO General, Inc.

King Kong vs. Godzilla (1963)—but it's a man in a monkey suit. © Toho International

Dino de Laurentiis' *King Kong*—in this shot, an inert, fur-covered styrofoam giant. © Paramount Pictures

with which to work. Kong was a deity toppled from his throne because of affection for Ann. Sure, other giants have fallen from heights for the love of a woman or man. But never had it been an exploited animal, something that gave Kong a headstart in the race for audience sympathy. And seldom did the film permit Kong to be other than proud and just, rarely having him attack a native, sailor, or dinosaur unless provoked. Yet, in itself, this broad character outline was not enough to make King Kong a classic screen personality. After all, Dino de Laurentiis used the same story, but his Halloween party ape evoked more laughs than sentiment. O'Bie, on the other hand, used his skills as a stop motion animator to wring *life* from the cotton and latex model.

Perhaps the greatest quality that O'Bie brought to *King Kong* was the entirely appropriate gift of melodrama. The stop motion gorilla was able to make such exaggerated movements as beating his chest while roaring or pounding the ground with his fist when angry—gestures that would have appeared ludicrous if undertaken by an ape actor. The epic role of the mythological god *called for* the robust and highly stylized caricature of an ape. However, what gave this framework its more sensitive depth were such distinctive stop motion touches as Kong's fangy snarl, erect human gait, fully expressive face, and the unavoidable borrowing of O'Bie's own mannerisms. This made him a character of considerable pathos and hubris. Add to that his scriptural status as the victim of greedy circumstance, and you have a figure of genuinely tragic dimension. Indeed, it would not have been so far out of line to award O'Bie a Best Actor Oscar for his surrogate performance as King Kong!

Had O'Bie's contribution to the special effects of *King Kong* been nothing more than this vivid and eloquent animation, the work would still have been classic. But O'Bie was also involved with the miniature designs and multiple exposure techniques. Supervising Delgado on the character models, Larrinaga and Crabbe on the glass paintings, assistant animator E.B. Gibson, and technicians Fred Reefe, Orville Goldner, and Carroll Shepphird, he created the rankest jungle and most virtuoso scenes of a monster on the loose

that the cinema has ever seen. To do this, however, required no small amount of ingenuity.

One of the more important processes devised for *King Kong* was a variation of rear-screen projection known as *miniature-screen projection*. Instead of creating a huge image of a background scene, a small screen was placed in a miniature set, onto which the full-scale settings and actors were projected a frame at a time. With the prefilmed action frozen on the miniature screen, the model was posed, a single frame of raw stock was exposed to record the entire setting, the miniature-projected footage was advanced another frame, the model was again manipulated, another exposure was made, and so forth. In this fashion, it was possible to shoot long shots of Fay Wray tied to the native altar as Kong came crashing through the trees, or to insert the actress in scenes of Kong battling miniature-projected and wire-supported model biplanes on the scaled-to-size Empire State Building set. Even the mattes were much improved over what had previously been done, *King Kong* benefiting from the newly invented *optical printer*. A camera-projector unit, the optical printer simultaneously and precisely exposed both the positive of the background footage and the opaque matte of the new element to a fresh negative. This negative recorded the background save where the matte had left it unexposed. Then, on a second pass through the optical printer, the new negative was exposed to the positive of the element being superimposed, thus completing the composite.

However, the optical effects crew wasn't alone in treading new ground. For Delgado's part, he had more to do than build the miniature models. Although Ann Darrow in Kong's grip was usually executed with a four inch long stop motion figure, the sculptor helped build a full-size working replica of the ape's hand. Operated by studio technicians positioned off-camera, this intricately geared mechanism was used for close-ups showing Fay Wray being held by the monster. For example, it figured prominently in the scene where Kong snatches Ann from her New York hotel room. With stop motion footage of the scowling Kong rear-projected behind one window, the mechanical paw was shoved through a second window,

Robert Armstrong bandages The Son of Kong's finger—wounded in their defense—with a piece of Helen Mack's slip.

A rear-screen shot from *Son of Kong.* The rear screen meets the floor of the soundstage just above Miss Mack's shoe.

A publicity shot from *Son of Kong* featuring Robert Armstrong, Helen Mack, and a styracosaur.

brushing actor Cabot aside and snatching up the girl. The hand was also used in a marvelous scene wherein Kong, sitting on a ledge outside his Skull Island cave, examines his fair-skinned bride, peeling off her clothes and sniffing them with natural curiosity. In this sequence, the footage of Ms. Wray in the paw—her clothing actually being torn away by wires—was miniature-projected behind the Kong model. The ape figurine was positioned in profile so that its own right arm was not visible, the life-size mock-up appearing to be an extension of the miniature. For this scene, it was imperative that O'Bie plan the movements of the model Kong's fingers to coincide with the stripping away of Fay Wray's clothing.

Delgado also worked on two other mechanical props: the life-sized head of Kong which, with its rolling eyes and grinding jaws, was used in a few menacing close-ups—most notably, the rather grotesque scene wherein Kong plucks a New Yorker from the battered train, chomps him to pulp, and spits him out—and a full-scale model of Kong's foot, briefly seen as it ground a Skull Island native into the mud. Among the sculptor's other

43

responsibilities were to help dress the sets with miniature props and trees, including the log from which Kong shook the brave men of the *Venture*.

The special effects in *King Kong* were all crafted with the kind of attention to detail that we mentioned in our discussion of *The Lost World*. Small, atmospheric touches made Kong's jungle come alive: stop motion birds flitting through the trees, a steaming pool of lava sitting almost unseen beside a stream in Kong's cave—the water itself being the Los Angeles River matted into the miniature set—lesser animals feasting on the remains of the smitten tyrannosaur as Driscoll edges by, and so on. The animator's New York miniatures were filled with matted extras screaming from apartment windows or scurrying underfoot, and there was even a promotional banner for Cooper's movie *Chang* attached to the elevated train.

Carefully and lovingly crafted, the heavily advertised *King Kong* saved RKO from bankruptcy. Accordingly, delighted studio heads gave Cooper their approval to shoot a sequel. However, he was given only nine months to ready the film for Christmas 1933 release and, for some mysterious reason, was allotted less than *half* the budget of *King Kong*! Cooper was alarmed. While the special effects would, of course, improve with the experience gained on *King Kong*, there was no way to recreate the grandeur and drive of the original film for $250,000. But the executives were adamant. So Cooper and Ruth Rose decided to approach the new film, *Son of Kong*, as a light-hearted fantasy, telling the tale of a twelve foot tall, white-furred Skull Island ape.

Truly, success seemed to be a curse for O'Bie. It was always followed by a decline rather than an improvement in his fortunes. When he protested to Cooper that the new film would fail as a pseudocomedy, he was told that this was how it must be. Extremely resentful about what amounted to a take-it-or-leave-it attitude, O'Bie took it, feeling all the while that without Kong's "chutzpah," the puppy-pure, wide-eyed Son of Kong would never win public approval.

The plot crafted by Cooper and Ms. Rose had Denham (Robert Armstrong) and Englehorn (Frank Reicher) flee to the China Seas to avoid the many lawsuits spurred by King Kong's tear through New York. Using the *Venture* to carry freight from island to island, they learn about a treasure hidden on Skull Island. Hastening to Kong's home—and carrying a stowaway, a young entertainer named Hilda (Helen Mack)—the crew finds the kindly Son of Kong, whom they rescue from quicksand and who, in turn, saves them from various prehistoric animals and helps them locate the treasure. However, an earthquake strikes and, while Denham and the gorilla are gathering up the wealth, the rest of the party hurries to a rowboat. Skull Island begins to sink, and the ape's foot is caught in a fissure; unable to save himself, the Son of Kong holds Denham above the churning waters until Englehorn can row close enough to save him. With enough money now to pay his creditors, Denham plans to marry Hilda, something made possible only by the self-sacrificing gorilla.

Although the animation and *Son of Kong* was slick, and the composite work even better than it had been in *King Kong*, the picture lacked the grit, romance, and soul of the original. And, as O'Bie had predicted, the film was only a modest box office draw. However, the creative bind that had grown at RKO was far from O'Bie's most pressing concern. O'Bie's son William had been left permanently blind by a tubercular infection in his eyes, and Hazel, it was learned, had both tuberculosis and cancer. Her physicians prescribed a variety of drugs, which dulled both the pain *and* her judgment; as a result, on October 7, 1933, she took a gun and shot both her sons and herself. William did not live long enough for the ambulance to reach him, and Willis Jr. died en route to the Santa Monica Hospital. Only Hazel survived, crying to her doctors, "My husband is not to blame in any way. I just couldn't sleep, and there was no one to leave the kids with." As the hours crept by, it became clear that the gunshot wound had drained Hazel's diseased lung and actually *prolonged* her life. Since this was the last thing that the woman wanted, she refused to eat and had to be force-fed by hospital interns. Shortly thereafter, she was moved to the prisoner's ward of the Los Angeles General Hospital. Despite pressure from the district attorney's office, the county grand jury would not indict her until she was well enough to appear in court. Her trial was scheduled and postponed numerous times. Then, on November 16, 1934, Hazel O'Brien took a sudden turn for the worse and died. A day later, O'Bie married Darlyne Prenett, whom he had been dating since March.

The marriage to Darlyne kept O'Bie from dwelling on the tragedies of the past year. Professionally, he busied himself with Merian C. Cooper's *The Last Days of Pompeii* (1935), for which he masterminded the climactic cataclysm. But the film was a short-lived respite from his disappointments. After contributing to the special effects of *The Dancing Pirate* (1936), O'Bie spent the next two years out of work. Then, a summons from Merian C. Cooper, who had since moved to MGM, involved the animator in a potential blockbuster adventure film entitled *The War Eagles*. Based on an idea by Cooper, *The War Eagles* told the tale of historian Hiram P. Cobb who is convinced that there are Vikings alive in an unexplored region of the North Pole. Since he hasn't the backing for a substantive expedition, Cobb hires pilot Jimmy Mathews to fly him to the Arctic. When their plane is crippled by a fifteen-foot-tall white eagle, the explorers set down in a surprisingly warm region at the top of the world, where they discover Nordic peoples living as they had centuries before. While Mathews is busy falling in love with a young lady named Naru, Cobb learns that eagles like the one they had encountered are flown to the Valley of the Ancients, where the Vikings gather soil for crops. Mathews joins his hosts on one such hunt, during which they are attacked by an allosaur. Dispatching the monster, they fly off and are engaged by a pteranodon. Defeating this second creature, they return to the settlement. Meanwhile, having repaired the plane radio, the pilot learns that Germany has subjected the United States to a ray that neutralizes all electrical impulses. Hearing that enemy planes and zeppelins are attacking the crippled American continent, Mathews and Cobb stir the Vikings to action. Mounting their war eagles, the primitive warriors speed South, engaging and defeating the foreign air force in the skies over New York.

As always, Cooper needed a test reel to sell the film to his money people. To do this, he had Marcel Delgado build models of several eagles and the allosaur, and O'Bie filmed a ten-minute sequence from the Valley of the Ancients episode. Cooper was thrilled with the footage, but *The War Eagles*

was destined never to be made. When Hitler invaded Poland in September of 1939, and pushed mankind into the abyss of a new World War, Cooper reenlisted in the air corps. *The War Eagles* was put on a back burner. By the end of hostilities, the critical plot element of American-German antagonism had become dated, and the picture was dropped. However, O'Bie had learned always to have several irons in the fire at any given time. So while waiting for word on *The War Eagles*, he had been working on another project, an original scenario entitled *Gwangi*.

Gwangi was the story of a group of cowboys who discover a tyrannosaur living in the Grand Canyon. Roping the monster, they plan to display it at the Wild West Show to which they are attached. Placing the beast in a reinforced cage, they learn that dinosaurs are extraordinarily powerful: during a show, some lions escape and attack the tyrannosaur. Laying ruin to his prison, the monster batters the felines and terrorizes the small southwestern town. He is finally forced from a cliff by a truck. *Gwangi* went into production at RKO, and Delgado and O'Bie spent almost a year building models of the tyrannosaur and lions and drawing storyboards, respectively. However, the picture was dropped in 1942 so that the less costly *Little Orphan Annie* could be accomodated on the production schedule.

Even the love and support of Darlyne did not lessen the hurt of the back-to-back demise of *The War Eagles* and *Gwangi*. Nor could the fifty-six-year-old O'Bie lose himself in work. Wartime Hollywood no longer had access to the lucrative foreign market, and was playing it safe with low-budget features—films for which the animator's skills were hardly needed. Thus, O'Bie was both frustrated and relieved when he was asked to move to Chicago in May of 1942 to produce classified films for the navy, a position he held until November of 1943. Upon returning to Hollywood, he found money so scarce that he was willing to accept any technical work he could find. On one occasion, he even rendered a glass painting during an artists' strike, sneaking the piece past a picket line to an RKO soundstage.

With the end of World War II came hope for a new prosperity. Cooper and Schoedsack had rejoined forces and were preparing to shoot a new gorilla film. They asked O'Bie to create the special effects. The picture was *Mr. Joseph Young of Africa*, later called *The Great Joe Young* and finally *Mighty Joe Young*, and it would win O'Bie the Oscar for Best Special Effects in 1949. It also gave young Ray Harryhausen his first feature film assignment, serving as O'Bie animation assistant. It is a film we will examine at greater length in Chapter Five. Following the movie's completion, plans were formulated to shoot *Joe Meets Tarzan*, pitting the ten-foot-tall gorilla against Lex Barker as Edgar Rice Burroughs' jungle hero. Unfortunately, *Mighty Joe Young* posted disappointing grosses, and the sequel was shelved. However, O'Bie had another film ready to roll, a property which had been bought by Jesse L. Lasky and Paramount Pictures. In 1944, O'Bie and Darlyne had written a story entitled *Emilio and Guloso*, which they renamed *El Toro Estrella*, the saga of a twelve-year-old Mexican boy named Emilio, who takes a bull as a pet. The lad becomes very fond of the animal, and is understandably crushed when his impoverished father sells it to one Señor Garzon to fight in the ring. Resolving to strike a deal with Garzon, Emilio has him promise to return the bull and pay 1,000 pesos if he and his Indian friends can capture a dinosaur that is alleged to inhabit a primordial valley. Garzon agrees, and the young adventurers track down and snare the creature, a tyrannosaur. However, as the monster caravan nears the village, the beast escapes and causes considerable damage. Faced with no alternative, Emilio frees Guloso, who kills the dinosaur but is himself mortally wounded. His head cradled in the young boy's arms, the brave bull dies. In a subsequent treatment of the story, Garzon reneges on his promise and it is Emilio himself who frees the tyrannosaur.

By April of 1950, a great deal of preproduction work had been completed on the film, which was now known as *The Valley of Mist*, after the dinosaur's home. A script had been written by Richard Landau, and both O'Bie and Ray Harryhausen had done detailed drawings of key scenes. However, Lasky was unable to muster the necessary funds for what was planned as a multimillion-dollar color production, and the property was optioned by producers William and Edward Nassour. They retitled the work *Ring Around Saturn* and had a new script written, but the project died a few

months later. Following the collapse of this film, O'Bie developed a number of new and most unusual properties, including a proposed motion picture in which the Marx Brothers discover a giant Pelican, and a monster epic called *The Leviathan*. This latter film ironically anticipated the *King Kong* remake, as an oil company goes searching by submarine for new sources of fuel and accidentally unleashes incredible beasts upon the world. When these projects dissolved, O'Bie was called back to work by Merian C. Cooper, who asked him to come up with a screen treatment for *Food of the Gods*. The picture was canceled early-on.

Then Cooper became involved with the travelogue *This Is Cinerama* (1952)—the first film to use the wide-screen process—and put O'Bie on the payroll to create a few special effects, but primarily to explore the possibility of remaking *King Kong* in the audience-participation system. However, the success of the travelogues—there were five in all—killed *King Kong* as well as delayed the creation of fiction films in Cinerama until 1962 when, ironically, MGM and fantasy filmmaker George Pal released *The Wonderful World of the Brothers Grimm*, an effort which relied heavily on stop motion photography (see chapter 17). Yet, there were even more dulling blows to come. O'Bie's drawings and an outline for a television series were examined and rejected by a variety of producers. Dubbed *The Westernettes*, the show was about giant children riding the range astride equally large ponies. O'Bie had as little success selling plans for a pair of amusement park rides. The first of these was to have featured mechanical horses on which youngsters would "chase" rear-projected bank robbers. The second idea was submitted to Walt Disney, who was just beginning the construction of Disneyland. The animator suggested a simulated trip to the moon: passengers seated in a mock spaceship would watch the sights of space and our natural satellite on a wrap-around motion picture screen. Naturally, this footage would have included an appearance by the monstrous Lunasaur. Unfortunately, Disney already had a similar attraction in the works. Returning to film, the animator wrote a story called *The Beast of Hollow Mountain*, about rival cattle ranchers Hank Oliver and Jim Larkin. When Oliver

The Giant Behemoth.   © Allied Artists

is found murdered, Larkin is the natural suspect. However, he claims that the deed was done by a tyrannosaur which lives in a nearby cavern. Sheriff Dean Roberts checks out Larkin's claim and discovers the monster; trapping the beast, he and his men bring it to town to prove Larkin's innocence. However, the dinosaur works itself free and, after ravaging the countryside, is skewered by Roberts on a huge stake. Since the Nassour brothers had shown an interest in his previous monster story, O'Bie brought them the property. And they bought it, shooting the film in 1956. However, looking for a shorter production schedule than O'Bie's meticulous work would have required, they hired Jack Rabin and Louis De Witt to handle the stop motion, with only fair results (see photograph in chapter 17).

After this barren and bitter seven-year period,

O'Bie found it satisfying to work with Ray Harryhausen on *Animal World* (1956). An early effort by producer Irwin Allen—who went on to mastermind such top-grossing pictures as *The Poseidon Adventure* and *The Towering Inferno—Animal World* was a documentary about the evolution of life on earth (see Chapter 8). This was followed by a pair of uninspired monster-on-the-loose films, the shoestring productions *The Black Scorpion* (1957) and *The Giant Behemoth* (1958). *The Black Scorpion* was a giant arachnid freed from its subterranean cavern by a volcano; it went on a destructive spree in Mexico City before suffering a fatal fire-bombing at the hands of the military. *The Giant Behemoth* was a member of the brontosaur family who took out his aggressions on London, eventually succumbing to a radioactive torpedo. Both films were animated by O'Bie and Pete

47

A mechanical model of *The Black Scorpion* used exclusively in close-ups. © Warner Communications

Peterson, an associate from *Mighty Joe Young.* However, the pictures' budgets were so limited that the stop motion scenes for each were completed in a mere three months, many of the sequences being shot in Peterson's garage! Yet, even these pictures were a godsend compared with what lay ahead.

For obvious reasons, both *The Lost World* and *King Kong* held a special place in O'Bie's heart. Thus, it was particularly agonizing for the animator to mark nearly a half-century in motion pictures with disappointments involving these two films. In 1960, O'Bie was signed to oversee the special effects on a color remake of *The Lost World.* O'Bie was delighted with the prospect, and drew dozens of sketches showing the monsters in action. Then he

learned that producer Irwin Allen intended to have living lizards portray the ancient reptiles. Allen knew from *Animal World* how long stop motion photography takes, and didn't want *The Lost World* to be tied up in over a year of postproduction special-effects work. Nor would the climax feature a brontosaur razing London; the picture was to end with Professor Challenger (Claude Rains) grabbing a baby dinosaur and leaving the Lost World. Allen was saving the original conclusion for a possible sequel. O'Bie objected, but his sensible argument that lizards with plastic frills do not look like dinosaurs went unheeded. It was then the animator realized that he had been hired for the prestige of his name, and made only a minimal contribution to

The Beast from Hollow Mountain

© United Artists

The Giant Behemoth threatens London's Westminster Abbey.

© Allied Artists

49

One of the lizards used to represent a dinosaur in Irwin
Allen's remake of *The Lost World.* © Twentieth Century Fox

the film. Hard on the heels of this upset, O'Bie decided that enough was enough. He would create his greatest work, teaming two classic monsters in *King Kong vs. Frankenstein*. O'Bie's plot had a descendant of the infamous Dr. Frankenstein build a fifty-foot-tall monster in an African jungle laboratory. When the gartantuan creature escapes, his reign of terror reaches the ears of some shrewd San Francisco hucksters. Realizing that there is money to be made on the giant, the Californians have him captured. Simultaneously, an expedition to Skull Island finds and snares King Kong. Like the showmen who have caught the new Frankenstein monster, the ape's captors intend to show their find in the Bay Area. Thus, plans are made to display the monsters together in an outdoor stadium. Inevitably, the leviathans burst from their cages and fight one another to the death.

Completing his text and art presentation, the first thing O'Bie did was to bring it to RKO's Daniel O'Shea, who handled the licensing rights to King Kong. O'Shea thought the film had promise, and suggested that O'Bie take it to producer John Beck. Beck put a writer on the project, changed the name to *King Kong vs. Prometheus*, and promised to keep O'Bie informed on the status of the script and the financing. Months passed, and the next time that O'Bie heard of his project or Beck was when he read in *Variety* that the producer was making *King Kong vs. Godzilla* at the Toho studios in Japan, with King Kong being portrayed by a man in an ape costume! It was a shattering turn of events. Fortunately, O'Bie had little time to dwell on it. Both he and Marcel Delgado had just been hired to execute a clutch of stop motion sequences for Stanley Kramer's Cinerama comedy *It's A Mad, Mad, Mad, Mad World* (1963). The segments involved long shots of the featured players as they balanced precariously on a fire escape and a ladder.

On the afternoon of November 8, 1962, shortly after joining the Kramer film, the seventy-six-year-old O'Bie left the studio early, complaining that he did not feel well. O'Bie went home and took a nap, ate dinner with Darlyne, and then settled down to watch television. Moments later, Darlyne heard O'Bie gasp and saw him fall to his side. She called the hospital and an ambulance arrived within minutes—but it was too late. A heart attack had taken the life of Willis O'Brien. His body was cremated and his ashes placed in Los Angeles' Chapel of the Pines.

"When I first met O'Bie," Darlyne O'Brien told me, "I did not know what his work was. And when he asked me if I had seen *King Kong*, I shuddered and said, 'Ugh—*no*! I *hate* those horror pictures!' He sort of smiled and said, 'Oh, I don't think you'll hate *King Kong*.' Nothing more was said about it, and it was about six or eight months after we were married that it was running in a small theatre on a side street. We went to see it, and I loved it. I'm so sorry he didn't realize how great *King Kong* had become before he died—but I'm sure he knows now."

At best, Willis O'Brien was a man who handled his medium with the same genius that moved Michelangelo to bear a hammer and chisel or Chopin to draw blood and tears from a piano. He used his articulated figurines to personify brilliantly the emotions that filled his spirit. Likewise, O'Bie suffered because his values were out of joint with those of the rest of society. He placed too much trust in unimaginative producers, people who put the dollar before the dream. Yet, *sticking* to those values, O'Bie was able to accomplish that of which most of us only dream: he developed an art form, and in *King Kong*, created an artistic masterpiece.

Of course, our adoration of *King Kong* cannot erase the defeats O'Bie endured. But it certainly justifies the faith he maintained in both himself and in his art. We can only hope that Darlyne O'Brien is right: "I'm sure he knows now."

Ray Harryhausen today, posing before preproduction drawings from his various films. Photo taken in Mr. Harryhausen's home by the author.

CHAPTER FOUR

Ray Harryhausen

"I first saw *King Kong* quite by accident. My aunt was a nurse and she was taking care of Sid Grauman's invalid mother. She was given three tickets for an afternoon performance of some strange film called *King Kong*. I didn't know what it was about—I was young and hadn't read too much about it. So my aunt kindly invited my mother and myself to see this film at Grauman's Chinese Theatre. I haven't been the same since."

In most every facet of life today the term "inspiration" is generally as meaningless as its companion terms "quality" and "professionalism." Yet, these traits still have value to Ray Harryhausen, who cut his eyeteeth on the motion picture that may very well be the supreme definition of inspired filmmaking. Indeed, because of *King Kong's* towering example of excellence, both the film and its creator became Ray's heroes. "I know that the word "hero" is considered an old fashioned and useless word today, but O'Bie was my hero and I still think that the idea of the hero has enormous value. Of course, it's very difficult to think back that far and recall all the details, because it was 1933. But I remember that *King Kong* left a strong impression that I don't think one can really analyze. I suppose part of the fascination was that you couldn't quite figure out how it was done. You knew it wasn't a man in an ape suit. But *however* it was done, it haunted me for a long time. I was in awe of the fact that O'Bie could produce, on the screen, the illusion of life, that these fabulous prehistoric creatures could walk around by themselves in beautifully crafted jungles. These marvelous dinosaurs that you'd seen in storybooks, and this gigantic ape that performed extraordinary feats of strength simply overwhelmed me. It was all so dynamic and vivid.

Of course, like most young boys, I'd always been interested in prehistoric life. As a hobby and for school projects I used to make little dioramas of dinosaurs and particularly of mammoths and saber-toothed tigers found in the La Brea Tar Pits. But after seeing *King Kong*, I saw how you could bring these animals to life by using a camera. It was much later that I discovered first-hand the wonders of stop motion photography."

Ray Harryhausen has spent nearly forty years animating screen fantasies. In that time, he has created fifteen feature-length motion pictures and several short subjects, all of which have won him a legion of devoted fans and have considerably broadened the boundaries of film art. His work is meticulous, his stop motion creatures brilliantly designed and animated, and his special-effects processes near-flawless. A genuinely modest man of taste, morality, and splendid good humor, all he has ever wanted to do since the age of thirteen was to create astonishing visions on the screen. However, he has done more, becoming the greatest special effects artist in film history. But no one achieves a goal without years of painstaking study and experimentation, and Ray was indeed a long time in polishing his skills.

Born on June 29, 1920, Ray went to school in southern California, attending Audubon Junior High School and Manual Arts High School in his teens. Ray's scholastic endeavors were hardly what one might term extraordinary: "I wouldn't say that I was an outstanding student. I enjoyed certain courses and I felt miserable in other courses. Mathematics never seemed to be my favorite subject. I got through it, fortunately, and I regret not putting a little more effort into it and the other subjects that I didn't find enjoyable. But everybody looks back and says, 'Gee, if I had only done that, why, I would have been better off.' However, I'm happy to say that in later life I found use for even the most disagreeable subjects." However, apart from these typical academic travails, Ray had that frustrating passion for *King Kong*. "My school chums and I, of course, used to all go together to the so-called "flea pits" and see a reissue of *King Kong* or *The Most Dangerous Game* or *She* or *Dr. Jekyll and Mr. Hyde*—the unusual pictures of that period. Unfortunately, at that time, I couldn't find any kindred souls who thought as much about *King Kong* as I did." It was a fortuitous day for him, therefore, when in 1937, he asked the manager of a second-run house that was showing *King Kong* if he could borrow the large stills from the film that were on display. The exhibitor told Ray that the shots belonged to Forrest Ackerman. Visiting the young Ackerman, a fantasy memorabilia collector—and today the editor of *Famous Monsters of Filmland* Magazine—Ray was introduced to a science-fiction club that met once a week at the Little Brown Room of the Clifton Cafeteria in Los Angeles. There, he met fellow fans of imaginative films and, most notably, aspiring author Ray Bradbury. That Harryhausen was inspired by these people after his own heart is clear in what Bradbury later wrote about his early relationship with Ray: "Harryhausen and I, at seventeen, were like most teenagers. But unlike many, we had large dreams that we intended to fulfill. We used to telephone each other nights and tell the dreams back and forth by the hour: adding, subtracting, shaping, and reshaping. His dream was to become the greatest new stop motion animator in the world, by God." Sufficiently fired by his new friendships to try to emulate his hero O'Brien, Ray would get home from school and experimented every day with wooden armatures, making models like the famous Cave Bear, which was his first stop motion creation.

The Cave Bear is familiar to Harryhausen's fans not only because it was his premier model, but because he sliced up his mother's fur coat in order to make it. And, while apocryphal stories have risen from the event—about how Ray was severely punished for his indiscretion—in fact, he was never even disciplined for the action. "It was hanging in the closet, and it hadn't been worn for some time, and so I decided upon my own that perhaps I could use it for the Cave Bear. Of course, after I had taken the plunge, I decided to ask for permission and ultimately my mother said that she didn't want it anymore. So I hope that doesn't disillusion anybody that I was whipped to death or beaten to the point of insensibility by my mother for taking her fur coat!" Needless to say, because of its extended worth, the garment was a modest investment in Ray's career.

Ray's first test footage of the bear was only a modest success from a technical standpoint. But seeing this creature that he had built come to life on the screen was an incomparable thrill. "At the time, I didn't have a place to do these experiments. I had no lights, so I built the sets outside in the sunlight, and then borrowed a 16-mm camera from a friend of mine. He kindly came over and we shot a number of scenes. We weren't sure whether we'd get one frame or not: you'd touch your finger on the camera and maybe two or three frames would go by. But when we got the film back a few days later, the excitement of actually seeing this bear move was quite satisfying, which encouraged me to do more. Of course, the one thing I'd forgotten was the fact that shooting outside, taking several hours, the sun would move. So you'd see all the shadows changing. But still, that didn't dissuade me."

What Ray had first filmed, early in 1938, was a sequence in which the bear chased an appropriately scaled human figure about the miniature set. In the case of subsequent tests with the Cave Bear, Ray actually matted himself and his German Shepherd named Kong into the picture. The monster was seen lumbering from a cave and, as Harryhausen and his pet stood behind a tree, the animal took a swipe at them. Missing, the bear turned disgustedly and ambled back into its cave.

If Harryhausen were a fanatic about stop motion before, becoming involved with it firsthand was a dream come true. And it had the telling effect of teaching Ray about determination and dedication. "I wanted to do stop motion so badly that it became a hobby. But I was still in school, and wondered if my hobby could develop into a profession. It was such a limited field that I was not quite sure how far I could go in it. You know, how many pictures do they make using stop motion techniques? I think these were my very subconscious thoughts at the time. But I so much enjoyed working with the jointed miniature figures, that I'd spend all of my spare time doing it. I even began to go to night school to take classes at U.S.C. They had just started their series of film courses: editing, art direction, and photography. I studied with Lou Physioc, who was one of the photographers in Hollywood who was teaching a cinematography course at night. All phases of trick photography, from matte shots to double exposure were discussed at length. I didn't quite know what I was going to do with all of this information, but I knew I was intensely interested in it. If you believe in Destiny, you'd say that it was an accumulation in preparation for some unforseen future event. But the immediate result of these efforts was that I began to take learning and life very seriously—what I knew of it. I mean, it *is* a serious thing, to be alive, if you think about it. It's quite a miracle. And I had this strange notion—and, as I look back, maybe it was somewhat distorted—but that I was wasting time if I weren't doing something constructive every minute. And when I didn't find too many people who felt like this, I began to think I was a little abnormal. But every waking hour I felt that I should be doing *something*, either studying or experimenting. I suppose that that was part of my driving force. But to apply this drive, a small area was set aside on our back porch for my workshop, and I would work until two o'clock in the morning on various projects. It would take weeks to make a prehistoric animal and then you'd have to tear it down if it didn't look right. At times it was discouraging. There seemed to be so many dead ends and little, if any, helpful information to be found in print. But once you passed that discouraging aspect, you were likely to reach your goal. And a lot of people get discouraged during that period; for some reason, I just didn't. I can't put my finger on just *why*—but I felt compulsion, I suppose, to keep making these things. It's what makes me want to believe in Destiny. Of course, I don't want to make it sound *too* idealistic: by that time, I really was trying to figure out what I was going to do when I got out of school."

Wrapped in his work, pensive about life, and concerned about his future—Darlyne O'Brien would later say of Ray, "he was always an extremely serious boy and seemed to have the weight of the world on his shoulders. I seldom saw him smile,"— Ray kept plugging away with his models and test reels. He even got a little workshop of his own: "My dad and I built a studio in the back of our garage. It was a big one in which I could leave things set up without having to take it all down when the cars were run into the garage at night. So that new studio really helped and encouraged me. My parents, God bless 'em, were always very interested in what I was doing."

With a place to work and a sense of roots, Ray's endeavors became more ambitious. He took night courses in drawing and sketched out scenes for such elaborate projects as *David and Goliath*, while building new models with more durable metal skeletons. His first three monsters of this type were the prehistoric stegosaur, triceratops, and agathaumas. Actually, this latter creature was listed as a monoclonius on the film itself. The creature was rechristened only when Harryhausen realized that it didn't exactly resemble a monoclonius, whereas paleontologists had not yet uncovered the skull of an agathaumus. In any case, with muscles of cotton and rubber skin, the models were put through brief paces, the triceratops pausing to lunch on a stop-motion man in one abbreviated take. Ray followed these tests with scenes of an allosaur marching through a glade, grabbing a Harryhausen look-alike by the arm, and swallowing the writhing, tortured soul one limb at a time. When I first heard about this sequence, I suggested, in another of my books, *Movie Special Effects*, that Ray was gleefully avenging the ruthless murder of King Kong in scenes such as this. But laughing his vibrant laugh, he set the record straight: "It's not a question of my personally getting a delight in seeing somebody devoured. I made these rather gory scenes in my early tests purely for experimental reasons, to see how convincing they could be. There was no other reason for it: it just turned out to be rather horrifying!"

One of Ray's favorite creatures from this evolutionary period was his "creature from Jupiter." A visual pastiche, designed in 1939 from illustrations in contemporary fantasy magazines, which Ray explains was "work that hadn't been put on the screen to any extent," the Jovian is a humanoid animal with a saurian head, four tentaclelike arms with webbing strung between them, a pair of squat legs, and a tail. For the animal's screen debut, it is shown in an intimidating close-up, roaring innate defiance. Moments later, a cylindrical spaceship whizzes into the frame behind the creature, who spins about and grabs the craft. The beast examines it, then tries unsuccessfully to eat it. The interlude worked out so successfully that Ray decided to revive the Jovian in a number of succeeding productions, having it tangle with a pterodactyl, a brontosaur, the agathaumus, a woolly mammoth, and a man whom the monster consumes!

As we have noted, Ray is a firm advocate of Fate and Destiny. This will become more evident when we discuss *Jason and the Argonauts*. Ray believes that, although we are unaware of the course, our existence is neatly plotted out for us by some force greater than we. If this is so, then it was indeed Fate that drove Ray to tackle an overly elaborate project called *Evolution*. By 1940, he had come to own a single-frame camera and wanted to consolidate his special effects experience in one stunning feature-length film. And he *did* intend for it to be stunning: "Naturally, when one embarks on a project like *Evolution*, you think oh gee—I'm going to show them all. Nothing like the story of *Evolution* has ever been done in motion pictures before, so I'm going to show the stop motion origin of the world and the origin of the species. Well, it finally became very ambitious, out of hand, really. But I suppose it's very good to place something beyond your reach as a goal, because just striving for that you learn far more than if you place your goal too low. So I managed to buy a 16-mm camera, and through hit and miss, I started this rather grand project hoping that it would be released to schools and possibly be used as a documentary film of some sort."

Making a rough outline of the film, Ray had intended to tell the entire story of life on earth, from the birth of the stars through the coming of Homo sapiens. Unfortunately, beyond the awesome scope of the film, there was just one problem. "I had begun *Evolution* before I saw Disney's *Fantasia* (1940). Of course when I saw the picture, I realized that it was quite inane to continue, because he did it all in *Fantasia*, in the sequence *The Rite of Spring*, and so beautifully." However, as we shall see, the year he lavished on *Evolution* was not wasted.

Harryhausen shot a great deal of color footage for the film, the most staggering of which was the build-up to an unrealized fight between an allosaur and a brontosaur. In misty, atmospheric shots worthy of *King Kong*, the brontosaur is seen snaking along a beach—which was really the waters of Lake Malibu matted into Ray's miniature set. The spray surrounding the monster as it waddled through the surf was animated. Pterodactyls flit past the mountainous beast which pauses in its march as it suddenly sniffs danger in the air. Suddenly, an allosaur leaps into the frame and the giants square-off, the carnivore confidently stalking its prey. Other sequences involved Harryhausen's triceratops, a dimetrodon, and additional monsters.

When *Evolution* evaporated because of *Fantasia*—not to mention the sheer bulk of the project—Ray decided that the time had come to engage in more practical enterprises. For one thing, as his experiments and schooling had left no time for Ray to hold a part-time job of any sort, he wanted to get involved with movies that would generate an income. As Ray summarizes the situation late in 1940, "I thought I had better start directing my forces and not spend so much time on epic-scale productions like *Evolution*. The scope that it encompassed was far too great." Gathering up the tests from his abortive epic, he showed them to a producer newly arrived in Hollywood from Europe, a man whose stop motion shorts known as Puppetoons had just begun and were creating quite a popular stir. Viewing the amateur footage, George Pal—who recently described Harryhausen to me in one word: "brilliant"—hired the twenty year old to work on his eight-minute-long pictures.

Thirty thousand individual frames went into the making of each Puppetoon, although it was not the kind of stop motion animation on which Harryhausen had been raised. "It was a different type of animation because it was very stylized in the design of the figures and the sets. And, similar to the technique of cartoon animation, separate figures were used for each frame of film. Twenty five individual puppets were used to make one step in a walk cycle. And then you would reuse them in another cycle. There were also at least twenty-four heads for each puppet in order to give it a variation of expression and form the vowels of speech. If a great amount of dialogue were used, each head had to progressively change to form each word. Depending on what was said on the soundtrack, you would choose the appropriate head by a number on a cue sheet. In some cases, the whole head was substituted; in other cases, you would have to change only portions of the face or mouth. In this way, you get a certain type of smooth animation as it was all precalculated in the form of drawings. But you end up with an extreme design type of figure rather than a naturalistic figure. They all, of course, had stiff bodies, highly designed, because they were made for short subjects. Creatively, it was not as enjoyable as doing freehand animation with a single jointed model, although sometimes such a figure was used. But we had a lovely, very small group of interested, devoted people consisting of animators, set constructors, two or three painters for the many puppets, and a cameraman. It was a very harmonious atmosphere in which to work. It was my first job working professionally with animation, and it was a great pleasure. My initial assignment with George was to animate a character named Jim Dandy, one of the first characters he created when he first went to work producing the Puppetoons for Paramount. Later came Dipsey Gypsy and then Strauss and Jasper. And it was, as I've said, very enjoyable."

The Puppetoons won an Oscar in 1944, began stumbling shortly thereafter due to rising production costs, and were finally discontinued in 1947. However, Ray's tenure with Pal ended abruptly in 1942, when Harryhausen was handed a job by Uncle Sam, to serve for three years in the Army Signal Corps. "Fortunately, I was placed in a film unit after showing them some of my experiments, and I was able to make some animated sections for orientation films, as well as acting as an assistant cameraman on live action shooting. So I was at least able to do something I was qualified to do, and not tossed in a big circle of infantrymen, which I was certainly not cut out to be!" However, apart from animating miniature tanks, jeeps, and other military vehicles for the training films, Harryhausen sculpted figures for the photographed covers of *Yank* Magazine, featuring the cherubic caricature of an enlisted man named Snafu, which is an abbreviation for "Situation Normal: All Fouled Up"—although variations on the phrase have appeared from time to time.

Discharged after World War II, Ray headed for Southern California visiting, Florida, Cuba, and Mexico en route. Returning to his parents' home, Ray decided not to burden the floundering Puppetoon staff with an additional animator, electing, instead, to produce some short films of his own. Setting up shop in his old garage studio, Ray went searching for appropriate subjects to shoot, although throughout, what he was really longing to do lay far afield from his current endeavors.

In 1939, Ray had realized his long-standing dream of meeting Willis O'Brien. "I first called him when he was making *War Eagles* at MGM. A school friend of mine knew him, and she said he was a very understanding man, and just to call him up. So I called him up, told him how much *King Kong* meant to me, and told him that I'd been making dinosaurs all my life. I also said that I would be enormously honored if he would view them. So he kindly invited me to the studio and I brought them out to MGM in a suitcase. Of course, when I saw his office with all these hundreds of beautiful drawings for *War Eagles*, I almost went out of my mind. The walls were *covered* with them! Some were painted in glorious water color and others in oil, but the majority of them were drawn in a bold charcoal technique. It wasn't easy to recover from this sudden and overwhelming exposure to all I had dreamed about for years. But I managed to compose myself and, although I didn't show him any of my movies, I took my animals to him and he studied them carefully. Then he made some very kind comments about my mammoth, eryops, and stegosaur, things like my stegosaur had legs like a sausage. But he said it in a very nice way, and it didn't hurt me. It was in a way that encouraged me. In fact, I have never forgotten his first words: 'You've got to get more character into your animals.' And I suddenly realized how emaciated they looked. Now he didn't mean to stylize them—

he meant stronger accentuation of the muscular structure under the skin. More design to them. If you were to stylize them, they'd look like cartoons, too simplified."

As a result of getting together with O'Brien and having had him actually take the time to show concern, to criticize his work, Ray redoubled his efforts to perfect his craft. It was at this time that he first conceived of *Evolution*. "I went back, working feverishly away, trying to put more character into my animals. In the meantime, I went to see every reissue of *King Kong*, to study the animals and see what he meant by character. And I realized that it was the understructure of the detail that went into the animal. To improve them, I realized that I should study sculpture more seriously, and learn how to make plaster casts. My mother took me to Barnsdale Park to learn how to make casts and molds. This occurred during the summer vacation period. Then I went to some classes in ceramics and learned how to sculpt from a model. Some stage acting courses came later. Then I felt that I should study life drawing much more and went to classes, some during the day and some at night. I drew from the model to learn muscle structure and general anatomy, which is very important in this field. This covered a number of years, of course, and it is rather strange how development can be so gradual that one is unaware of the knowledge being stored for the future. I knew that it would still be difficult to establish a career in stop motion, but at least this training would be useful in gaining work in advertising, commercial art, or architecture." All the while, Ray kept going to see movies, studying the grandeur of *King Kong* and Cooper's other films, as well as those of Alexander Korda—most significantly *Things to Come* (1936) and *Thief of Bagdad* (1940)—and literally immersing himself in melodramatic screen fantasy. As a result, it is not surprising to learn that, although practicality and finances forced Ray to produce short subjects immediately after the war, his heart and ambitions lay in feature-length motion pictures.

Unlike Pal, whose Puppetoons were either allegories or light-hearted fantasies such as Dr. Seuss' *And To Think I Saw It On Mulberry Street* (1944), Harryhausen decided to film the great fairy tale classics, in all the splendor with which they were originally written and illustrated. He would employ O'Bie's stand-by process—as he had in *Evolution*—of using panes of painted glass to create lush, multileveled foregrounds, as well as to build detailed and evocative sets and more realistic puppets than those of Pal, while having his mother Martha sew a beautiful wardrobe for the characters. And, true to form, Ray wanted to make these films as faithful to the source material as possible. But the problem, as his research revealed, was that he could never seem to find a definitive version of any given fairy tale. "When I first started my fairy tales, I had in mind the schools and educational authorities, because, at the time, they didn't have any subject matter like that in 16-mm. They were all commercial cartoons. So I wanted to try to do the fairy tales as they were originally written. But there were so many interpretations, some of which were unusually gruesome. So I decided to visit various schools asking principals and visual education authorities what they would like to see. I was trying to do it in a methodical way. But I got such a variety of answers that I became confused. But I had this film left over from the war, some Kodachrome that was outdated, and I decided that I would just do something to please me, since everyone seemed to have a different point of view as to what these films should be. So I made a picture that *I* thought would be workable and interesting. It actually began as four three-minute subjects that I thought could eventually go on television, which was just budding on the horizon. If I had a following, splendid. If not, I had no one to blame but myself."

What Harryhausen shot was a picture called *Mother Goose Stories*, a ten-minute-long film starring a stop-motion Mother Goose in a framing story that introduced the tales of *Little Miss Muffet*, *Old Mother Hubbard*, *The Queen of Hearts*, and *Humpty Dumpty*. The picture was in production for several months, and when it was completed, Ray proudly took the 400-foot-long effort to the various academic officials whom he had contacted earlier. He wasn't certain quite how to market the film, and if the scholastic personnel couldn't actually buy the film for their schools, perhaps they could recommend some outlets. But as soon as he began showing *Mother Goose Stories* around, Ray ran into trouble. The people who had maintained various versions of the stories actually expected to see *their* interpretation on the screen. As a result, they became stupidly critical, as is the wont of many so-called teachers in the United States. As Ray laments, even now, "One lady—she was a principal—saw Humpty Dumpty fall off the wall and said, 'Why isn't there a *yolk* on the ground?' Another felt the red background of the titles would excite the children too much." Comments such as these quickly discouraged Harryhausen because his viewers were nit-picking; they refused to see the fine and sincere production that *surrounded* these controversial details. Fortunately, things got better before they got worse, or landscaping may have gained a house designer at the expense of film losing an animator. "Finally, a very dear teacher friend, under whom I had studied puppetry, suggested that I go to Bailey Films. Bailey was a man who distributed unusual motion pictures to schools and universities and had a good reputation with the school boards. So I brought them to Bailey and upon the first viewing he decided to release *Mother Goose Stories.*"

With the money he received from *Mother Goose Stories*, as well as what remained of his mustering-out pay from the army, Ray set about producing other fairy tales for Bailey, although these were ten minutes *each*, rather than an omnibus of shorter episodes. The first of the four pictures was *Little Red Riding Hood*. Ray's New York-based author-director-actress friend Charlott Knight wrote a narration for the film, and a musical score was added to the finished short. *Little Red Riding Hood* was followed by a three-minute television commercial about *Kenny Key* for a Los Angeles housing project, after which, in answer to a prayer, Ray was transported from his garage studio to the RKO lot at Culver City. He was about to work on his first feature-length film.

A rare poster from *Mighty Joe Young*. This was designed before the name of the picture was changed. Notice the glib approach to this film as opposed to the more dynamic renderings of *King Kong* in Chapter Three.

A preproduction sketch of the roping of *Mighty Joe Young*.

CHAPTER FIVE

Mighty Joe Young

"I had kept in touch with O'Bie over the years. Progressively, he had seen my various films and experiments, and he seemed impressed. Finally, in 1946, he started preparing and designing a new ape picture called *Mighty Joe Young*. Moving his home office to the RKO Pathe Studio in Culver City, he asked me if I would be interested in assisting him doing bits and pieces like keeping his drawing pencils sharpened, cutting mattes for his sketches, making character drawings of the gorilla, and so forth. Of course, I was delighted and went to work on the film."

Mighty Joe Young was an attempt by Cooper, Schoedsack, and O'Bie to recapture the success and lost glories of *King Kong*. And, in the end, they had indeed created an exciting, Oscar-winning motion picture. Unfortunately, the Hollywood unions saddled O'Bie with a lot of unnecessary people to perform various functions in the special effects department, which made the budget inordinately high. O'Bie was rightfully annoyed, but filmmaking had changed since the days of *King Kong*. In addition to this, as Ray explains, "the studio had changed hands. Howard Hughes had just bought it, and very few films were being made there. So *Mighty Joe Young*, being a resident of the studio for two years, was burdened with the bulk of the studio overhead. This made the picture appear to cost an enormous amount, over two million dollars." As a result, the film was unable to make money, and as Ray observes pertinent to O'Bie's subsequent string of disappointments, "many producers shunned animation for a long time not because of O'Bie's material, but because of what *Mighty Joe Young* had cost."

In the screenplay by Ruth Rose, based on a story by Merian C. Cooper, we are introduced to Mr. Joseph Young when he's a baby. Two native bearers are passing through the Young plantation of Africa when seven year old Jill Young (Lora Lee Michael) stops them, asking to see what's in their basket. The men show her the baby gorilla—a real monkey, not a stop-motion model—and the precocious Jill decides that she must have it. Trading a jack-in-the-box, some trinkets, and a flashlight for the ape, the girl hides it in her father's bed. Naturally, when he enters the room, Mr. Young (Regis Toomey), a widower, is startled to find Joe amidst the sheets. But he allows Jill to keep the gorilla, who is lulled to sleep by the tune *Beautiful Dreamer*. Years pass, and in the Manhattan office of Max O'Hara (Robert Armstrong), the entrepreneur is busy planning for an African safari. The purpose of the hunt, in which he will use cowboys to capture wild animals as well as provide a unique press angle, is to gather attractions for his new Hollywood nightclub *The Golden Safari*. Hiring cowboy Greg Johnson (Ben Johnson) to help lasso the animals, O'Hara is busy organizing last-minute details of the all-important newspaper coverage. It is all that his media secretary Windy (Frank McHugh) can do to keep up with the fast-talking O'Hara.

After spending several weeks in Africa, with cages of lions to show for his efforts, O'Hara is preparing to break camp when the settlement is invaded by a rather salty gorilla. The ape attacks a caged lion while O'Hara's aides run for safety. However, the showman sees dollar signs on the veldt, and deciding to capture the ape for his nightclub, rides boldly out with his men, lariats in hand. A frenzied battle ensues as the gorilla snaps the cowboys' ropes and smacks at any horse or rider

Joe tugs a miniature projected cowboy from his horse.
© RKO General, Inc.

that comes within range, finally scaling a cliff, snatching O'Hara from his mount, and preparing to dash him to the ground. With no time to worry about taking the ape alive, Greg grabs a rifle and draws a bead on the rampaging monster; suddenly, a young woman bursts from the bush and slaps the gun down. She calls to the ape, and when he hears her whistling the tune *Beautiful Dreamer*, gently lowers O'Hara to the ground. Turning to Greg, she yells at him for daring to encroach on her property, and with that, Jill Young (Terry Moore) and Joe walk off. Hobbling to Greg's side, O'Hara, who is quaking, nonetheless has the presence of mind to mutter that he must sign the girl and her pet to perform in his Hollywood showplace.

Venturing out to Jill's plantation, which she has managed ever since the death of her father, O'Hara sweet-talks the girl into signing a contract.

She and Joe are then transported to Hollywood for the opening of the nightclub. Wrought in a lush African decor with the captured lions kept in glass cages behind the bar, *The Golden Safari* is packed for the debut of the mysterious Mr. Joseph Young. No one knows who or what he is, and Windy has a difficult time keeping the curious press under control. Finally, however, the curtain rises and O'Hara introduces Jill, who sits at a piano and plays *Beautiful Dreamer* as the house lights dim.

Illuminated by a spotlight, the platform on which Jill is seated suddenly rises, floating above the stage as if by magic. Then the lights spring back to life and Joe is seen holding the scaffold aloft. The audience is awed by the giant ape, and Joe is an immediate hit.

In the weeks that follow, O'Hara devises a number of different acts for the monkey, which include a tug-of-war with world-famous strongmen such as Primo Carnera, Man Mountain Dean, the

Mighty Joe Young attacks Max O'Hara's African camp.

The drunks pay Mighty Joe Young a visit. © RKO General, Inc.

Mighty Joe Young about to sample his first liquor.

Joe Young breaks from his cage in a December 3, 1947 test shot that did not appear in the finished film.

An unidentified lass with the Mighty Joe Young model
which, by now, has molted and decayed.

Swedish Angel, and others, and a setting wherein Joe, the monkey to Jill's organ grinder, retrieves large-numbered coins thrown to the stage by diners, Joe's selection entitling the owner to a free bottle of champagne. However, by their seventeenth week in Hollywood, Jill realizes that it was a mistake to come to America. Joe is kept in a cage, the only window of which looks out on a garbage-strewn alley; the ape quickly grows lethargic in his prison. Angry with herself for having bought O'Hara's pitch, Jill has dinner with Greg and announces her plans to return to Africa. However, she has fallen in

One of the coins tossed at Mighty Joe Young during the organ grinder sequence.   © RKO General, Inc.

love with the cowboy and asks him to come with them. Greg agrees, but Fate has other plans. Bored with festivities at *The Golden Safari*, three drunken patrons sneak into the cellar of the nightclub to treat Joe to a drink. The ape guzzles down their liquor and signals for more. Insulted by the monkey's ingratitude, one of the visitors pushes his cigarette lighter into Joe's hand and triggers the flame. Outraged, the intoxicated ape pounds down the reinforced iron door of his cage, crushes it to rubble as an afterthought, and pursues his antagonists up the stairwell. The men go screaming into the main hall of the club, and customers have a good laugh at their fumbling antics—until Joe comes after them, pushing through the wall of simulated jungle foliage that is part of *The Golden Safari's* design. Climbing to the rafters, where he demolishes the hut-like orchestra stand, Joe grabs a vine and swings across the dance floor, overturning

panicked guests and furniture; grabbing hold of a balcony, he tears at the thatched roofing and some debris falls to the bar, cracking the glass on the lion cages. Freed, the felines prowl about the room feasting on patrons—including one of the drunks—while, looking for any outlet worthy of his wrath, Joe attacks the cats. Hurling them across the club or beating them insensate, Joe finally turns his attention to the main support pillar of the building. Pushing it down, he causes the ceiling to fall in and is beaten into sobriety by crumbling pieces of structural matter.

By this time, Jill has arrived and ushers Joe back into his cage. However, the gorilla's future is in the hands of the court. And, despite Jill's fervent pleas to allow her and the ape to go home, Joe is declared an untenable menace and a warrant is issued for his death by gunfire. But O'Hara refuses to accept the verdict. Aware of what the gorilla means to the girl, he bribes a freighter captain to transport Joe to Africa. The only problem is getting the ape past his police guard to the boat. Pretending to pay a last visit to Joe, O'Hara suddenly announces that he is having a heart attack and is helped to his office by Joe's warden. As soon as the men are gone, Jill runs into the cellar, opens Joe's cage, and escorts the ape into a waiting van. Greg speeds away just as the firing squad arrives. When the police realize that they have been deceived, they set out after Joe on a tip from O'Hara—which, needless to say, sends them in a wrong direction. This leaves the ape free and clear, until Greg stops to get air in one of his tires. When a derelict tries to sneak aboard the van, he spots Joe and alerts the police. Although Greg transfers Joe to another truck, the police pick up their trail and follow them through a swamp, where everyone gets mired. Fortunately, Joe is able to free the truck and our heroes speed off.

Upon leaving the marshland, Greg happens past a burning orphanage, and stops to see if he can be of any assistance. One of the women manages to choke out a plea to save several children who are trapped on the top floor, and Jill rushes in to rescue them. The steps catch fire behind her, and Greg is forced to meet her upstairs by roping an ornament and scaling the outside of the building. However, there is no way that Greg can evacuate both the children and Jill before the ledge on which they're standing collapses, so Joe makes an appearance, scaling a tall tree to deliver his mistress from danger. Meanwhile, Greg wraps the children in a blanket and carefully feeds the bundle earthward, climbing from his perch only when the youngsters are safe. Just then, a small child appears on the uppermost ledge of the orphanage. Greg tries to ascend, but his rope catches fire and breaks; Joe is forced to climb the tree, and pulling the baby to his breast, begins his descent. Unfortunately, burning rubble sets Joe's tree afire, and as the flames climb higher and higher, so does Joe. Finally, the tree collapses. Hugging the tot's body close to his own, Joe takes the full brunt of the fall. He releases the child, and it begins crawling toward a waiting attendant. But before anyone can reach the baby, the blazing structure finally buckles under the flames. Although dazed, Joe sees the danger and hurries to the frightened child, using his own body to shield her from the sudden rain of timber and brick. Joe is wounded but alive and, as Jill and Greg realize while hastening to his side, after this selfless display, no one would dare take a gun to the ape.

Weeks go by, and one morning Windy greets Max in his New York office with a surprise. He has just returned from Africa where he took home movies of Jill, Greg, and Joe. He rolls the film. While the ape shows off newfound manners—whereas he used to swallow bananas whole, he now peels them—the newlyweds wave to Max. Mimicking their gesture, Joe joins in the greeting, and for the first time in a monster film, all ends happily.

Mighty Joe Young was released in 1949, and as we noted earlier, earned O'Bie an Oscar over the modest competition of exploding oil wells in *Tulsa*. However, Oscars are not easily won, and just designing and planning the special effects for *Mighty Joe Young* had actually taken up most of O'Bie's time. He was able to animate only a few scenes, with the late, very talented Pete Peterson and even Marcel Delgado contributing some stop-motion work of their own. However, most of the show-stopping animation in *Mighty Joe Young* was done by the twenty-seven-year-old Harryhausen. Naturally, one would expect that this promotion from pencil sharpener to stop-motion technician caused Ray to shudder with ecstasy—but such was not the case. At least, not at first. "I had hoped to do

animation, of course, and I knew that was really why O'Bie hired me. All the test and fairy tale animation I had made had not been in vain, as it was quite smooth and proved that my work was far more fluid than the work of many professionals in that field. O'Bie also seemed to think I had a knack with characterization. But after the time I spent aiding in the preparation of drawings and various other things, when I finally got around to doing the animation, there wasn't the thrill that I thought there would be. It was all so gradual. It sort of progressed until, well, you were *hoping* for the day when you could animate and get your hot little hands on a gorilla, and see what you could make him do. But it all came so gradually because the picture was on, then it was off, on, off; should we make it or should we not; could we get the money or could we not? So this went on, as it does in most pictures, until finally, when you get to that point—the reason you were hired—it all comes about so normally that you take it in stride. I *did* feel excited when the picture was finished, more so than actually entering it. Once you become involved in it, it becomes sheer hard work."

Apart from the physically exhausting hours the film required, Ray found that the most difficult part of animating a realistic character like Joe—as opposed to the Puppetoons or even his comparatively simple fairy tales—was the mental attention it demanded. "You have to concentrate all through the scene. That's why I prefer to work alone, personally. It helps to avoid distraction. If you're not always aware of what you're doing, you can make mistakes which can't be corrected except by starting over again. Once you start a scene, which may last two days, you have to keep your mind focused on what you're doing. After each movement of the figurine you have to ask yourself if you have taken the pliers out of the shot; have you left something in there you shouldn't have? You do one frame after the other, and finally, after the ten-thousandth frame, it becomes easy to take things for granted. You move the model, click, move the model, click, so you have to keep your wits about you all the time, or you make terrible mistakes. It's even difficult to break for lunch. When the projector is switched off, there is a change in temperature making the projector or film or both shift a small

Ben Johnson (in black cowboy hat) with, seated from left to right, Ernest B. Schoedsack, Merian C. Cooper, and Willis O'Brien. © RKO General, Inc.

amount. And the fact that you're projecting the image from a distance means that a microscopic move will make the background jump out of its position. Then you see the film the next day and you say, 'Oh gosh, why didn't I foresake a wretched, mundane thing like lunch and continue with the scene.' But, unfortunately, we have to eat, and I didn't really want to take intravenous injections. Sometimes, of course, I eat on the set. That's what I often did on *Mighty Joe Young*. In fact, to get in the mood for the picture, I would eat carrots and celery all day." Ray adds that this diet almost became permanent: "I went through this period when I

thought I should be a vegetarian. I had gone through the Swiss Slaughterhouse and I thought, 'Good lord.' Then I started reading about how all carnivores have short intestines and we've got long intestines, so we shouldn't eat meat. But I lost so much weight that I had to go back to eating meat."

As with any motion picture, the story of *Mighty Joe Young* went through many changes during the months of planning that preceded the actual production phase. Ideas were suggested and discarded, often inspired by O'Bie's renderings of a gorilla in various and unusual circumstances. For instance, in one version of the scenario, it was

69

Ray Harryhausen with one of the models of Joe Young.
© RKO General, Inc.

planned that another gorilla would break from his display case in *The Golden Safari* and, King Kong-like, go after Jill. Hearing her screams, Joe was to have exploded from captivity and engaged the antagonistic ape in a tremendous struggle. This sequence was replaced by Joe's drunken spree in the nightclub. Another version of Joe's tug-of-war had the monkey matching his strength against that of an Indian elephant rather than the strongmen. In still another early outline, Jill wasn't a plantation owner but a Tarzan-like savage who had been raised by apes. However, during the various story conferences attended by Ray, O'Bie, Cooper, the Schoedsacks, and even in the earliest stages of production, John Ford, these various alternatives were considered, and for one reason or another, rejected.

After the story had been agreed upon, continuity sketches or storyboards were drawn. These thumbnail renderings represented each shot of the picture and were created, as they are for most every film, so that such time-consuming details as blocking, lighting, and camera placement had already been thought out by the time a full complement of film craftsmen joined the payroll. Meanwhile, Ray and O'Bie designed the first armature for Joe, which they had Harry Cunningham construct and Marcel Delgado dress with cotton and foam rubber. The metal skeleton, which was made up of some 150 articulated pieces, was tooled at a cost of nearly $1,500. Joe's fur, which was made of lamb's wool, was applied by taxidermist George Lofgren. The ape's teeth were enamel-covered metallic pieces, and the eyes were made of glass. The finished figure stood sixteen inches tall. The craftsmen then built four duplicate models and two smaller apes, one ten inches tall and the other five inches in height—both used for the long shots—so that worn models could be repaired—torn skin patched or sagging limbs tightened—without causing Ray, O'Bie, or Peterson a delay in

their stop-motion work. Delgado also built a number of stop-motion lions, men, horses, and figures of Jill for such sequences as the roping of Joe, the nightclub rampage, and the orphanage fire. These figures enabled O'Bie to design certain shots with greater impact than if he had been forced to use their real-life counterparts. We'll be discussing these and other technical aspects of the film later in this chapter.

As strange as it may seem to the lay reader, Ray had his favorite of the four larger Joe models, and it was the only one with which he really felt comfortable. "I think it was the appearance of the model, along with your concept of a gorilla. Somebody else may have a different concept; as you know, three or four people can look at the same object and see it in a different light, just as you get different opinions when people have viewed an accident. Certain people stress certain points, and

Willis O'Brien animates Joe and a model of Jill Young on the tree during the orphanage episode. Courtesy of Darlyne O'Brien. © RKO General, Inc.

other people stress different points, which gives a variety of concepts as to what actually happened. Anyway, for my preliminary research, I had read, of course, *Toto and I*, which was a book about a woman who raised a gorilla from its birth to adulthood. Then I studied pictures of gorillas in zoos. I remember I photographed them to see how they walked and their little idiosyncracies, which came in very handy. We didn't try to copy the movements, but they gave us an inkling of what a gorilla would do in his emotional pauses, so to speak. But this one gorilla model was the first one, the one I had designed with O'Bie. Of course, we had gone through various changes in our concept of a gorilla: high forehead, low forehead, and so forth. Nor, in fact, were the models all the same. If you look carefully at *Mighty Joe Young* and *King Kong*, you'll see entirely different physiognomies. For instance, the shape of the head of the Kong on the cliff was entirely different from the Kong fighting the allosaur. They were rebuilt so many times, and it is difficult to rebuild them quite the same way. But I got attached to this one model because I felt that it looked like the gorillas I had seen. You could put him in poses that gave you that feeling of dynamic quality." Pet model or not, the first stop-motion footage created by Ray had to be a very sobering experience: it was the sequence in which Jill leads the ape back to his cage. Because of Joe's reluctant, fractional movements, the fifteen-second shot took a taxing three days to animate.

Fourteen months were lavished on the special effects of *Mighty Joe Young*. And, although the RKO treasurers would no doubt have disagreed, aesthetically speaking, the expenditure in time and money were well worth it. The animation, of course, was breathtaking. Ray, O'Bie, and their associates made an absolute scene-stealer of Joe. Sometimes this snatching of the limelight was worked through virtuoso process shots, and at other times, by portraying Joe as a helpless victim of human greed. Personalitywise, he was always involved in very expressive mugging. During his nightclub debut, the camera holds tight on Joe's face as he supports Jill and the piano above his head. With a visage that radiates childlike innocence, eyes wide and brow coyly furrowed, Joe is constantly glancing up at the platform and reinforcing, for the audience, his continuing concern over Jill's welfare. Conversely, the more tragic end of the ape's emotional range comes to light in his cage at *The Golden Safari*. Joe gazes forlornly into the alley at a man filling a trash can. His appetite spoiled, the ape pathetically nudges a tray of food to the floor. Then there's poor Joe's confusion, which was carefully sketched by O'Bie and Ray to emphasize the gorilla's role as the exploited one: led onto the stage for the tug-of-war, he picks up the rope and, uncertain just what to do with it, tries to hand it to Jill. Laughing, the strongmen jerk at the rope and pull Joe off balance; roaring in anger, the ape retaliates by not only defeating his opponents but picking up the last one, Primo Carnera, and heaving him into the audience. A less extreme expression of Joe's bewilderment came during the escape, as the gorilla is shown sitting in the back of the truck, staring into space and absently drumming his knees, while his future is bandied about by a succession of individuals.

Of course, some of Joe's attributes are a bit more theatrical. During the roping scenes, for example, he corners one of the cowboys against the face of a cliff and, standing back, picks up a large rock and actually *winds up and pitches* the stone at his tormentor. Even more suggestive of human ire was the scene in the fleeing truck as Joe, sitting in the open-back vehicle, spits disdainfully in the direction of the pursuing police. However, even these very elicitory scenes notwithstanding, one of the most striking examples of Joe's highly affective nature occurs at the very end of the film. It shows, as we shall explore later and in Ray's own words, that every movement in animation is carefully calculated to get the most in appropriate personality from a character. Watching Jill and Greg wave to Max in Windy's home movies, Joe tries to ape their actions, as it were. At first, he manages only to flip his fingers open. Finally, however, he gets the hang of it and grins, evidently enjoying his newfound skill almost as much as he thrills to being able to peel a banana. And, while there are those who may quibble that this is an overly intelligent reaction for a gorilla, the gesture serves the purpose of drama without being *so* absurd as to make Joe or the scene appear ludicrous. It's fanciful and, yes, it's cute. But, like all of these sequences and character traits, it reaches the audience, which is really the name of the motion picture game.

Apart from the intricate and challenging character animation in *Mighty Joe Young*, O'Bie's special-effects set-ups were among the most complex ever designed for a motion picture. There were, of course, his many-layered glass shots, exacting static and traveling mattes, and a wealth of miniature props—including the burning orphanage, a five-foot-tall plaster model realistically shaken apart by a vibrator platform and filmed at high speeds to give the fire a roaring mass. But there was also the grueling animation of the four- to eight-inch-tall supporting players, such as the stopmotion men and horses.

During the roping scenes, most of the shots of Joe and his assailants were accomplished through miniature screen projection. On the set, the cowboy actors had been tossing their lariats at a large tractor, which Joe's body blocked from the singleframe camera during animation. However, Ray and O'Bie were still able to show the ropes actually going *around* the ape by animating thin wires dressed like the lassoes and carefully matching them with their miniature projected counterpart. Shots of Joe overturning horses and their riders were accomplished through "shadowboxing": the stuntmen would force their steeds to drop as if they had been tripped by an ape. Then, back in the stop motion studio, Joe was animated to conform to the on-

screen action as though he were "causing" the fall. However, in a handful of shots, O'Bie simply found it practical to employ stop motion horses and cowboys. For instance, in the scene where Joe yanks Max from his mount, it was a long shot done entirely on a miniature set with stop motion models. At other times, to effectively communicate the intense hounding of Joe by the cowboys, O'Bie thought it best to literally *surround* the gorilla with antagonists. Thus, miniature projecting a cowboy or two behind Joe, he also animated figures on the ape's camera side, as though the men were pursuing Joe in a circle. The results were most effective in maintaining the credibility and pounding pace of the entire sequence, as well as providing for a variety of interesting shots. Likewise, the nightclub melee benefited from stop-motion lions, as O'Bie was able to have them actually *leap* on Joe—something that would have been impossible to do with miniature screen or matting processes.

It's quite possible that the technical crew on *Mighty Joe Young* had less trouble with the miniature lions than they did with their live counterparts. In one sequence, for example, Joe picks up a stop-motion lion and hurls it across the room, an episode that concludes with a shot of a real lion sliding across the polished floor, spilling tables and chairs in a wild skid. To get the one brief shot of the lion's rough landing, the filmmakers had to dismantle the nightclub set used for the actors and

Ray Harryhausen animating *Might Joe Young* during the roping sequence.   © RKO General, Inc.

rebuild it on a twenty degree incline. Then, importing a lion from Billy Richard's World Jungle Compound in Thousand Oaks, they placed the animal on a specially constructed chute that was supposed to spill the beast to the slanted surface. Unfortunately, when placed atop the slide, the lion refused to budge. This, his trainer, Mel Koontz, crept to the animal's side to urge him along. Needless to say, both Koontz and the lion lost their balance and went slamming onto the set, destroying all the carefully arranged and constructed breakaway props. An entire day was lost rebuilding the set, after which the lion obligingly took his fall and was sent home.

Ultimately, the various problems were surmounted and the completed film, running ninety-four minutes, made for an unusual entertainment. The performances of the *live* actors left something to be desired: they knew the story was far-fetched and made a point of telling the viewer that they really weren't taking it seriously. This self-parody hurt the overall product enormously. Thus, while Ben Johnson was fine as the droll Greg—the character, as it was written, didn't take *anything* very seriously, so the teasing performance was appropriate—Howard Hughes' flame Terry Moore made Jill a superficial figure with little range other than to smile radiantly or pout, while Robert Armstrong overplayed O'Hara to the point of creating a blustering caricature of his gutsy *King Kong* impresario. Fortunately, Joe was able to hold up the show for them all, although, as Harryhausen himself has opined on numerous occasions, the tongue-in-cheek approach was terribly detrimental to the finished film.

CHAPTER SIX

The Beast from Twenty Thousand Fathoms

"There was a difficult period after *Mighty Joe Young* where O'Bie had *Valley of Mist* and Cooper didn't seem very interested in it, in fact, he didn't really want to do it. So O'Bie took it to Jesse Lasky, who seemed interested in it. Cooper was involved so thoroughly with John Ford and then Cinerama that he really didn't have too much time to think about it. But O'Bie felt it was a very unusual story, and the type of thing that he was best at. So I joined him in association with Mr. Lasky. A screenplay was written, and William Lasky was going to be the coordinator. They hoped to release through Paramount. But there was a long, drawn-out argument about financing, and how much it should cost, and the picture finally disintegrated. It was just terrible for O'Bie. I don't know how he bore up under his personal financial problems, but he continued the long and drawn out procedure of developing other ideas. As for myself, after waiting around for eight months on *Valley of Mist*, I had to either get out of the business, get a job somewhere, or do something on my own. You see, on a lot of these pictures, you get but a small retainer when they're being developed, which isn't substantial enough to keep you going. The producers just want to be sure that you'll be with a project when it actually hatches, and one understands that. So I went back to the fairy tales. I shot *Hansel and Gretel*, *Rapunzel*, and *King Midas*. I was about to embark on a sixth, *The Tortoise and the Hare*, when a friend of mine introduced me to Jack Dietz, who wanted to make a monster movie."

Jack Dietz's *The Monster from Beneath the Sea*, as it was originally called, was Ray's first feature-length venture on his own, most fittingly a screen adaptation of pal Ray Bradbury's *The Beast from Twenty Thousand Fathoms*, a tale which had recently appeared in *The Saturday Evening Post*. The story, retitled *The Fog Horn* when it was published in the Bradbury anthology *The Golden Apples of the Sun*, tells of a dinosaur rising from the depths of the ocean in answer to what it thinks is a mating call, only to learn that it is the bellowing of a lighthouse fog horn. Disappointed beyond imagining, the primeval creature destroys the tower and returns to the sea. Naturally, there was hardly enough material in the 2,500 word piece from which to draw a feature film, so Harryhausen and screenwriters Lou Morheim and Fred Freiberger incorporated the tale into an already existing first-draft screenplay, devising—long before it became fashionable—a subplot about the dangers of atomic weapons, along with romance, a tragic death, and an assault by the antediluvian monster on Manhattan. Produced for the remarkably low sum of $200,000, *The Beast from Twenty Thousand Fathoms* was released in 1953 and became the surprise hit of the year.

At an Arctic outpost, scientist Tom Nesbitt (Paul Christian) and Col. Evans (Kenneth Tobey) supervise the detonation of yet another in a series of American nuclear tests, this one being exploded far from where it can do mankind any harm. Still, some people at the base are wary. When a radar attendant exuberantly declares that each explosion makes him feel like science is writing the first chapter of a new Genesis, Nesbitt cautions him to be certain that we don't end up writing the final chapter of the old Genesis. Moments later, months of preparation come to an end as the weapon is fired. The radar operator sees a huge blip move slowly across his screen, but by the time he calls someone else to the

The Beast from Twenty Thousand Fathoms razes the lighthouse in a wonderfully atmospheric scene.

© Warner Communications

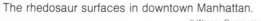

The rhedosaur surfaces in downtown Manhattan.

© Warner Communications

The rhedosaur in New York.

© Warner Communications

A rear-screen shot of New York's finest trying to stop the
Beast.

2A- BEAST FROM 20 THOUSAND
        FATHOMS #3

S-820

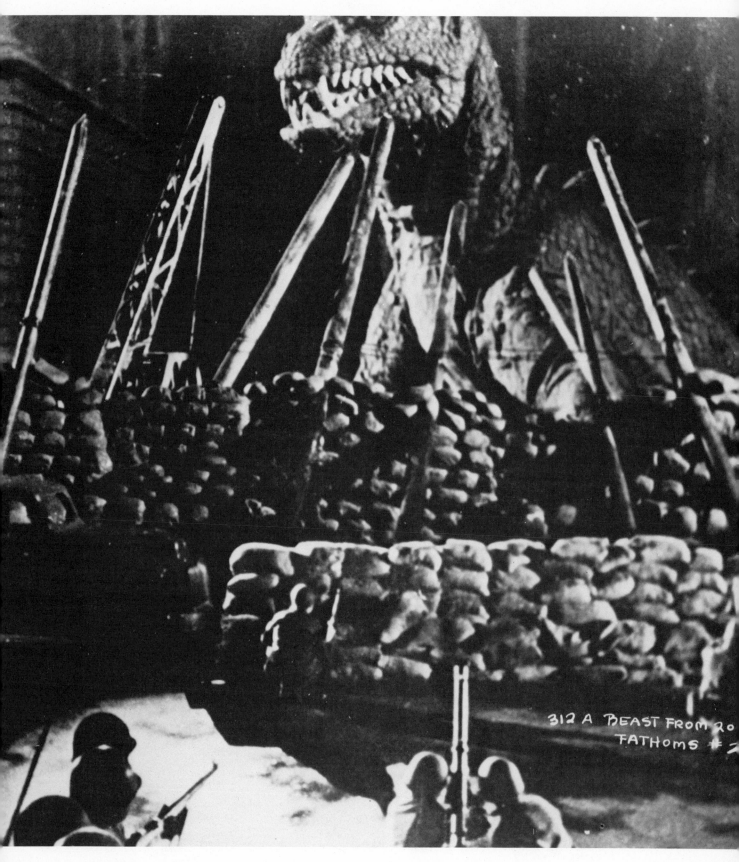

The rhedosaur runs into an army barricade.

scanner, the object is gone. They decide that the blast must have flung a large chunk of ice in front of the antenna.

Meanwhile, with mountains of age-old ice breaking up from the heat of the nuclear test, Nesbitt and an associate don cold weather gear to examine the environmental effects of the detonation. Escorted to a check point by soldiers who will stay behind in case of an emergency, the men go their separate ways. No sooner has Nesbitt gone than his fellow physicist is startled by the appearance of a huge prehistoric quadruped. Although the monster is in view for only a moment, the shock is sufficient to send the scientist tumbling into a crevasse. He fires a shot from his pistol and Nesbitt arrives shortly thereafter. However, while the newcomer prepares to rescue his companion, the monster reappears. With a nonchalant swish of its tail, the dinosaur sends tons of snow and ice thundering toward the scientists. Only Nesbitt survives the avalanche, and staggering from the downpour, discharges a pistol shot before collapsing. The soldiers hurry to his aid.

Back at the outpost, neither Evans nor the base medic put any credence in Nesbitt's tale of a monster. They believe that he hallucinated the beast, since the soldiers who returned to the site tried to reconstruct what happened and found neither a dinosaur nor any trace of a dinosaur, including tracks. Nesbitt asks them to explain away the monster's low, guttural roar: the doctor says that it was probably the wind. But Nesbitt is unconvinced. "No wind ever made a sound like that," he mutters under his breath. The scientist is sent to a New York City hospital to recuperate.

It is a stormy night off the Eastern coast of Canada, and a fishing boat is carefully riding out the squall. Suddenly, the pilot Jacob (Jack Pennick) releases the wheel and gasps: there is a huge reptilian head rearing from the choppy seas. Moments later, the monster's forearms come crashing down on the boat, and in a matter of moments, the vessel has vanished beneath the waves.

Back in Manhattan, Nesbitt notices an item in the newspaper about the sinking. Printed in the comic section, the article quotes the captain as having said that his ship was destroyed by a sea serpent. Although a nurse tells Nesbitt that the article is "right where it belongs—on the funny pages!" the scientist believes that it is a lead worth pursuing. Sneaking from the hospital, he visits the distinguished Professor Elson (Cecil Kellaway), a paleontologist attached to a local university. The elderly professor refuses to take the sighting seriously; after all, he tells Nesbitt, "if all the reports of sea serpents were placed end-on-end, they'd reach the moon!" But Elson's secretary, Leigh Hunter (Paula Raymond), who has long been an admirer of Nesbitt's research on radioactive isotopes, and now that she has met the physicist, is also taken with his continental good looks, enters the discussion on Nesbitt's behalf. She points out that if Stone-Age mammoths have been discovered in Siberia, perfectly preserved, why not a dinosaur? Elson admits that he would accept the possibility, save for one critical aspect: the elephants were dead, whereas Nesbitt claims that this beast was alive. The physicist comes up with a different approach to the problem. He proposes to browse through a selection of illustrations showing various dinosaurs. If he finds the monster, he will contact the captain of the fishing vessel and show him the same batch of sketches. If they *both* choose the identical creature, then that will prove the animal exists, or that the two men shared the same hallucination. Elson admits that the suggestion has merit, and Nesbitt arranges with Leigh to visit her apartment and go through the drawings.

Poring over the hundreds of renderings, Nesbitt becomes frustrated, wondering if he would recognize the monster even if it appeared at Leigh's window. However, his fears are unfounded; he spots a drawing that looks vaguely like the beast and, rummaging through the collection, Leigh pulls out a picture of a rhedosaur—a fictitious monster invented for the film by Harryhausen. It is indeed the creature that Nesbitt saw in the North Pole. Unfortunately, when the couple telephones the Canadian sea captain, he refuses to join in their experiment, claiming that enough people have already called him 'mad' for swearing to have seen a sea serpent. Desperate, Nesbitt tracks down his first mate, Jacob, who agrees to come to New York and look through the drawings. He, too, selects the rhedosaur. Elson is no longer an amused skeptic. He calls Col. Evans, who has returned to the States, and says that he is willing to stake his reputation on the fact that the monster exists. In addition, he asks Evans for reports of any bizarre happenings along American coastal waters, and the colonel agrees to gather the information.

That night, two men are singing dirges in their lighthouse when a dinosaur lumbers from the sea and destroys the stone structure. The next day, Elson, Nesbitt, Leigh, and Evans meet to review the coastal data. Fishing is poor in the Northeast, and people who visited certain beaches have been reported missing. But the most astonishing things are the inexplicable razing of the lighthouse and the obliteration of an entire New England fishing village. Charting the course of these disasters from the Arctic, Elson believes that they are the work of the monster, who is making its way to ancestral breeding grounds in the Hudson submarine caverns, where the only known rhedosaur fossils have been found. Determined now to locate and actually *see* the dinosaur, Elson asks Evans if it would be possible to recruit a diving bell. The colonel arranges the expedition.

Descending with an able seaman, Elson is thrilled by the view and watches, with interest, as an octopus and a shark do battle. But the fight is never completed, since the rhedosaur arrives and gobbles up the combatants. Elson radios an enthusiastic description of the animal to Leigh, but the broadcast ends abruptly when the creature turns on the diving bell and swallows its occupants. Leigh is heartbroken and Nesbitt blames himself for not having gone in Elson's stead, but there is little time for remorse. Within hours, the monster has come ashore at New York's downtown docks. Marching through the streets, it decimates buildings and automobiles, even snapping up a wildly kicking policeman who has paused to unload his gun at the rhedosaur.

By nightfall, Evans has moved troops into the Wall Street area, and they assault the dinosaur with heavy artillery. The creature is wounded and retreats, bleeding profusely from a neck wound. However, as the military learns too late, the animal's blood is the harbinger of some mysterious contagion from earth's antiquity. People begin dropping like leaves in autumn, and Evans realizes that the rhedosaur will have to be dealt with in

some manner other than shellfire. He suggests burning the creature, but Nesbitt argues that the smoke will spread the ancient bacteria hundreds of miles in every direction. The scientist suggests, instead, that they fire an isotope into the monster and kill it through radiation poisoning. Evans agrees to give the plan a try. The men move quickly when they hear that the rhedosaur has come ashore again, at the Coney Island amusement park. Nesbitt orders the rare isotope and has it secured in a projectile, while Evans assigns his top marksman, Corporal Stone (Lee Van Cleef), to fire it. Their target: the wound in the monster's neck.

Donning radiation suits, Nesbitt and Stone go to the amusement park where they find the dinosaur making a shambles of a roller coaster. But the vantage point from the ground is a poor one, and the corporal tells Nesbitt that he can't guarantee a hit. The men decide they'd have a better shot from the top of the roller coaster, and they reach their goal via one of the attraction's carriages. Thus poised, Stone is able to drive the missile home. However, the beast does not die immediately, and lashes at the roller coaster with a vital rage. Butting the superstructure and tearing down portions of track, the monster causes the men's train to slip away. Plummeting from the tracks, it explodes and begins a fire. Faced with immolation, the men climb down the ride's weakened support struts and manage to reach the ground safely. Meanwhile, the rhedosaur, screaming from pain and defiance, pushes down an entire side of the roller coaster and emerges on the beach. There, after long and agonizing throes, the being from a long-gone era collapses and dies.

The reason that Ray Harryhausen was able to create the awesome spectacle without incurring an expense similar to that of *Mighty Joe Young*, was by working alone and contriving less expensive means of creating visual effects than had ever been used in a film of this type. And his revolutionary processes have seldom been accorded the public or professional recognition that they deserve. However, before we examine these techniques, let's look at the rather interesting—but entirely characteristic effort and thought that Harryhausen applied to the production.

"The Beast from Twenty Thousand Fathoms

The Beast, amok in Coney Island, levels one wall of the roller coaster. © Warner Communications

was a creative challenge, since I had to devise ways and means of doing it to prove that these pictures could be made for not a fantastic sum of money. So it made me think in different ways than I had worked with O'Bie, where we created scope using glass shots like they did in *King Kong*. Of course, I went through terrible pangs of 'Can I do it or can I not?' and I had to always prove it to myself first. I got into a state of mind that almost bordered on neurosis. I used to go into my little garage studio and do experiments in 16-mm before I would open my mouth and say I could do it. You see, no one did this type of thing at that time, and if you wanted to, one could really get away with murder on the screen. Many a low budget film used very second-rate composites incorporating men in suits or obvious mechanical dummies. But I just didn't want to do anything that was inferior to *King Kong*. It was a high precedent to set, and you never reached it, but it was something that you tried to fight for. However, as it *was* my first solo venture, I had to take a stand that I had to do the best I could do under the circumstances, which I tried to do. I was rather proud of the fact that I was able to complete a rather complicated project under rather negative circumstances—I had only six or seven months to do the animation—as well as the lack of a suitable budget." However, Ray's "neuroses" aside, he was glad to have a feature motion picture on which to work, rather than short subjects or an assignment outside the field. So he approached the film with great vitality, designing a monster-on-the-loose epic that, if it's not *King Kong*, is second to none in its technical ingenuity.

Ray's novel technical development for *The Beast from Twenty Thousand Fathoms* was to be able literally to drop his stop-motion model into real settings by using what commentators through the years have referred to as 'a reality sandwich.' It is the basis of the process which Ray employs even in his current films. Broadly, it involves shooting the live-action background with the shadowboxing performers, then miniature projecting this footage and animating the monster as one would in any stop-motion film. However, Ray's innovation was to matte out those elements which he wanted in the foreground—buildings, cars, or people behind which the monster was to move—and then matte

The front screen projection process. If we wished, for example, to superimpose Ray Harryhausen and his model of the hydra on the street scene above, we would first photograph the street and thread it through the projector (a). This footage would then be shown on the reflective side of a two-way mirror (b) and, following the path of the arrow, thereby shine onto a screen (c). With Harryhausen standing before the screen, the camera (d) sees both the animator and the background through the window side of the two-way mirror. The two are thus photographed and composited.

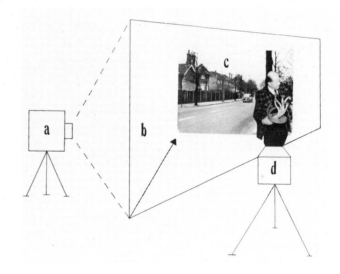

them *back into* the negative containing the miniature-projected stop-motion footage. Thus, the character could be inserted into the scene with the original, monsterless footage perfectly reconstructed. Previously, even in *King Kong* and *Mighty Joe Young*, one could never show the

83

monster behind anything but a miniature setting, a glass painting, or a matted-on element that was not a part of the original plate. The trouble with miniature settings and glass paintings, as Ray has observed, is the cost of creating them, while the problem with the matting-on method is that it's very difficult to get a composite where the lighting is perfectly matched and there are no matte lines, black borders that surround the superimposed object if the contours of the opaque internegative do not precisely match the shape of the matted element. Thus, Ray's trick, which could be accomplished in an optical printer, was both slick, less expensive, and more realistic than these other methods of superimposition.

Another process used and developed by Ray in *The Beast from Twenty Thousand Fathoms*, but pioneered by O'Bie, was front-screen projection, a technique which gained its greatest recognition when it was used extensively by Stanley Kubrick in *2001: A Space Odyssey* (1968). Although Ray's format was somewhat less sophisticated at the time of *The Beast from Twenty Thousand Fathoms*, all forms of front-screen projection work roughly as follows. Unlike rear-screen projection, where the camera and projector are on opposite sides of the screen, front screen projection allows the effect to be executed on the same side by using a mirror. With the camera perpendicular to the screen, and the projector forming a right angle with the camera, a two-way mirror is positioned so that it bisects the right angle at its vertex, the reflective surface facing the projector. When the background footage is run through the projector, it is bounced by the mirror to a screen made of some highly reflective material such as millions of tiny glass beads. This surface flashes a crisp image back to the camera, whereas the comparatively dull stop-motion model sitting on a table-top in front of the screen does not. And, as the two-way mirror is transparent from the camera's vantage point, the entire set-up is re-photographed with no obstructions whatsoever. Aesthetically, the benefit of this process over rear-screen projection is that, not having to pass *through* a screen—which tends to dilute and haze the image—the background footage is presented to the camera with remarkable clarity even on a very large projected image. Variations on

this process include the use of reflective white cardboard or plastic cutouts to place elements of the background plate in front of the stop-motion character. Trimmed to the exact shape of the foreground objects and set between the model and the camera, they allow the figure to walk amidst the front-projected terrain without the use of optical mattes, while presenting the two-dimensional eye of the camera with what appears to be a still unbroken image.

Technically then, *The Beast from Twenty Thousand Fathoms* represented a landmark in the creation of special visual effects. For in conjunction with the standby processes of old, such as a handful of miniature New York street sets as well as rear-projected sequences of the rhedosaur charging frightened citizens, the picture was a veritable textbook of stunning optical monster making. But what was the result of Ray's prodigious screen wizardry? Does the film's drama live up to the polish of its technique? Happily, it does.

Given the fact that the rhedosaur is a cold-blooded lizard and not a sympathetic or generically expressive mammal like Joe Young, Ray chose to emphasize the theatricality of the moment rather than of the monster. For instance, the destruction of the lighthouse is done entirely and brilliantly in silhouette, with the tower's probing beacon and the rolling surf adding tremendously to the desolate, eerie mood of the sequence. Contrarily, the attack on the amusement park is filled with fire and frenzy, with a huge crowd gathered about the roller coaster as the beast chews it to matchsticks. The monster's confrontation with the military in Manhattan is also superbly realized, the creature snapping at its attackers, and failing to stop their barrage, turns and slaps at them with its tail, unable to progress, but unwilling to retreat. Not surprisingly, most of these scenes were both conceived and designed by Harryhausen.

As ever, Ray was deeply involved with the film from its inception, contributing narrative threads and storyboard sketches. Thus, "it was my desire to do the lighthouse in silhouette because I thought it could be more effective and different, to give the picture variety. And of course a lighthouse doesn't really show up unless it's photographed at night. As for the roller coaster, the producers were trying to figure out an ending to take place in an amusement park. Everybody was trying to think up ideas about how to end the picture so that it had a spectacular climax. So I came up with the idea of the leading man and his assistant having to get up on top of the highest part of the roller coaster to get the proper aim to shoot this isotope into the beast. From there you get the release of the roller coaster, so you have this excitement of something moving and happening all through the end of the picture. We didn't want it just to be bang, crash, and the beast writhes and drops dead."

In terms of character, the rhedosaur performs more or less as one might expect a dinosaur in a modern metropolis to behave: it ate, it reacted to aggression, and it took out what must have been anxieties left over from Bradbury's original tale by devastating everything in its path. And while the beast's alienation could have been better expressed with one or two scenes such as O'Brien included in

A British advertising gimmick for Ray Harryhausen's first solo film. Courtesy the British Film Institute.

The Lost World, with the brontosaur nipping curiously at a street lamp, it was malevolence and not inquisitiveness that Harryhausen and Dietz were selling. Only in the film's concluding moments is the creature allowed any pathos, as Ray puts the beast through a tortured reaction to the burning pain of the isotope. Otherwise, the rhedosaur is simply a creature that inspires awe and apprehension. Its appearance, from the nasty little eyes to the cruel lizard's mouth, says a lot about the monster at a glance, and its rattling roar is especially unnerving. Ray even sneaks in a touch of the grotesque: the beast's feasting on a policeman. I mentioned this scene to Ray, asking if he still weren't trying to even the score with humanity for the death of *King Kong*. Once again, he denied it. He created the scene for the same reason that "every gangster picture has people being mowed down with a machine gun. You're dealing with a theatrical proposition, and you have to devise ways where human life is in danger, which is the essence of drama. Maybe that's why, for some time, I've been known as a human disaster. I've destroyed Washington D.C., the Golden Gate Bridge, Manhattan, and Rome. But those are all devices for melodrama. It's the same reason that people go through their normal, everyday lives and never see a murder, yet if you turn on the television, every other picture, or sometimes *every* picture, has somebody being murdered. Now you can say that one of the most horrifying shots, and one that they had to remove, in *King Kong* was when he picked people off the streets and stuffed them in his mouth. But that's what an animal would do that size. And a beast that would knock a ship over and knock a lighthouse over would certainly get hungry. So if he saw a little thing running down the street, he'd pick it up and chew on it. At least we didn't show layers of sausage hanging out from the policeman's stomach, and blood dripping down all over the pavement, or heads and severed arms, which they get away with today."

Naturally, Ray's animation was fluid and properly accented the rhedosaur's hostile personality, from its destructive, bearlike gait to its wicked little snarls. However, there *were* two brief shots in which close-ups of the animal were executed with other than the stop-motion model: when the beast gazed into the window of the ship, and later, when it growled at the men in the lighthouse. Ray tells us what was used for those shots and why. "We built a little hand puppet that was about twice the size of the model, so that we could get more detail in the face. Of course, when you're doing so much animation in a picture, you try to find corners to cut, and when there's just a small part of the animal showing, you try to get away with it. The fact that you're working with an economic situation, a limited budget, if you can save a week's worth of animation by building a big, detailed head, then you build it."

Special effects aside, *The Beast from Twenty Thousand Fathoms* was the first film of the fifties' famous monster-on-the-loose craze that continued with the Japanese *Godzilla* leveling Tokyo in 1954, Ray's own *It Came from Beneath the Sea* splintering San Francisco landmarks in 1955, an outer-space giant destroying Rome in Harryhausen's incredible *Twenty Million Miles to Earth* (1957), and countless other films. But *The Beast from Twenty Thousand Fathoms* was the first film of this genre to combine the monster-amok storyline with a warning to temper our liberal testing of atomic weapons. There was no preaching as in Robert Wise's *Day the Earth Stood Still* (1951), when an alien being put a forcible halt to earth's nuclear experimentation. Harryhausen's film simply used the bomb as a catalyst and let us draw our own conclusions. Only *Godzilla*, with roughly the same plot, made the same point with more sickening immediacy, coming as it did from the only nation ever to suffer the fury of an atom blast. Of course one must be careful not to overintellectualize what is primarily a contemporary plot device, but in both films the cautionary subcurrent is definitely there.

The performances in *The Beast from Twenty Thousand Fathoms* were all quite good, particularly those of Cecil Kellaway as the personable, white-haired Elson, and Kenneth Tobey as the very martial Col. Evans. But, as in *Mighty Joe Young*, the monster and its eye-filling reign were the film's real stars, and they were tough ones to upstage!

CHAPTER SEVEN

It Came from Beneath the Sea

In Hollywood, unless you win an Oscar or direct a *Jaws*, no one comes rushing with fistfuls of dollars to finance your next film. However, if the coming of Charles Schneer wasn't a mad rush, it was at least an auspicious development in Ray Harryhausen's career.

After *The Beast from Twenty Thousand Fathoms*, Ray drew huge black-and-white renderings and wrote two twelve-to-fifteen page outlines for new films, *The Giant Ymir* and *The Elementals*. He set them both in Europe because, as he noted in his *Film Fantasy Scrapbook*, "I felt myself getting restless and had a longing to go to Europe. At the time, I did not have the money for a proper vacation, so I thought I would try to dream up a story idea for a film that required European locations." *The Giant Ymir* was about a satyrlike monster from Venus running loose in Rome, while *The Elementals* told the tale of batlike men invading Paris. Ray even made a short color reel for *The Elementals* to prove that he could, indeed, create the wonders described in his outline. And Jack Dietz bought it, turning Ray's treatment over to a writer who then drafted a screenplay. But months passed, and when Dietz was unable to find backers for the film, *The Elementals* was dropped. At a loss for what to do, Ray considered going back to his fairy tales.

"I had visions, though again my imagination carried me away, of making twenty-five ten-minute subjects for television, and I thought well, I've got five of them. So I tackled *The Tortoise and the Hare*, realizing halfway through it that working alone one does have a tendency to get depressed a lot. You have problems, and you say to yourself, 'Is it all worth it?' Somehow you have to whip yourself

into getting up and doing things you don't particularly want to do. Then you see the things you've got to do, like six-hour scenes, and all the props. You can't buy them, so what do you do? You have to make them. And you also have to have some pocket money. I had money left over from the army, which kept me going for a while, and from *The Beast from Twenty Thousand Fathoms*, albeit a very little because I needed a break. But I started thinking of the two to three years of hard work all by myself that I couldn't very well afford because I was doing a lot of these on speculation. The thought of financing it all myself, without any advance money, was depressing. I couldn't even go to work for George Pal on his new feature films because I knew that he was involved at a studio, and it's very difficult to work at a major studio unless you belong to a union. So it was all quite complicated." Fortunately, a young producer by the name of Charles H. Schneer decided to contact Ray through a mutual friend. He had seen *The Beast from Twenty Thousand Fathoms*, and although he hadn't yet considered the specifics of plot, Schneer knew, as Ray tells it, "that he wanted to make a picture of a giant octopus pulling down the Golden Gate Bridge. The story developed from that. I thought, 'Well, that'll be an interesting challenge.' I'd always wanted to do something with the San Francisco Golden Gate Bridge, but I didn't know what. Besides, I felt I had to make a living, so I'd better not turn down any work. So I got to know Mr. Schneer better, and George Worthing Yates developed a story. Again, for a while it was all talk and I thought, 'Oh Lord, this'll go on again like the other pictures where months will go by.'"

But the project's formative period was

Donald Curtis (left), Faith Domergue, and Kenneth Tobey.
© Columbia Pictures

relatively brief, as Schneer has never been one to let his engine idle. First exposed to motion-picture making in 1942, when he was drafted and assigned to the Signal Corps, the twenty-six-year-old went to work at Universal Pictures in 1945 and for Columbia the following year. Rising quickly to the status of producer, he was not only responsible for Ray's second feature film, but produced ten of the twelve Harryhausen pictures which followed. Although Schneer became an independent produc-

er in 1957, most of his output has been released through Columbia.

Like all of Ray's films, the story for this new picture, *It Came from Beneath the Sea*—a name selected after Universal enjoyed tremendous returns on Ray Bradbury's *It Came from Outer Space* (1953)—was in great part the work of Ray Harryhausen. For one thing, he had always been interested in sea serpents, and wanted to retain the essence of that enthusiasm as a point of reference for animating his antagonist, the huge octopus. "Ever since I can remember, I was fascinated by strange animals and forgotten lands. Hyperboria and mythology has always struck a note in me that I think you'll find recurs in most of our films. So I used to delve into concepts about sea serpents in books, like the kraken and other monsters that have been sighted. The discovery of the coelacanth (a prehistoric fish believed extinct but discovered in 1938 off the shore of southern Africa—JR) substantiated a lot of these theories that Conan Doyle dreamt about in *The Lost World* and those types of things. Also, because I was exposed to such animals in my early youth, like those in *The Lost World* which I remember seeing—the brontosaur falling from a cliff into the mud stood out in my mind for years—they left an indelible impression. Of course, the more you are exposed to it, the more you try to read about it. And when you discover that other people are quite involved in these things, you begin to believe that they *could* possibly exist." However, apart from making certain that the scenario embodies the mystery and wonder of sea serpents which had so fascinated him, Ray was, and remains involved in the plotting of his films. Only he knows the limit of his special-effects camera.

"I always make contributions, and I say that with modesty—not because I'm a particularly modest person, because you can't afford to stay in Hollywood if you're modest—but I'm always contributing to our stories. I have to, because the average writer does not know what can and can't be done in a way that is economical. So I usually make twelve key sketches of situations that I feel I can do within reason on a given budget. Then we try to showcase these in the story. Indeed, the story is written around them. In the following story conferences, everybody contributes. It's seldom one person that makes a film. Even Orson Welles. He had Mankiewicz and several others, although you can always spot a Welles trademark, which is a marvelous thing. Unfortunately, film involves so many people that it's very difficult for one person, outside of a Hitchcock, a Welles, or a David Lean to say, 'this is *my* product!'"

The picture which emerged from these discussions and nearly a year of live action and stop motion photography, was another antibomb monster-on-the-loose saga. Cruising through the depths of the Pacific, a submarine commanded by Peter Mathews (Kenneth Tobey) is suddenly stopped dead in its course. Radiation levels climb, and regardless of the drive or escape tactics employed by Mathews, he cannot free his vessel. Finally, whatever force was holding the submarine simply vanishes.

Back at the San Francisco port, naval investigators examining the submarine find a chunk of flesh lodged in the ship's mechanism. Unable to identify it, they call in marine biologists Lesley Joyce (Faith Domergue) and John Carter (Donald Curtis). Working for days without sleep, they announce their dramatic findings to the authorities: the sample belongs to an octopus. A giant octopus. Accepting the report with tongue-in-cheek, the military representatives excuse themselves, and the scientists are rightfully annoyed. Only Mathews remains objective, trying to retain his position as a liaison between the mind and the muscle.

Meanwhile, crossing the Pacific, a huge freighter is attacked and sunk by a monstrous octopus. There are a few survivors, but they refuse to tell rescuers what actually happened for fear of being ridiculed. Fortunately, Dr. Joyce is able to win the confidence of one young sailor and he tells her about the octopus. The naval executives are now inclined to put stock in the scientists' claims,

A publicity sketch for *It Came from Beneath the Sea*.

It Came from Beneath the Sea for food—and found it in a freighter. © Columbia Pictures

although it is difficult for them to believe that such a beast can really exist. Joyce and Carter explain that sightings of giant octopi are not *new*: they have persisted through the centuries. As for why the creature has elected to surface just now, the researchers can only speculate that our atomic tests in the Pacific have killed its natural food sources, forcing it to the surface in search of alternate supplies. A decision is made to try to find the monster by keeping close tabs on any unusual goings-on in the Pacific.

After exploring various leads, Mathews, Joyce, Carter, and a local law enforcement official meet at a northern-California beach to investigate a missing persons claim. There, they find the impressions of large suckers in the sand—moments later, the octopus strikes. It kills the sheriff's aide, and our heroes hurry to San Francisco to report that the beast is in their midst.

To prevent an assault on the region's most populated area, Operation Sea Beast goes into effect, as San Francisco Bay is barricaded both above and below the water. Sonar and radar are employed to identify every object moving through the bay and before long, a great mass is detected moving in from the open sea. The navy's precautions notwithstanding, the enormous form presses on into the harbor, and moments later, a huge tentacle bursts from the water. It begins crushing train carriages and other items scattered about the docks, and even smacks a helicopter from the sky before turning its attention to the Golden Gate Bridge. Coiling about the pillared base of the suspension bridge, the octopus yanks the span asunder and slides back into the water. Moving inland, the monster resurfaces, wrapping itself about the famous Market Street tower. The landmark crumbles beneath the weight of the cephalopod which, the military now realizes, is trying to pull itself ashore, where food is most plentiful. While the tentacles raze building after building in search of nourishment, Mathews has his men don flame throwers and attack the beast. Fortunately, their fire repels the octopus, and the animal withdraws to the floor of the bay.

Elsewhere, Mathews has armed his submarine with an electric torpedo and the projectile, capable of generating intense voltage, is fired into the monster's brain. However, the missile fails to detonate. Slipping into a Scuba outfit, Mathews leaves the submarine and tries to trigger the blast. Lashing out, the octopus knocks him unconscious. Afraid that this opportunity to kill the beast may elude them, the anxious Carter dons an underwater suit and rushes to Mathews' aid. Repairing the torpedo, he scoops up the unconscious officer and swims away. Seconds later, the weapon comes sizzling to life and the prehistoric predator is destroyed.

If the reptilian rhedosaur did not lend itself to the ready conjuration of personality, the octopus presented an even greater challenge. For, as Ray laments, without a face through which to communicate pain, outrage, and other feelings, "you had to put emotion, if I may say so, in a tentacle." Not that the emotional range of the octopus is particularly broad: it is called upon to eat people without remorse, to act belligerent, to register agony, and to die. Still, it has many interesting character traits, and certainly more personality than a real octopus. As Ray notes, "You could never make a real octopus do anything. And this *is* one way of making a motion picture. But Charles had seen *The Beast from Twenty Thousand Fathoms*, and he saw what variety you could get with animation, and I suppose he felt that we could do much more with a synthetic octopus."

In order to build his monster's persona, Ray first had to mimic the most important aspect of a cephalopod's being, that of a slimy, undulating mass. He did this by coating the monster with glycerin and by constantly having one or more of the beast's tentacles in snaking, pulsating motion. This created the illusion of life. Mastering these movements, Ray was then able to work on the elements of drama. To this end, he let the tentacles speak for the monster. They roll with languor when the creature is fed and contented, as in the scene on the beach; they dart and seem to sniff the streets while prowling for sustenance; they convulse and retreat when shocked by the flame throwers; and in a remarkable use of personification, one tentacle even appears to have 'eyes' as it rears back, crashes through the window of an office building, and, hovering above a desk, studies the room in search of people to eat. Indeed, not only is this last sequence a deft use of the tentacle, but it is one that Ray had always wanted to shoot.

"That was a hangover from *The Lost World*. I remember vividly the scene where the brontosaur's head came through a window. Of course, things like that always stick in your mind, and you say to yourself, 'Here's a chance to make something similar.' Not that you try to copy the idea, but it was a situation that could look startling. And I thought the tip of this tentacle sort of feeling around, to see whether or not there's anybody in there, could be quite horrifying." The shot was executed with a miniature tentacle and some full-sized settings: "Of course, we couldn't afford to make a big tentacle on the kind of budget we had to shoot the picture. To build a mechanical thing that hardly functions outside of a few simple movements is enormously costly. Besides, you can never get anything really active out of it without it looking mechanical. At least, that's my belief, and maybe someone will prove me wrong. But even the marvelous bust that they built for the first *King Kong* had its limitations."

Making the octopus interesting beyond its innate hostility was not the only new problem faced by the animator. Being an aquatic creature, the cephalopod had to be shown both beneath and upon the sea. Although *The Beast from Twenty Thousand Fathoms* had a few brief underwater sequences, showing the monster's attack on the diving bell—shot "dry" with a painted miniature backdrop—the entire climax of *It Came from Beneath the Sea* was set at the bottom of the San Francisco Bay. As a result, Harryhausen had to devise a means of simulating the haze that would surround an observer on the ocean floor. For the live action sequences, this wasn't a problem: "We took a few shots of some men in Scuba gear paddling right to left and left to right." However, placing the octopus underwater involved more complex optical techniques. Obviously, these scenes could not have been filmed underwater: even if the stop-motion model *were* seaworthy, the position of the water would change from frame-to-frame causing it to jerk unnaturally on the screen. One answer was to combine the finished animation with footage of water via an optical printer. A second

method was to shoot stop-motion scenes through a distortion glass, a plate which ripples the setting for the camera and creates the impression of being submerged.

Other considerations in such scenes are, first, the pace of the model. Since an octopus that size would be held to a crawl by water resistance, "the animation is especially difficult because of the microscopic movements that you have to make to cause the tentacles to flow and look like they're in the water." No less complex were shots of the animated tentacles slithering from the real San Francisco Bay. Although the composites were achieved through Ray's standard special-effects processes, he elected to increase both the realism *and* his work load by superimposing foam wherever the tentacles broke the water. This frothing effect lent bulk and power to the octopus' every move, and was of tremendous value to the overall illusion.

When it's so easy, in Hollywood, to simply recycle one's successes or to peddle mediocrity, it's reassuring to note that Harryhausen took pains to make his second monster-on-the-loose film different from the first. Technically, of course, the basic stop-motion and process methods used in *The Beast from Twenty Thousand Fathoms* were employed to shoot *It Came from Beneath the Sea*. Conceptually, however, the two films were worlds apart. True, the antagonists were both giant animals from the dawn of life. But that broad generalization fails to consider the entirely different creatures that Ray presented onscreen. Let's compare, for example, the sinking of both the fishing vessel in *The Beast from Twenty Thousand Fathoms* and the freighter in *It Came from Beneath the Sea*—scenes which more or less sum up the distinctions between the beasts. Although both sequences occur at night and were, of course, created for their exciting screen values, the rhedosaur's assault was presented as an exhibition of mindless force. Resurrected by a holocaust, the dinosaur courted brute violence from the destruction of the ship and the lighthouse through the dismantling of Manhattan through its own fiery death. The octopus, on the other hand, slithered from the dark and mysterious ocean not to thrash the ship but to *pull it under*. It was an approach that resulted from Ray's knowledge of maritime lore: a long-standing

Harryhausen's model of the Golden Gate Bridge is about to feel the crunch of the quintopus. © Columbia Pictures

nightmare of sea-faring men has it that *something* will one day crawl from the deep and unknowable ocean to do away with trespassers. Everyone praised the vision of human vulnerability captured by the shot in *Jaws* (1975) where the shark tugged a young boy from his rubber raft and dragged him down; Harryhausen had been doing scenes like that twenty years earlier! While the rhedosaur's ferocious appearance before the small boat is staggering, the coming of the octopus preys on our inherent fears to give us a good old-fashioned scare.

While one can expect and even foresee certain unusual difficulties in the making of any film, *It Came from Beneath the Sea* presented Ray with three rather unusual obstacles. The first of these was the fact that he could only afford to build a five-tentacled octopus. Motion pictures are made with money that is generally borrowed from a bank—and must be repaid with interest. However, there is no way that one can rush a stop-motion film, which usually leaves backers biting their nails and impatiently waiting for a return on their investment. As Schneer told me recently, "We're always under pressure, but I would never sacrifice quality. And if a distributor doesn't have the sensitivity, which most of them don't, and the understanding, which none of them do, then we have to make them understand that the final result is worth the time, effort, and enormous bank interest." But there are, as we shall see in most every Harryhausen film, corners one can cut, and that includes something as radical as the elimination of three tentacles. Not only did it save money in the building of the model, but it gave Ray several limbs less to animate, thus reducing the length of the production schedule. For this reason, Ray always tried to show the monster at least partially submerged, leaving alert viewers to surmise that the other tentacles were simply underwater.

A second unique challenge for Ray occurred when *It Came from Beneath the Sea* was first being developed. It was Schneer's notion to shoot the picture in 3-D. At the time, theatre revenue was taking a severe beating at the hands of that new kid on the block, commercial television. Then, in November of 1952, Arch Oboler's *Bwana Devil* gave exhibitors a new lease on life—as well as on their theatres—by offering the public something

that they couldn't get on the small home screen: polaroid glasses with which to watch specially created motion pictures in *Natural Vision* or 3-D. And when *Bwana Devil* became a huge hit, along with such subsequent 3-D efforts as *House of Wax* (1953), *It Came from Outer Space* (1953), and *Creature from the Black Lagoon* (1953), Schneer saw added commercial clout in a 3-D octopus. Thus, he had Ray perform experiments to see if the process would work in conjunction with his special-effects techniques. Harryhausen executed the tests with the rhedosaur model and found that the whole thing was feasible—*if* Schneer were willing to finance a special-effects schedule that would have to have been extended threefold! The idea was dropped, and propitiously so: by late 1954, while *It Came from Beneath the Sea* was still before the cameras, the 3-D craze had worn off.

Finally, Ray was faced with the odd and potentially disastrous circumstance that arose when San Francisco city officials decided that they didn't *want* their Golden Gate Bridge destroyed in a motion picture. While the span was, of course, reconstructed in miniature for scenes showing the octopus actually tearing it down, the film crew needed stock shots of the bridge to use in rear and miniature projected sequences. As Ray tells the story in *Film Fantasy Scrapbook*, "In order to obtain permission and cooperation to photograph the various landmarks in San Francisco it was necessary to present the script to the 'City Fathers' for approval. We were astonished to be confronted with a big 'No' on the matter of the Golden Gate Bridge. We supposed they felt that any suggestion of destruction on film, even in a fantasy, might undermine the public's confidence in the soundness of its structure. We had of course gone too far into production to be defeated by this decision." Thus, the necessary footage was shot on the sly, from the back of a bread truck and other clandestine locations. The film was tremendously popular in San Francisco.

While *It Came from Beneath the Sea* features striking visual effects, tells an involving tale, and perfectly captures the mystique of humankind's relationship with sea serpents, the script and performances lag far behind those of *The Beast from Twenty Thousand Fathoms*. Tobey and Curtis vie for the spot of leading man, with neither character sufficiently well developed to hold the spotlight. They are even competing with the very liberated scientist of Faith Domergue, who is actually the strongest and most interesting of the players although she is put in a subservient position simply because she's a woman. And, unlike the screenplay of *The Beast from Twenty Thousand Fathoms* which allows for color in Nesbitt's almost fanatical determination, Elson's tragic demise, and

Evans' smug confidence that tales of a monster are just so much bilge water, *It Came from Beneath the Sea* uses its characters solely as unrounded pawns to further the action. Fortunately, the picture survives these deficiencies thanks to the superb values contributed by Ray Harryhausen. It all goes to underline what Schneer suggested in his comment about quality: backers who don't believe that Ray is worth his weight in interest had better consider what this film would have been like without him!

Careful lighting flawlessly combines the miniature saucer
with this footage shot on the streets of Washington, D.C.

© Columbia Pictures

CHAPTER EIGHT

Of Saucers and Saurians

There was a flying saucer picture in Ray's stars, so to speak. True, George Pal's Oscar-winning *War of the Worlds* (1953)—transferred from nineteenth-century England to Los Angeles of the 1950s—had done very well at the box office, and UFOs, first sighted in 1947, were constantly in the news, two factors which undoubtedly convinced Charles Schneer and Columbia Pictures that *Earth vs. the Flying Saucers* would be a sound financial proposition. But if Ray's heart had been anywhere in his budding years as an animator, it was with dinosaurs...and flying saucers.

Back in 1949, predating the science-fiction film flurry which began with *Rocketship XM* in 1950 and *The Thing* and *Day the Earth Stood Still* a year later, Ray had tried to convince Jesse Laskey to produce H.G. Wells' *War of the Worlds*. "I'd shown him ten big drawings that I'd made. This, of course, was long before *War of the Worlds* was actually made at Paramount by George Pal. I had wanted to stick to the Wells concept of saucerlike creatures on tripod legs which may or may not have worked. And I wanted to keep it in the Victorian period, like we later did with *First Men in the Moon* (1965). Unfortunately, there was a revulsion on the part of many financiers about doing period pictures, because you had to have period buildings, and you would run the budget up tremendously. Of course, I thought what George Pal did with *War of the Worlds* was marvelous—but I still think there's room to do it a different way. As a matter of fact, I made test footage in 16-mm with rear projection, showing the smoke and the big capsule, and then the cylinder turning by itself. I was also going to try by using a traveling matte, to put real people in the foreground, but I never got to that. The film I was

using, 16-mm, just isn't accurate enough. So I gave that up. But I shot the background plate of the screw turning and falling out, and then one tentacle comes out, searching around the edge, then the second tentacle comes out—just as Wells described it. I even went so far as to put music with it. I used Shostakovich's *First Symphony* which, to me, suggested the scene. In fact, I even tried to show it to Howard Hawks when they were making *The Thing*, because I thought they could use this type of scene. But nothing ever came of it. Of course, it was very effective the way they did *The Thing*, but I wouldn't have done it that way. Maybe it would have been less effective. Until you actually do it, you can never tell. Obviously, he knew what he was doing. But I still have this footage, although some of it's deteriorated. I had a 35-mm blow-up made of it and I was horrified when I opened the can and found a liquid mess."

The rest, as they say, is silence.

Perhaps Ray may one day film *War of the Worlds*. Until then, *Earth vs. the Flying Saucers* is his tribute to the Wells masterpiece, if not in plot and setting, then at least in its cataclysmic scope. Driving to the Skyhook facilities with his new bride Carol (Joan Taylor), Dr. Russell A. Marvin (Hugh Marlowe) is tape recording some observations about the American space missile program. Suddenly, a flying saucer appears before Dr. Marvin, knitting through the air and humming at a high-pitched frequency. The rapidly spinning disk paces his car for a short while, and then, as quickly as it had appeared, the saucer shoots skyward.

Arriving at Skyhook, Marvin replays the tape, hears the saucer noise, and is still mystified. However, everything is about to become painfully

97

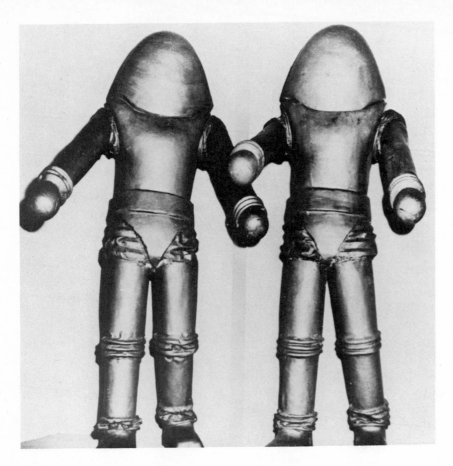

Wearing suits made of solidified electricity, these aliens prepare to speak with Hugh Marlowe onboard their flying saucer.

© Columbia Pictures

A flying saucer in London, with Joan Taylor and Hugh Marlowe aided by an ambitious studio publicity person.

© Columbia Pictures

clear. Early the following day, the saucers land at the military base and a humanoid figure emerges from the ship. Its features entirely hidden by a metallic space suit, the alien lumbers forth and is shot by trigger-happy soldiers. An energy field appears around the saucer as similarly accoutered beings come forth to retrieve their fallen companion; one of the creatures raises its arms and fires a ray which causes the troops to disintegrate. Turning, the outer-space visitor proceeds to destroy weapons and set buildings ablaze, reducing the Skyhook installation and its personnel to ashes. The only survivors are the base commander, captured by the aliens, and the Marvins, who had been in a cellar when the holocaust occurred. Unfortunately, their sanctuary may also become their tomb, as Dr. Marvin finds it impossible to open the debris-blocked door. With both the air and electrical power fading, he tape records an account of the attack. However, rewinding the spool, the scientist hears the saucer sounds from the day before, but slowed by the failing output of the generator. And what had previously been unintelligible noise was now a message from the aliens announcing that they would be landing at Skyhook the following day. Unfortunately, they had inaccurately transcribed the address from their accelerated time reference to our own. Hence, the tragic debacle which followed.

Since the attack on Skyhook could hardly have passed unnoticed, rescue workers are quick to arrive and the Marvins are saved. Brought before an investigative committee in Washington, D.C., Dr. Marvin plays the tape recording and asks that he be allowed to contact the aliens. After all, he notes, the Skyhook catastrophe was due to a misunderstanding and nothing more. But the military says no, and assigns the scientist a bodyguard, Major Huglin (Donald Curtis), to make certain that he doesn't sneak off on his own. However, Marvin is determined: speaking with the aliens from his hotel room, on a radio frequency described in the tape, he requests a meeting on a deserted beach. The creatures agree to the rendezvous, and Marvin steals to the garage. When Carol realizes that he has gone, she and Major Huglin follow.

At the appointed location, the trio is welcomed into the saucer which promptly speeds skyward. Once in space, the aliens usher out the captured

Harryhausen's superb miniature of the Capitol about to be destroyed by a stricken saucer.   © Columbia Pictures

Skyhook officer, display a device with which they have read his mind to learn about the human race, describe the gyroscopic propulsion system of their spaceships, and explain the reason that they have come to earth. With their home planet dying, the aliens' only hope for survival is to migrate to a new world. And they have selected earth, informing Marvin that permission must be granted for relocation wherever the extraterrestrials wish, or our planet will be taken by force. Left to reflect upon the ultimatum, Marvin and his coterie are returned to the beach.

Carrying the aliens' demand to leaders of the American armed forces, Dr. Marvin suggests an alternative. He asks for a remote research facility at which to design and build a specialized antisaucer weapon. The officers agree, and Dr. Marvin goes to work. Drawing up plans for a gun that will upset the crafts' aerodynamic stability, Marvin and his staff soon become aware of a globe of light hovering in a far corner of the laboratory. Realizing that it's an alien spying device, the researchers shoot it down and gather up their materials. Minutes later, the invaders arrive in force. With ray guns that come snaking from the saucers' bellies, the creatures set the laboratory afire and, as punishment for this betrayal, mercilessly toss the kidnapped soldier from the ship.

Setting up shop in Washington, D.C., Marvin builds his guns, the army monitors intersaucer transmissions, and the aliens take their case to the people of earth. Appropriating space on every broadcast and communications medium, they promise several days of natural disasters unless we submit to their will. And the cataclysms do indeed occur—floods, storms, and fires—although scientists are quick to assure everyone that these upheavals are due to explosions on the sun and not anything the aliens have done. Thus, while humankind bends, it refuses to break. Faced with no alternative, the aliens descend upon Washington, D.C., where Marvin greets them with his antisaucer artillery. In a spectacular rain of destruction, weapons and people are vaporized, saucers are hit and plunge out of control into the Potomac River and various buildings, and one disoriented saucer even dives earthward slicing through the base of the Washington Monument, destroying the landmark. Finally, with only a handful of guns and saucers left, the last leg of the showdown begins. On the steps of the Capitol, Dr. Marvin courageously holds his ground, blasting the two remaining saucers: one of them falls and rides up the Capitol, leveling the Senate, while the other goes tumbling into the Dome and explodes. The city has been destroyed, but earth has won the battle royal. And, for his part in the fray, Dr. Marvin is awarded a Nobel Prize.

The making of *Earth vs. the Flying Saucers* was a memorable experience for Ray. Technically, as we'll see in a moment, it created problems of an entirely different nature from those he had encountered in his first two solo efforts. However, Ray found researching the subject matter almost as fascinating as the challenge of the special effects. As with any film he makes, Harryhausen gathered together as much resource material as possible. But this film was unique in that it allowed him to actually discuss the subject with people who claimed to have seen or traveled on UFOs. And while Ray wasn't convinced that any of these people had ever really flown through deep space, the interviews impressed on him the plausibility, if not the actuality, of UFOs. Schneer wasn't buying the argument: "Ray may believe in flying saucers, but

I'm still an agnostic. I don't say he's right, I don't say he's wrong. I just say I don't know." But the important thing is that Harryhausen, stimulated by these talks, his studies, and periods of personal reflection on the vastness of the universe, was able to translate the essence of this modern-day mythos to the screen.

Flying saucers are synonymous with movement and mystery, and *Earth vs. the Flying Saucers* works hard to maintain both of these qualities. Ray had his discs constantly in motion and performing, spinning like tops while in flight and executing swoops, dips, turns, and climbs as though cellularly alive. But apart from poetic truth, Ray says, "I had the saucers dip and dive in a conscious attempt to give the film variety. There was a challenge in rounding out the saucer, which is inanimate. I mean, what do you do? You have the same problem you had with the tentacle in *It Came from Beneath the Sea*. There's no character outside of a long, tubular object, and you've got to try to make it look interesting and vary it so that in every scene it doesn't do exactly the same thing. We even tried to get a variety in the ray gun, by having it go in and out. That's a big problem in any feature film to get enough variety to keep the picture interesting." Conversely, the aliens, unlike their transports, are an enigma—stiff, clumsy, and always hidden in their opaque metal space suits. It's a marvelous contrast, albeit, the result of compromise.

Early on, Charles and Ray had decided that to make the UFOs interesting, they had to be shot in stop motion. Unfortunately, after establishing the cost of animating the saucers and their decimation of Washington, D.C., there was little money left in the budget for the aliens. Hence, the script was conceived so that the creatures would be seen only on rare occasions. "I hate to keep harping on this, as it sounds so strange," Harryhausen says, "but we *don't* have unlimited money, and the budget dictates a lot of what you're going to do. So there simply wasn't the funds to animate the aliens. But we didn't want to get into the realm of having midgets dressed in green suits coming from the saucers, so we simply limited the appearances of the people and made certain that when you *did* see them, they would be concealed in a metallic suit of some sort. Anyway, we thought there'd be more intrigue if you didn't see too much of them, although we didn't really want to create menace and horrify somebody like they did in *The Thing*."

Overall the energetic saucers and their unfathomable, lumbering occupants play well off one another. Likewise, the development of the terrestrial characters was a return to the substance of *The Beast from Twenty Thousand Fathoms*. Hugh Marlowe plays Dr. Marvin as a loving husband, a devoted scientist, and a man of fortitude. He is confident and headstrong and, indeed, has his best scenes when bucking the authorities, like Major Huglin who, himself, dislikes being a babysitter almost as much as the scientist resents having him around. Unfortunately, there's little to say about Joan Taylor's performance as Carol Marvin for, unlike Faith Domergue's role in *It Came from Beneath the Sea*, she serves solely as window dressing.

This whole question of characterization is an important and controversial one for Ray, who recognizes its value as well as its drawbacks. "We try to put characterization in a film as long as it doesn't stop the story. We constantly run into this problem in these types of films, and we're criticized many times by various people who say, 'If you only had better actors or better directors, you'd have a better film!' There *is* a point where that's important. But character takes time to develop. And when you're trying to tell a tale such as we do in the saucer picture, you either spend the time trying to develop characterization, or you spend the time developing the destruction, which is what these pictures are all about. Sometimes, of course, people don't always agree with the sacrifices you make. That picture, I thought, had good, rounded characterizations in it. But no one tore the ivy off the walls trying to see the film because of the characterization, or commented about it. We just wanted the picture to be popular and effective." And how did Ray define those quantities? "Spectacle. When the picture was made, disaster films were very popular. That was before the third time around, in recent years. But to get any kind of recognition, you had to have a total disaster. So basically, while it may sound crude, one just had to think in those terms."

One can dispute the impact that characteriza-

tion has on the box office performance of a film like *Earth vs. the Flying Saucers*, although, speaking from a strictly aesthetic point of view, the picture undoubtedly is more interesting because Marvin is fleshed out to a greater degree than, for example, John Carter in *It Came from Beneath the Sea*. However, one can't disagree with Ray's statement: action is of prime importance to *Earth vs. the Flying Saucers* or any of these pictures. And the climax of *Earth vs. the Flying Saucers* is nothing if it isn't crammed with eye-filling destruction, all of it remarkably executed by Ray in stop motion with an aerial brace.

We mentioned briefly the aerial brace in our section on *The Lost World*, a device which keeps an airborne model both aloft and steady during animation. Specifically, for each item that must be suspended above the set, the aerial brace apparatus consists of a spindle that can be rotated horizontally, a bar that runs parallel to the set and is supported by stands situated beyond the working area, and as many thin, strong wires—nylon thread or some similar substance—as is necessary. Fastened to the armature of the model before it is built up, the wires are attached to the spindle which, itself, is clamped out-of-frame to the overhead bar. Like the model, the spindle can be moved incrementally about its own axis or along the overhead strut so that, during animation, the model can be made to move or simply hover above a scaled set or before a miniature screen. The wires themselves are too thin to photograph or, if they happen to reflect the studio lights in a particular position, can be handpainted from the individual frames.

All of the saucers in this film were given flight by an aerial brace, but Ray employed the wire and spindle units for more than just the ten-inch-long metal spaceships. Since the budget of *Earth vs. the Flying Saucers* wouldn't allow for the costly destruction of miniature buildings using high speed photography—which would have slowed their collapse to give them the mass attendant to a life-size structure—Harryhausen had to work their destruction in stop motion *animating every piece of falling debris at the end of an aerial brace*! That included everything from the entire top half of the Washington Monument to the smallest bits of stone chipped from the pillars of the Senate

Ray Harryhausen holds the ceratosaur seen in the
'carnage' shot. © Warner Communications

Two of the mechanical models built for *Animal World*.
© Warner Communications

A scene of carnage from *Animal World*.   © Warner Communications

Building by the crash of the saucer. When one considers the careful manipulation of what amounted to dozens of wires per shot, and the fact that Ray seldom makes notes when he works, the full range of his concentration and talent becomes dramatically evident.

However, comparatively inexpensive and easy to choreograph though it may be, there is one serious drawback to the use of animation in scenes of destruction such as these. If one were to examine footage of a live-action disaster, falling chunks of brick and wood appear as blurs on film. In other words, they are not frozen in space with each click of the camera's shutter. And this seems perfectly natural on-screen: in real life, the object would also appear blurred, falling, as it is, faster than that one-tenth of a second needed by the brain to clearly register an image. But in stop motion, there is no blur as each frame records the clear and distinct position of an object. Even if the animator were to increase the size of each segmentary movement, the object would fall *faster*, but no truer to life. Thus, there is a touch of *strobing*, or jagged unreality to such scenes. But Ray doesn't trouble himself unduly with this problem. Although animator Jim Danforth has experimented with means of achieving a natural blur (see chapter 17), Ray feels that only the sharpest eyes ever catch the flaw. And while Harryhausen would be the first to agree that one should strive for perfection in *any* case, there is a limit to how much polishing, experimentation, and reworking one can do on a tight motion-picture schedule and budget. "Years ago I used to worry about it, but I don't any more. Again, you have to be practical. And most of the processes that you have to go through to create an illusion of blurring, in the final result, I don't think are worth it. Our buildings look like they're crumbling and, in later films, our pterodactyls look like they're batting their wings. It's in the movement of the figure, I think, rather than in the strobe effects that give the illusion that something is falling or flying. But you can go to so much trouble to do a thing like that, and it can defeat your budget; it can defeat many things. Sometimes we get criticized for it, and everybody's entitled to their opinion. But it just isn't worth the effort, we don't think." According to some producers, filming critical moments of your own movie isn't even justified when you can avoid it: the producers of a monster-on-the-loose effort known as *The Giant Claw* (1957) had a budget so restricted that they used disaster footage from Ray's 1956 saucer picture during their own creature's onslaught. Likewise, segments from Ray's next film were destined to see double duty, this time in the motion picture *Trog* (1970). When star Joan Crawford peers into earth's dim past through the mind of a captured caveman, she sees prehistoric animals that had originally performed in the 1956 Harryhausen-O'Brien collaboration *Animal World*. And, just as these scenes were the highlight of *Trog*, so were they the featured attraction of Irwin Allen's documentary about the evolution of life on earth.

Ray began *Animal World* shortly after he completed *Earth vs. the Flying Saucers*, both films being released within weeks of one another. When producer-director Allen won an Academy Award for his 1953 feature-length documentary *The Sea Around Us*, based on Rachel Carson's best seller about the history of marine life, he decided to shoot a sequel describing the genesis and development of all terrestrial animals, from microbes to dinosaurs. The result was a longer motion picture—eighty-two as opposed to sixty-one minutes—composed of segments which are related only in that they each focus on one of the earth's principal life forms. Initially, Ray's involvement with the project was to have been extremely brief. "Irwin Allen had seen some of my dinosaur footage, and he called me in to talk at first about just using still pictures in the film, making models and dioramas and photographing them as examples, since it was just a small part of the overall picture. And he really didn't want to go into too much animation because you had the problem that there weren't any humans involved. So you couldn't make any amount of dramatic qualities as we know them, other than just having animals fighting one another." But Ray convinced the producer that living dinosaurs would make the film more commercial than still photographs, and Allen put *both* Harryhausen and Willis O'Brien on the picture. His instructions: to create an effective sequence in as brief a production period as possible. Thus, the animators' involvement with the twenty-minute prehistoric episode lasted a mere six weeks, during which time Ray "did all the animation and

An *Animal World* allosaur.   © Warner Communications

O'Bie did the designing of the animals and the sequence. He also did the layouts of the glass shots and the miniature trees; the models were all built in the studio prop shop, including some large models, some mechanical heads and necks, which Mr. Allen used to try to cut down on some of the animated footage."

As Harryhausen has suggested, the purpose of the dinosaur segment was to show life as it really was in primitive times. This included scenes that covered the entire prehistoric spectrum, from the laying of eggs and the birth of dinosaurs, to awesome scenes of death and brutality. Fights between the monsters were especially grisly. As

105

The ceratosaur munches on the plates of a stegosaur.
© Warner Communications

Ray observes, "We tried to make the sequence very gory at first, natural to animals. You saw many scenes in the rest of the picture where, for example, a tiger tore animals to pieces and quivering paws and legs all covered with blood were seen. We tried to do the dinosaur sequence in the same vein. When the stegosaur was killed, the ceratosaur, I believe it was, tore big hunks of dripping flesh from him and started chewing it. But when the picture was previewed, we received so many negative remarks about the bloodletting that a lot of it had to be removed in the final version." The climactic volcano was equally gruesome, and more than one critic condemned the eruption for what Ed M. Clinton Jr. of the Scottish magazine *Nebula* described as being, "barbarous rather than documentary (as) terrified dinosaurs flee and are destroyed by...crevasses opening in the earth, (one) trapped creature screaming in agony as lava slowly burns him to death."

However, if they quibbled with the tastelessness of individual vignettes, most reviewers praised the overall realism of the prehistoric saga. And there was much in it that was both striking and original. For one thing, as the sequence was shot entirely on tabletop without the use of process photography, it could be filmed in color. Thus, it was a picture book come to vivid life. And while Ray was concerned about the segment lacking focus due to an absence of human players, the uniqueness of this bygone era abetted by O'Brien's raw panoramas and realistic colors, was in itself quite sufficient to hold one's attention. Then there were the monsters. Except for close-ups of the stiff, mechanical models,

106

A brontosaur succumbs to the heat during the *Animal World* volcano.   © Warner Communications

peacefully grazing when an allosaur leaps from where the cinematographer would be standing, over the camera and into frame, angrily swishing its tail at the viewer. The creature's appearance is at once ferocious and startling, and it establishes the ravenous pace for the struggle that follows. Artistically, it was a proven maneuver: Ray explains that, "I had done that same shot with the test footage I had made for *Evolution.* In *Evolution,* I had the allosaur leap over the camera because I had used the music to *Firebird Suite.* And there was a key chord which, when I heard it, I said, 'I've just *got* to make an allosaur jump in to that music!'" Recalling the effectiveness of the aerial-braced jump, he decided to recreate it for *Animal World.*

Although *Animal World,* as a whole, wasn't as popular as *The Sea Around Us,* Ray and O'Bie distinguished themselves admirably in their dramatic summary of prehistoric life. Unfortunately, the picture is rarely seen today, a sad result of the decline of the documentary film form as a whole. However, Ray is well-represented in the media by new movies, past and upcoming reissues of his more recent work, and wide television exposure of his early motion pictures. One of these latter films has an especially wide following: *Twenty Million Miles to Earth.* A favorite of both TV and science-fiction retrospectives, it was his next picture and one that many Harryhausen scholars consider to be his finest effort to date.

the dinosaurs were all smoothly animated and incredibly realistic. Though Ray himself is merely modest about the segment—"Well, for what it was in relationship to the entire picture, it certainly was adequate; it served its purpose"—it contains some of his liveliest work. The red-tinted volcano scenes and resultant dinosaur stampede are both frightening and exciting, and the battles between the animals are inspired. Indeed, one particular shot is nothing short of brilliant: a herbivore is seen

A pteranodon from *Animal World.*   © Warner Communications

Although Ymir was dismantled so that Ray could use his armature for the cyclops in *The Seventh Voyage of Sinbad*, he made this plaster cast as a record of his handiwork. Courtesy the British Film Institute.

CHAPTER NINE

Twenty Million Miles to Earth

"At the time I wrote *The Giant Ymir*, not only had I wanted to see Europe, but filmmakers were running out of locations in America. So what could we destroy *except* Europe?"

After completing *Animal World*, Ray went through his files to see if there were any old properties worth reviving and trying to sell. He came across *The Giant Ymir* and sent his outline to Charlott Knight, the writer with whom he had collaborated on *Little Red Riding Hood*. While Charlott rewrote the story, Ray drew new sketches replacing his horned, devil-like Ymir of old with a revised, reptilian creature, and took the entire presentation to various Hollywood producers. Most of them felt that the picture would be too costly; some doubted that Ray could really work the wonders he described in his treatment. Obviously, they hadn't seen his earlier films. However, Schneer, who was in the throes of becoming an independent producer, saw promise in the project and undertook its production.

Ray was thrilled with this opportunity to go to Italy first to scout locations, and later to actually shoot the picture. But the aspect of *Twenty Million Miles to Earth* which most excited him was that, "Kodak had just developed a film that was very fine grain. The grain problem has always been a big bugaboo for duplication, particularly through rear projection and optical effects. And they had just refined this new film, which we used for the first time in *Twenty Million Miles to Earth*, so that you could hardly tell, unless you were very critical about it, where the original negative left off and the duplicate negative began, which I felt was a big advance in our type of photography. It caused you to be less aware of the sudden approach of a trick shot,

and made the overall pattern much more believable."

The vehicle that gave Ray an opportunity to perform some of his most dazzling film effects and animation began, innocuously enough, in the small Sicilian fishing village of Gerra. Young Pepe (Bart Bradley) and his father are working the nets from their small boat when a huge rocket comes screaming from the sky. Crashing in the waters of the Mediterranean, it begins to sink, but not before Pepe's father has entered the craft and rescued two men, whom he brings to shore.

When the leader of the ten-man space flight, Col. Calder (William Hopper), awakens in an Italian hospital, he hastens to speak with his companion, Dr. Sharman. Calder's physician, Marisa Leonardo (Joan Taylor), urges the astronaut to bed, but he will have none of that. Although Sharman is dying from a fatal disease which everyone but Calder contracted on the planet Venus, the colonel pressures his crewmember about an unborn Venusian that they carried from the planet. He wants to know how long it can survive in its protective cylinder. Unfortunately, Sharman dies before he can hazard a guess. But Calder needn't have worried about the specimen. Elsewhere, playing Cowboys and Indians in a seaside grotto, Pepe finds the drifting cylinder, and hurrying from his village, sells the artifact to Dr. Leonardo (Frank Puglia), Marisa's grandfather and a zoologist who travels about Italy via trailer. Opening the canister, the scientist is puzzled by its contents, a jelly-like mass inside of which he can vaguely discern a small, humanoid figure. But there is work to be done and, leaving the curious find, Dr. Leonardo goes about his business. That night, the being in the egg-like sac claws its way to freedom. And no sooner has the foot-tall creature climbed to its feet than Marisa returns from the hospital, enters the trailer, flicks on the light, and frightens the animal almost as much as it startles her! She calls her grandfather, who grabs the strange beast and places it in a large cage. The next morning, the scientist pays a visit to his prize, and is shocked to find it grown to the height of a human being. Breaking from its prison, the new-born alien ambles into the surrounding forest.

Meanwhile, working in cooperation with the Italian government, Col. Calder and his military superiors have succeeded in tracing the whereabouts of the all-important container through Pepe, and arrive at Dr. Leonardo's trailer shortly after the Venusian Ymir has fled. They set out after the animal who, wandering about, has made his way to a barn, which he enters in search of sustenance. However, no sooner does the creature arrive then he is set upon by a dog. The two thrash violently about the floor, the Venusian ultimately slaying its adversary. But the sounds of their struggle have alerted the farmer, who enters the barn just as Calder and his associates arrive. They spot Ymir in a loft and plot his capture: poking at him with a long pole, Calder lures the creature down and prods him toward a hay wagon. Unfortunately, the men are unable to force the creature inside and, after attacking the bitter farmer, Ymir smashes through a far wall of the barn and escapes into the night.

Since Ymir has not yet had time to feed, and knowing that its diet consists of sulfur, Calder and his men search the sulfur-rich Mt. Etna for the monster. When they find him holed up in a cave, a plan is formulated to capture the beast alive. Aware of the fact that Ymir's only known weakness is electricity, the colonel has a helicopter fitted with a metallic net. Dropping bags of sulfur outside the monster's lair, Calder waits until Ymir has taken the bait before approaching with the net. He releases it, and as a group of soldiers secure the mesh, one of their number runs a cable to a waiting generator. At Calder's signal, contact is made and the creature drops to the ground, unconscious.

Brought to the Rome Zoo, Ymir is kept in a cement building near the elephant house. Sedated by a constant flow of electricity, the creature, now over twenty feet tall, is studied by scientists. They learn some amazing things about the Venusian: that, for example, he has no heart or lungs, only a maze of small tubes running through his body. Thus, nothing short of a cannon would have an appreciable effect on the beast. They also determine that breathing the earth's alien atmosphere has been responsible for Ymir's astonishing rate of growth which, Calder assures the scientists, is not indigenous to the species.

After preliminary studies have been made, the day arrives for the first declassified glimpse of the monster and its new home. However, as Col. Calder conducts three reporters on the historic tour, a piece of equipment slips from a pulley and cuts the flow of electricity to the monster. Slipping from his stupor, Ymir breaks through a concrete wall of the makeshift laboratory, and assaulted by a frightened elephant, engages the pachyderm in a furious struggle. The two behemoths battle their way through the streets of Rome, crushing people and cars underfoot. Finally, Ymir's relentless pounding forces the elephant to its knees. Biting the fallen animal in the throat, the Venusian keeps gnawing until his opponent is dead. Continuing through the city, Ymir kills a handful of Italians before taking to the waters of the Tiber.

Hoping to recapture the monster, Calder tries to force it back on land by having his soldiers throw hand grenades into the river. The ploy succeeds: Ymir resurfaces, ripping apart a bridge in the process. Continuing its rampage, the monster demolishes the ruins of the Temple of Saturn and makes for the Colosseum. Climbing the ancient stadium, Ymir tosses huge stone pieces at pursuing troops, and it is now clear to Calder that the Venusian will have to be destroyed. Calling for bazookas and tanks, the colonel has them fire at the creature. Wounded, Ymir drops to his belly but retains his grip on the ledge of the Colosseum; unleashing a barrage at the monster's perch, the artillerymen bring down the entire top half of the wall. Tumbling to earth amidst a shower of rubble, the kidnapped Ymir has lost his battle to survive.

With the possible exception of *Mighty Joe Young*, *Twenty Million Miles to Earth* contains Harryhausen's finest character animation to date, as the hounded, lonely Ymir comes *alive* on the

Ray Harryhausen's model spaceship crashes in the Mediterranean Sea. © Columbia Pictures

screen. There are so many eloquent and seductive moments which sparkle with genius: Ymir emerging from his egg, and wraithlike, rising to his feet in the darkened room; the small creature burying its face in its arm and scratching at the air when Marisa turns on the light and rubbing his eyes as they become accustomed to the glare; the Venusian's battle with the dog, seen entirely in shadow on the barn wall; Ymir charging the camera—which represents Col. Calder's point of view—being entirely illuminated by sharp under-lighting; the alien accepting the bags of sulfur, cupping the food to his mouth while keeping a wary eye on the movements of the soldiers; Ymir's anguished reaction to his bombardment on the Colosseum; and several more. However, along with

the alien's gestures and mannerisms, his aggressive characterization, too, is a triumph for Harryhausen. Because the plot so thoroughly victimizes Ymir, Ray wisely refrained from playing *too* directly for audience sympathy. Any pathos which emerges from *Twenty Million Miles to Earth* has its roots in the genuinely tragic situation, rather than in Ymir's personality. To wit: a pawn of human progress, not only was he snatched from the womb and brought to a strange world, but death came to him a mere few days after he had been born. And what a life! Crawling from his gelatinous incubator, Ymir is shocked with a harsh light, brusquely grabbed from a worktable and shoved into a cage, attacked by the dog, stabbed in the back by the farmer with a pitchfork, poked and pushed

111

From left to right, William Hopper, Frank Puglia, and Joan
Taylor. © Columbia Pictures

against a hay wagon, chased and electrocuted,
locked in a zoo, tormented by an elephant, peppered
with hand grenades, and shot with artillery. There
was hardly a moment's respite for the poor
creature! Thus, like *King Kong*, the picture is
structured so that we cheer for the Venusian not
because he is a cuddly, self-sacrificing character like
Son of Kong, but because he is fighting for the right
to live. It's a dimension with which we can identify,
and in its bestial, active manifestation, gives the
picture flavor. However, if Ymir suffered, at least
there were creative and dramatic dividends!

Visually, the film unreels like an etching by
Gustav Doré, one of Ray's favorite artists. The
Roman settings give it a classical feel, while stark
brights and darks moodily underline the perform-

ance of the dragonlike Ymir. As Harryhausen
comments on the values of black and white, "I think
a colorful subject like Sinbad or an Arabian Nights
tale must be done in color. It would be very drab in
black and white. But I prefer black and white,
personally. I think it has a great deal of advantage
over color because I always *think* in black and white.
I find light and shade much more powerful than
color. You can achieve that magic and mystery up to
a certain point in color, I think, just as there are
certain things in color you can do that you can't do
with black and white. But in *Twenty Million Miles
to Earth*, we were trying to work with the black and
white to get a mood, to make the picture more
dynamic, visually. Of course, so many of the scenes
you design on the spur of the moment. For instance,

Ymir prepares to attack the soldiers by marching *through* the ruins of the Temple of Saturn.

Ray Harryhausen's preproduction sketch of Ymir toppling the Temple of Saturn... © Columbia Pictures

in the barn sequence, the key lights were so underlit that you had to try to complement it with the animation. But, as I said, decisions like that are all involved with the concept at the moment."

Beyond the Doré-esque atmosphere, a Harryhausen trademark which emerged in this film and was seen again in *The Seventh Voyage of Sinbad* (1958), *Jason and the Argonauts* (1963), *The Golden Voyage of Sinbad* (1973), and *Sinbad and the Eye of the Tiger* (1977), was a stylized walk adopted by his humanlike or bipedal creatures. As they move through their paces, the animals tend to hunch forward slightly, their arms drawn back as though preparing to strike. Human beings, of course, as well as the gorillas—when they're not

parading about on all fours—walk with their arms dangling at their side, swinging to and fro. It would be a pleasure to report that Ray invested months of experimentation in a search for the most dramatic way to position his creations, thus evolving this popular bearing. Unfortunately, this was not the case. As Ray has emphasized throughout the book, stop-motion filmmaking is an expensive undertaking. And the more time it involves, the costlier it becomes. Thus, the popular stance was developed primarily for economic reasons. To animate each arm swaying back and forth could add weeks to a film's production schedule, and the stylized pose was an alternative. However, before purists condemn Ray for having "compromised" on his art, it should be pointed out that he *did* have a rather remarkable precedent: Walt Disney gave Mickey Mouse only four fingers on each hand because, anatomy and aesthetics notwithstanding, it *was* two less digits to animate! Ray is constantly faced with the cruel realities of time and money, and must ever make do as best he can.

While schedule and economy are certainly among the most important aspects of commercial filmmaking, maintaining believability is equally vital. If the monster and the special effects are poorly executed, or the performances insincere, then the picture becomes laughable, particularly in the already incredible science fiction genre. And while Ray always works hard to uphold his end of the credibility, *Twenty Million Miles to Earth* was a backbreaker. Not only was there the single

character of Ymir, whose movements, reactions, and general patterns of behavior had to remain constant, but there were human figures, the dog, the elephant, and destruction to animate.

As ever, Ray felt that high speed photography would have showcased the feeling of the ruins to better effect. But he was once again faced with the limitations of his budget. "Every year that goes by, inflation makes it necessary to put more and more into a film. We had a little more money to spend on the special effects, but not a great deal, because we had the trip to Rome. And we had to budget ourselves to get the most out of Rome and all the monuments, which played an integral part in the climax. So I went over and picked all the locations and photographed them with a second unit, while Charles coordinated everything. We had doubles in

...and how that same scene looked in the completed film.
© Columbia Pictures

Ymir in the loft of the barn.   © Columbia Pictures

Ymir battles Ray's stop motion elephant...

...and ultimately slays the beast.   © Columbia Pictures

Rome, and when we got back to Hollywood, we brought the leading characters into the various Roman settings of our picture with process backgrounds. So once again, because of these other expenses, I had to animate the destruction. And it is terribly trying, as you don't feel like you've accomplished anything when you animate these scenes. No matter what you do, it always gives a different illusion than high-speed photography. But it's a necessity, and that's why you do it." However, these aerial braced scenes were a lark compared to the problem presented by the elephant. An animator *always* takes his life in his hands when he undertakes the stop-motion portrayal of a known creature, one about which audiences will be especially critical.

"I had always remembered O'Bie saying in the early days, when I first met him, that he hated to animate anything that could possibly be done in live action. And I quite agree with that, up to a point. But we ran across this problem in two pictures, both involving elephants—*Valley of Gwangi* (1969) and *Twenty Million Miles to Earth*—where we wanted a big elephant, an eleven-foot elephant, to make it look impressive. As Barnum and Bailey used to say, 'People won't go to see a flea circus, but they will go to see Jumbo!' So we wanted as big an elephant as possible. And around Hollywood, you could only get

about an eight- or nine-foot elephant at the most, trained. I often wish I had been born at the time of Jumbo. It would have saved me months of animation, except in the actual contact sequences between the monsters and the elephants." Fortunately, Ray was able to spare himself *some* animation by renting a normal-sized elephant and making him appear huge by hiring a four foot tall man to play the keeper.

Obviously, one's foremost consideration when animating any character, be it realistic like an elephant, a human, or a gorilla, or fanciful like the rhedosaur or Ymir, is that they carry themselves not like models, but as if they were living creatures. With an elephant or an ape, one must examine footage of the animal—as Ray did for *Mighty Joe Young*—to study their gait, facial expressions, muscle reactions, and so forth; even the smoothest animation will not sell an audience if the screen representation doesn't resemble animals they have seen. But to animate Ymir or any fictitious beast requires special things. "There are certain limitations that you have to accept with animation because of the structure of the model and the fact that you don't have muscle but rubber pulling against the armature, and that sort of thing. So you can't always do a naturalistic movement, per se. But you can *simulate* it. For example, you try to give the illusion that there's a shift in body weight. Otherwise they get off balance. I have this problem particularly with two-legged creatures. They always have to keep their center of gravity over their feet. Sometimes you even have to go through the gesture yourself, just to plant it in your mind. As for the real animals, I used to time them with a stopwatch, but I find that sometimes cumbersome and it gives you a false lead. It's better, after a lot of experience, just to *feel* it, because otherwise you get a stiff, mechanical illusion rather than the flowing motion that you are trying to achieve. So you keep in mind something you've seen. For the Ymir, I considered a tyrannosaur, what an animal would do that walked on its hind legs and had a tail. If he got up or swung around, the tail had to follow to prevent him from falling over. You have to keep those things in mind because you want it to look logical."

If the special effects in *Twenty Million Miles to Earth* were more complex than usual, the human

Ymir emerges from the Tiber. To give the illusion that the creature was wet, Ray coated his model with glycerin. This creates a problem in that, unless the animator is careful, the substance becomes tacky, causing the highlights to change from frame to frame. © Columbia Pictures

players brought no new intricacies to their roles. William Hopper did as much as he could with the strong, stern, but shallow Calder, and Joan Taylor, who might have created a character as interesting as that of Faith Domergue in *It Came from Beneath the Sea* really wasn't on-screen all that much. Thus, only Bart Bradley's Pepe had any real depth, preoccupied, as he was, with American Western movies and willing to help Calder find the missing canister only if he could buy a horse with the reward money. Yet, there *was* a performance in *Twenty Million Miles to Earth* that merits our close scrutiny, as it marked the beginning of an auspicious acting career—that of Ray Harryhausen.

"There is a photographer who runs up and is crushed by the elephant. Everyone thinks that's me, but it isn't. I was in another part of the picture, although I can never find myself. I was feeding peanuts to the elephant during the chaotic sequence where Ymir broke loose in the elephant house, and I only did it out of desperation. We had a lot of extras in Rome in the zoo, and we did a rehearsal where everybody ran. Then the director said, 'Good.

Let's start again.' Everybody went back to their places, but the man who had been feeding elephants wasn't there. He had apparently gone home. So I shot out there, grabbed the bag of peanuts, and started throwing them. When the director said run, I ran. So that was my initiation before the cameras."

In all fairness to the script and players, there is no doubt but that Ymir and Ray's marvelous special affects are what the 1957 picture is all about. And they do indeed carry the film most ably. As for Ymir being Ray's finest creation, it is certainly one of his best animated models, and its well-rounded character elicited viewer reaction. Stunning to watch, Ymir and *Twenty Million Miles to Earth* do indeed represent a tour de force exhibition of Ray's mastery over his medium. However, designations such as Best Picture and Best Character must be based on personal preference rather than absolutes. After all, there are just as many people who feel that Harryhausen's next opus, *The Seventh Voyage of Sinbad*, is his greatest effort to date. And, like fans of Ymir, admirers of the cyclops and his cinematic kin have the ammunition to support their claim!

Ymir came *Twenty Million Miles to Earth*—and ended his days at the base of the Roman Colosseum.

CHAPTER TEN

The Seventh Voyage of Sinbad

"You're in an awkward position today, in that even if you wanted to do a picture in black and white, you really can't—unless you're Mel Brooks and you insist. And he's in a position to insist. But the distributor feels that black and white makes the product very difficult to sell."

Times were changing and, as in mainstream moviemaking, the day of the black-and-white fantasy film was nearing an end. Thus, Ray began working on the perfection of color special-effects techniques, and considered what properties would be best suited to color. One such concept was *The Seventh Voyage of Sinbad*.

Like *The Giant Ymir*, *The Seventh Voyage of Sinbad* was not an easy property to sell. Harryhausen drew several large renderings and took them to a half-dozen producers, all of whom assured Ray that films based on the *Arabian Nights* meant death at the box office. This rather uninformed opinion was the result of the failure of several tongue-in-cheek Scheherazadean films, and Harryhausen couldn't convince them that his picture would be different, a serious adventure film. Disappointed, he filed the sketches away, never expecting the picture to be made. Surprisingly, Ray had not discussed the film with Charles Schneer. "I thought *The Seventh Voyage of Sinbad* would be too complicated. We were making films on a very inexpensive scale, in black and white, and in many of them we utilized stock shots to a great degree, stock shots of disasters that had already been recorded, both real disasters and miniature disasters. And I felt that it was too complicated a project to do on the type of budget that we had originally for doing these types of pictures. In fact, when you are making a costume picture, you have to build everything. Where do you

find a typical *Arabian Nights* city or palace? You have to build it, and get the costumes. You don't just tell an extra to show up in a baggy costume. It's furnished by the studio, and you have all those things to consider." However, several months after completing *Twenty Million Miles to Earth*, Harryhausen casually mentioned the project to Schneer, and the producer asked to see the sketches. Unlike his peers, Schneer saw the entertainment possibilities inherent in the project and almost immediately undertook its production. He hired Kenneth Kolb to develop a story from Ray's drawings, and then a finished screenplay—and after Ray had ironed out the various problems involved in converting his special-effects processes to color, the picture went before the cameras.

Not surprisingly, *The Seventh Voyage of Sinbad* continued the tradition that had helped make each of Ray's solo efforts a hit, the practice of opening the film with fire and brimstone. There's a confrontation with a monster a mere five minutes into the film, which Ray admits is not his favorite manner of moviemaking. "You have a decision to make. I prefer the slow build-up, because I was raised that way, having teethed on *King Kong* which I thought had a perfectly constructed screenplay. It gradually weaned the public from the mundane into the spectacular and utterly fantastic. Unfortunately, you can't make every picture that way. So the modern approach, which came from the technique of television production, was that you start the picture off with a wallop. You grab the peoples' attention and then, if manipulated properly, they'll continue to watch as you start to build again."

En route from the kingdom of Chandra to

The very expressive cyclops reacts to Sinbad's attack in the opening moments of *The Seventh Voyage of Sinbad.*

© Columbia Pictures

Bagdad, Sinbad's ship is blown off course. Onboard is Princess Parisa (Kathryn Grant), whose betrothal to Sinbad (Kerwin Mathews) had prevented a war between the two great powers. Since the couple is in love, the marriage of state is hardly an imposition. Pausing at an island to gather food and refreshment, Sinbad and his crew are alarmed to find prints of huge cloven hooves in the sand, as well as a monstrous cave carved in the shape of a head. Sinbad decides to investigate, and walking toward the huge stone mouth, is met by the magician Sokurah (Torin Thatcher), who is grasping a small lamp and running toward the sea. Pursuing the sorcerer is a horned, Pan-like cyclops who strides onto the beach, roaring defiance. The sailors throw spears at the giant, their weapons striking and enraging the brute. However, while the cyclops is distracted, Sokurah has an opportunity to rub his lamp and mutter the words that summon the genie. A stream of smoke pours from the golden vestibule and becomes the young djinn

Barani (Richard Eyer); since the slave of the lamp can restrain but not destroy, Sokurah orders him to build a barrier between Sinbad's men and the one-eyed beast. Transforming himself into a ball of fire, Barani goes whirling through the air at the wizard's bidding, erecting an invisible wall before the cyclops. And batter the impasse through he may, the monster is unable to stop Sokurah, Sinbad, and the sailors from reaching their launch and heading for the ship. But the giant does not give up. Grabbing a huge boulder, he heaves it into the sea and overturns the small boat. Since Sokurah can't swim, Sinbad comes to his rescue; in the process, the magician loses his lamp. The spell broken, the invisible wall disappears and the cyclops wades waist-deep into the ocean. By this time, Sinbad and his party have reached the ship, so the beast must settle for retrieving the lamp. Although it is useless to the monster, who cannot speak, he realizes that someone edible is bound to come after it. And sure enough, no sooner have they set sail when Sokurah

More action on the beach at the beginning of *The Seventh Voyage of Sinbad.*   © Columbia Pictures

visits Sinbad in his cabin and pleads that they return to the Isle of Colossa to recover the lamp. Sinbad refuses, claiming that he and Parisa are long overdue in Bagdad.

That night, at the Caliph's palace in Bagbad, Sinbad, Parisa, and the Sultan of Chandra are honored with a feast. And, for entertainment, the Caliph asks Sokurah to perform some magic tricks. The sorceror gladly obliges. Placing both Parisa's waiting woman and a snake into a large jug, Sokurah bathes them with a strange mixture. Breaking the great ceramic, he reveals the maid to have four arms and a serpent's tail. Performing an exotic dance for the assemblage, the green-faced creature seems to enjoy herself—until her reptilian posterior rebels and tries to strangle her human half. Exposing the devilish hybrid to a second formula, the wizard returns the servant to normal. Next, Sokurah requests a brazier of live coals with which to "read" the future. Predicting war between Chandra and Bagdad, he offers to dispel the evil omen at the price of an escort to Colossa. Perceiving that Sokurah's prophecy was a lie to achieve his selfish ends, the Caliph orders him to leave Bagdad or his eyes will be torn out.

Later in the evening, after everyone has retired, Sokurah steals to Parisa's bedroom window. There, he casts a spell shrinking the princess to doll size. The next morning, when Sinbad learns of Parisa's fate, he tracks the magician down— unaware of his guilt in the matter—and asks for help. Sokurah admits that he can, in fact, restore the princess, but only with a potion made from the egg of a giant bird known as the roc, which nests on the peaks of Colossa. Sinbad agrees to make the journey, taking care to build a huge crossbow in case it is needed against any of the island's monstrous denizens.

Since few of Sinbad's original crewmembers are willing to return to the accursed island, the prince is forced to recruit men from the jailyards of Bagdad. Guaranteed freedom for service, the prisoners set sail with Sinbad, though they have no intention of honoring their commitment. Once underway, the criminals mutiny, assuming command and locking Sinbad and Sokurah below deck. However, a driving storm puts the ship on a course for the island of the sirens, women whose wailing

A stop-motion hand of the cyclops retrieves Sokurah's magic lamp after the magician's boat was overturned.

drives people mad. And while Sinbad and the magician think to stuff cloth in their ears, the rebellious sailors foolishly take no precautions. Thus, screaming and tearing at their ears, the cutthroats free their captain and swear allegiance if he will save them. Taking charge, Sinbad pilots the ship back to the open sea and lands the crew safely on Colossa.

Dividing the men into three groups, Sinbad leaves one contingent behind to assemble the crossbow while the other two companies make their way to the breeding grounds of the roc. They will take different routes so that if either group is captured by one of the island's many cyclopes, the other group can come to its aid. Sinbad and Sokurah each lead an expedition. However, not long after the men have separated, the magician leads his charge to a river of wine, where the sailors become drunk. Pressing on alone, Sokurah heads for the cave of the cyclops who stole his lamp. Meanwhile, Sinbad has also stumbled upon the cave, which is stocked with incredible riches from centuries of ships crashed on the shores of the island. Despite the urgency of their mission, and Sinbad's command that they continue on their journey, the crew decides to steal this wealth and return to the ship. However, the one-eyed ogre has other plans. Arriving as a scuffle breaks out between Sinbad and his men, the horned giant removes the stone roof of his vault and gathers up the sailors, depositing them in a wooden cage. Then, selecting one of their number, the cyclops ties him to a spit and proceeds to bake the poor soul over an open fire. But help is near—or so Sinbad thinks. He spots Sokurah and calls to the magician for assistance; the sorceror merely laughs and enters the cave of the preoccupied cyclops.

Faced with no alternative, Sinbad must place his fiancee in danger. Reaching into his vest, he withdraws a tiny jeweled box. In it is Parisa. Depositing her on the lid of the cage, he asks her to dislodge the bar that locks the door. And, although the sturdy latch is like a log to the shrunken princess, she manages to push it free. The timing is perfect: no sooner has Parisa completed her chore than the cyclops hears someone rummaging through his possessions and goes to investigate. He finds Sokurah, who has located the lamp, and gives chase; Sinbad and his men are thus able to climb from their prison, free the roasting sailor, and hasten to save the magician, the only man among them who can return Parisa to normal. After a furious battle, in which the cyclops attacks and kills many of Sinbad's men with an uprooted tree, the prince and Sokurah are cornered by the monster in a rocky cul-de-sac. Fortunately, Sinbad had the foresight to pluck a flaming ember from the fire. When the giant peers into the cave, the Arabian knight blinds him.

The snake-woman dances for the court of the Caliph.

The cyclops removes the roof of his cave vault to find Sinbad's men stealing his treasures.

Running to the monster's side, Sinbad then taunts him, urging the sightless beast toward a cliff. The cyclops follows, groping at the air, and tumbles from the ledge, landing dead in a river. The only positive result of the incident is that Sinbad has gained possession of the lamp. And, although he doesn't understand its power, the prince decides to hold onto the lamp until the deceitful magician has fulfilled his part of the bargain.

Venturing into the mountains of Colossa, Sinbad spots an unhatched roc egg, but Sokurah suggests that they search for one from which the bird has already emerged. However, Sinbad's men are hungry, and breaking the giant shell, they slaughter the golden-feathered, two-headed chick within. As they cook the bird, the magician anxiously watches the skies.

Taking a piece of the shell and retiring to a secluded corner of the cliff, Sinbad admits to Parisa his distrust of the sorcerer. She, in turn, offers to give her lover the upper hand by slipping into the lamp and asking Barani for the words that will invoke his protective power. Sinbad agrees to the plan and, sliding down the spout, she enters a misty chamber. There the genie greets her and shows the

The cyclops attacks Sinbad's men
outside his treasure cave.

The cyclops roasts one of Sinbad's men in a blue-backing
shot. Note the monster's tongue as he licks his chops.

princess a promise of freedom inscribed on the wall of the lamp:

> *When the big that is small shall again become tall, into fiery rock, to rise, you must fall.*

Parisa tells Barani that she was once tall, and hopes to be so again; promising to help him, she asks only the mystic phrase in return. The genie recites the words: "From the land beyond beyond, from the world past hope and fear, I bid you genie now appear."—which Parisa relays to Sinbad. However, no sooner has she climbed from the lamp than the parent roc, seeing what has become of its child, attacks the sailors. Sinbad leaves the princess and joins the fray, a fight which sees more of Sinbad's crewmembers slain. The slaughter ends only when the roc seizes the prince in its awesome talons and

The cyclops tries to reach Sinbad and Sokurah, who are entrenched between the two huge boulders.

© Columbia Pictures

Although Kathryn Grant would be added at a later date via optical printer, this Harryhausen doll helped Kerwin Mathews play a scene with his shrunken lover. It is doubtful, however, that the writing on the crate on which Sinbad is sitting came from the hand of the one-eyed giant.

© Columbia Pictures

deposits him, unconscious, in a mountaintop aerie. Meanwhile, back at the campsite, Sokurah kidnaps the princess and makes for his castle near the beach.

When Sinbad awakens, he summons the genie who directs him to the cavern which houses Sokurah's sombre stone palace. Stepping into the dark recess, the adventurer finds a dragon guarding the entrance of the cave from cyclops. Edging past the great lizard, he enters the magician's laboratory, hands him the eggshell, and demands that he cure the princess. Sokurah does as Sinbad asks, placing the tiny Parisa in a coffin and filling it with a steaming brew. When he raises the lid, Parisa is once again her normal size. Having kept his promise, Sokurah now asks for the lamp, but Sinbad refuses to turn it over before they are safely on the beach. Unwilling to wait, the wizard casts a spell on the human skeleton dangling from a nearby chain, and the hellish figure comes to life. Grabbing a sword and shield, the ghoul engages Sinbad in a nightmarish duel. The two parry from room to room until Sinbad corners the skeleton on a tall, spiral staircase and knocks him to the ground. The demon of bone shatters, and grabbing Parisa, the prince runs from Sokurah's lair. However, the magician has not yet finished with the couple. Smashing a crystal ball, the wizard causes the only exit from his domain, a stone bridge, to collapse. With no way to cross the sea of bubbling lava that

Safe from the cyclops' reach, Sinbad prepares to put out the monster's eye.

surrounds them, Sinbad calls upon Barani, who hands him a rope. Sinbad and Parisa swing to the other side. However, once across, Parisa recalls her promise to the djinn. And, with a sea of boiling mud at their feet, she surrenders the lamp to the "fiery rock" that the boy might be freed. Seeing this, Sokurah cringes and sets out after the pair.

Sneaking past the fire-breathing dragon, Sinbad and Parisa leave the cave only to meet another cyclops. The monster pursues them into the igneous labyrinth, and desperately outnumbered, Sinbad frees the dragon. The two beasts have at one another, and the lovers are able to flee to the beach. Meanwhile, the cyclops puts up a noble struggle but the outcome of the battle was never in doubt. With the dragon's massive jaws locked about its throat, the one-eyed monster reluctantly succumbs, just as Sokurah comes running from the cave. Sinbad, however, has had time to prepare a welcome. With his men tugging on the huge crossbow, the prince waits until the dragon appears at the mouth of the head-shaped cave, and then releases the arrow. The shaft pierces the monster's heart and the leviathan falls, crushing Sokurah.

The baby roc is killed by Sinbad's hungry men.

The parent roc avenges the murder of its chick.
© Columbia Pictures

A studio artist had a field day with this shot! Notice the painted trees and other signs of retouching.
© Columbia Pictures

Sinbad, Parisa, and what remains of the crew return to the ship and, setting sail, are surprised to find Barani aboard. But true to the legend in the lamp, he is now a mortal. However, in a final act of magic, he presents his liberators with a wedding gift: the treasure from the cyclops' cave. Appointing Barani cabin boy, the Prince of Bagdad charts a course for home.

In shifting his efforts from contemporary subjects to a period costume drama, Ray not only forsook the present, to which he has managed to return only as far as the early 1900s in *Valley of Gwangi*, but he relinquished the self-satisfaction of working in black and white. However, if Harryhausen missed either Gustav Doré or the twentieth century, it was not evident in *The Seventh Voyage of Sinbad*.

The trend-setting 1958 film was an entertainment unlike any the screen had seen since *King Kong*. Not even Alexander Korda's classic 1940 spectacle *The Thief of Bagdad* had the sense of wonder embodied in this very concise—only eighty-nine minutes long—Sinbad film; the picture is literally awash with fantasy. Even in the few minutes they have before first landing Sinbad on Colossa, the filmmakers carefully begin crafting a mystical mood about the film. Not the slow weaning from reality which Harryhausen prefers, it nonetheless effectively establishes the tone of the movie.

After the title credits—which feature beautifully rendered artwork of scenes from the film—the camera follows Sinbad's ship as it passes slowly through a strange fog. Mentioning the mysterious winds which blew them off course, Sinbad expresses confidence that they will soon find land and refreshment. The crewmen are not certain they're *that* desperate for sustenance; one sailor notes that if they do reach land, it is such that "no man dare set foot upon." His shipmate corrects him: "Sinbad dares." Suddenly, and to everyone's surprise, the intuitive captain orders a sounding, and at four-fathoms-seven, they find land where there should be no land, and the men fear they've encountered a reef, or, as one of them worries aloud, a sea serpent. But it is Colossa and, just before the launch is lowered, Sinbad asks Allah that they find food and water. A wary seaman adds the postscript,

The roc deposits a stop-motion Sinbad in its nest. Notice the stork flying in the background. © Columbia Pictures

"...and may Allah grant that we find nothing more."

Thus, in one brief scene, *The Seventh Voyage of Sinbad* has skillfully summarized the supernatural fears under which people of this era labored, the kind and scope of the fantasy that lies ahead, and the bold nature of the picture's title character. And, having prepared the viewer for such a bizarre realm of possibilities, the picture immediately sets out to deliver them. Moments later, a landing party is on Colossa and battling the ferocious cyclops.

The cyclops is one of Ray's most popular creatures due, no doubt, to the beast's novel design, its ability to emote, and its perpetually turbulent and strangely enamoring disposition. "I was striving for something different," Ray says of the model, "and it went through several clay model stages. It started out with two horns, then one horn, then no horns. But I wanted to get the satyr effect which would make it different than the average Arabian Nights fantasy that was produced in the good old

The skeleton swordfight. Harryhausen took up fencing to enable himself to identify with the skeleton during animation.

The spiral staircase atop which the skeleton meets its doom. Notice the holes in the board beneath the skeleton's feet, through which the model was secured during animation. This platform was not visible in the finished film.

days of Maria Montez. I was also striving to give the
appearance that the cyclops wasn't a man in a suit.
And I thought that the cloven hooves and the lower
quarters of a goat would help to aid that." As for its
ongoing fury, which the animal constantly accents
by trumpeting like an elephant, it is in keeping with
the beast's human-eating nature. Yet, it's difficult to
feel antagonism for the carnivorous monster. Yes,
the creature was *meant* to be feared—if the cyclops
had been a tame, rather easy-going character, the
open-spit cooking of Sinbad's crewman would have
been comical—and when it's not running after the
Prince of Bagdad in the finest arms-back Harryhausen tradition, the one-eyed giant is snarling,
raging pop-eyed at spear-throwing sailors, grinding
its jaws, or some other appropriately melodramatic,
contemptuous gesture. However, one can almost

Kathryn Grant and Kerwin Mathews edge past the dragon in
Sokurah's cave... © Columbia Pictures

...the dragon being far from hospitable with intruders.
© Columbia Pictures

sympathize with his ire: to him, humans are simply food. And when they put up a struggle—well, no one likes to fight for their supper, not even a cyclops.

One of the marvels of stop motion photography vividly underscored by this film is the way it breathes life into otherwise impossible creatures. Prior to *The Seventh Voyage of Sinbad*, Ray's monsters had all been vaguely familiar: the rhedosaur was a stylized crocodile, the octopus was huge but not alien, the *Animal World* dinosaurs were figures we had seen in museums, and Ymir was semihuman in form and very human in temperament. But until *The Seventh Voyage of Sinbad*, the cyclops was the kind of monster that had only lived in book illustrations or in the mind's eye, not on the screen and in color. Thus, like *King*

Kong was to his day, Ray's horned beast was a revolution in the utilization of film to flesh-out one of our species' oldest and most important cultural inventions: the myth. It is unfortunate that, until now, this monumental event has gone largely unnoticed by so-called film historians, to whom film art is determined by subtle obscurities and vogue rather than by the grander issue of the human imagination.

However, if the cyclops tantalizes the eyes and mind of the viewer, how does Ray react to it, or for that matter, any of his beasts? Is there a point at which the fantastic nature of these animals and the story strikes the animator? "On the animals, it hits me during the drawing stage. What we're striving for is the unusual, and we try to get bizarre situations that still have a thread of credibility to

The cyclops and dragon meet in Sokurah's cave.

them. As for the story, it's not something that forms itself at once; it evolves from the innumerable story conferences that Charles, myself, and the writer have. Fortunately, we can afford to do this because the press of time only comes during production, when you've got one hundred people on the payroll, and not so much during the story stages. That's when the problems start. But in developing the script, we have story conferences and a lot of these ideas come out of what we call sweatbox sessions, when each one of us throws ideas out, and then we capture the best of them and the writer incorporates them into the script. They seldom come from any one source. That's why I make the drawings: they root out ideas from everyone, and I find that quite stimulating. It's a chain reaction, cause and effect, and it's a lot of fun once you get going. After this stage, of course, it's less a matter of awe for the subject than enthusiasm. That's why I try to stick only to subjects that I feel very strongly about. Because one has to keep up their enthusiasm long after the live-action production has ceased to be. There's always some sort of a fire going when you're in live-action production, because you have to be on the ball every minute of the day, picking locations and all the other things you have to do. It's very stimulating, and consequently, a tremendous letdown when that's over with and you have to start building up again for the animation period. So you have to be taken with the wonder of the subject to keep up your enthusiasm for the year where you're still doing what the essence of the picture is all about—the actual photography of all the trick effects."

The confrontation with the cyclops starting *The Seventh Voyage of Sinbad* off with a jolt, the film then withdraws to spin its plot. Thus, until Sinbad's next meeting with the one-eyed monster, the only stop-motion creature we see is the snake woman, who was included for color rather than to advance the plot. A scene showing animated, harpylike sirens attacking the ship was planned but deleted due to cost.

The effectiveness of the snake woman's performance is due to its low-keyed presentation. One of Harryhausen's favorite sequences in the film, it was conceived as a rebellion of sorts against a trite genre standard. "Not only in Arabian Nights but in Biblical pictures, including *Ben-Hur* and *Cleopatra* and the most lavish productions, down to the Maria Montez pictures, they all have a sequence with a dancing girl. These vary considerably: some are more inventive than others, and some go to bizarre extremes. But presumably, these have proven to be an attraction. And if it isn't too far out of left field, there is no reason, I suppose, why you can't have it. Although I don't think that people will go to see a movie *because* of that, it's all part of the Middle Eastern mystique, that aura and image that always associates the Middle East with belly dancers and exotic beauties. Now, in *The Seventh Voyage of Sinbad*, while we had a few dancing girls just to keep an atmosphere of a sultan's palace, we tried to break away from it by having something completely different, like the magician proving his powers by merging the girl with the serpent, which I think gave it a fresh approach." Exotic and mellow, it offers a fine balance to the driving excitement of the other stop-motion creations. And, if the dance is marred by occasional close-ups showing the grease-painted face of the real handmaiden, it is, overall, an unusual scene. However, Ray did "cheat" a bit in designing the episode: when Sokurah has completed the servant's transformation, he strikes the jug with an axe, and as it crumbles to reveal the mutant, *it vanishes*! Another example of the magician's powers? Yes and no. "That came about on the spur of the moment, from a practical point of view. I had to decide at the moment he broke the jar what to do with all the nasty pieces of pottery that we'd have lying on the floor, and how I'd have to get an animated figure to slither over them. So I thought, why not make them disappear? After all, it *is* a magic trick: just have the jar dissolve out. So I got rid of it for that rather mundane reason."

Between the salvation of the snake woman and the reappearance of the cyclops, *The Seventh Voyage of Sinbad* busies itself with the shrinking of Parisa and the distinguishing of the heroes from the villains, the build-up that Harryhausen mentioned must inevitably follow a tumultuous opening sequence. However, despite the friction which exists between Sinbad and Sokurah by the time they return to the island, the crew's second bout with the cyclops is so striking as to overshadow their personal conflicts.

In the episode on the beach, the one-eyed monster had just enough time to growl and swat at the encroachers before they were gone. Contrarily, from the moment the horned giant finds the men in his cave to his fall from the cliff, the cyclops serves as a showpiece for Ray's technical and emotive prowess. Perhaps the most memorable such display—a brief throw-away, really—can be seen in one darkly comedic moment which occurs after the giant has tied Sinbad's man to the spit and pulled up a stool. Summing up the creature's simple, culinary designs on the human, Ray has him rotate the helpless Arabian *while licking his chops with delight*! Gruesome, but succinct! Another quick but telling gesture occurs when the cyclops locks Sinbad and his men in the wooden cage. The monster doesn't actually *shut* the trapdoor on the roof of the cage; he casually brushes it closed with a backhand slap. If ever a monster were disdainful of his prey, it is the horned behemoth! This scorn is even more evident in the cyclops' attack with the uprooted tree. The monster hurries about with a brisker gait than he's used for the entire film, as though anxious not to miss the joy of crushing even *one* of the sailors! However, it is a tribute to Harryhausen's skill that this same single-minded brute becomes an object of pity when Sinbad puts out his eye, the cyclops' pained outburst and groping pursuit of his tormentor being sensitively realized by the animator.

Technically, this segment has many splendid touches, including a breathtaking shot in which the cyclops lifts Sinbad from the treasure vault *by his boot*! This effect was accomplished with wires and miniature screen projection. Rigged with cables so that he could be hauled aloft on the full-scale cave set, actor Kerwin Mathews struggled as though the cyclops were standing overhead. Some time later, miniature projecting this footage in his Hollywood studio, Ray placed the cyclops' hand in front of the screen, inserting a miniature boot between its fingers. This prop boot was carefully positioned so that the two dimensional eye of the camera saw it as a natural extension of Sinbad's leg. Ray then animated the sequence as he would any other, taking constant care to maintain the alignment of the model boot with Kerwin Mathews' miniature projected image. For the shot which follows,

showing the cyclops carrying Sinbad from the cave to the cage, a stop-motion figure was substituted for the actor. Other first-class illusions include the monster's drop from the ledge, executed with an aerial brace and using a special five-inch-tall cyclops model; the cyclops attacking the sailors with a stop-motion tree, the shadow of which was matted into the scene while every root was animated in response to the tree's movement; and a shot of the cyclops moving the cageful of men to a more convenient location. The cage stands waist-high to the giant, and he really looks as though he's laboring under a great weight when he lifts the coop.

Odd and captivating though the cyclops was, Ray came up with an equally bizarre being in his next stop-motion attraction, the roc. More menacing then the cyclops because of its lack of any semihuman features or idiosyncracies, it served soley as an avenging angel that swooped from the skies in response to the death of its cute and guiltless offspring.

As one can well imagine, flying creatures are a special nightmare for animators, and the parent roc was just such an animal. Suspended from an aerial brace, the creature had to be kept perfectly steady while Ray animated its two heads, wings, and talons. Clearly not a job for the maladroit or impatient! Fortunately, the bird came to rest after its first pass at the crew, landing on a boulder that was part of the animated set and flawlessly matched with the real terrain of the miniature projected image. Another outstanding and carefully executed bit of special effects wizardry was the monster's grabbing of Sinbad, accomplished by having Kerwin Mathews fall out of camera and laying low while the rock picked up his stop-motion double. As for the baby roc, Ray built a separate model for its few brief scenes rather than simply disguise the adult figurine. As a result, when the sailors spear the animal, its innocent, pullet-like design gives the picture a brief moment of pathos.

The only possible reason that *The Seventh Voyage of Sinbad* did not win—or indeed was not even nominated for—a special visual effects Oscar is that the electorate are ignorant of what constitutes good and innovative special effects. No doubt they thought that Schneer had gone out and

A studio artist's interpretation of the cyclops-dragon
confrontation. The photographs of the sailors are from
shots of the beach scene at the beginning of the picture.

The cyclops and dragon have at one another.   © Columbia Pictures

The dragon, moments before he is impaled by a giant
arrow.

The dragon in a final moment of menace before his death.

hired himself a descendant of *The Odyssey's* Polyphemus to play the cyclops, or dressed a large eagle to portray the roc. Indeed, Ray has *never* been nominated for an Academy Award, although O'Brien took the Oscar for *Mighty Joe Young* in the name of all his assistants. Accordingly, before we look at one of Ray's most electric screen effects, the sequence which, more than any other, calls our attention to Harryhausen's genius, and the short-sightedness of the Academy, let's allow Ray to put this subject of Oscars and awards into perspective. "Of course, I was quite upset that *The Beast from Twenty Thousand Fathoms* wasn't nominated, because there was nothing out at the time. But there seems to be an aversion to this type of picture. I mean, *The Beast from Twenty Thousand Fathoms* had things in it that were quite remarkable for that period. *Jason and the Argonauts*, certainly had some fantastic things in it that had never been seen on the screen before, and presumably, were all very convincing. But then, I must be prejudiced. Anyway, I have a great deal of freedom right now, and I don't think an award would change my situation financially. It would be pleasant to win it, but that

isn't the purpose of making these pictures. I've long since left that behind. You don't go out and make a picture because you think it's going to get an Academy Award: you just make the picture the best way you can with the facilities and the budget we have."

More than any sequence in the film, the skeleton swordfight, executed with an eight-inch-tall stop-motion model and miniature screen projection, exemplifes the suspension of disbelief that is rampant in *The Seventh Voyage of Sinbad*. There, in the cellar of a murky castle, a human skeleton is actually doing battle with a living man! Two hundred years ago, Ray Harryhausen would have been burned at the stake for creating such visions. Today, he is simply ignored at Oscar time. However, there was anything but a sorceror's conjuration used to put the encounter on film.

The live-action element of the duel, with Kerwin Mathews slashing at thin air, was filmed in a cave in Majorca. Mathews would rehearse his blocking and thrusting with Olympic fencing master Enzo Musomeci-Greco, their fight would be shot so that Ray could refer to Musomeci-Greco's movements while animating his skeleton, and then, while the steps were still fresh in Mathews' mind, the cameras would film his shadowboxing the imaginary skeleton, which wouldn't be added "in the flesh" until months later. Obviously, this form of moviemaking imposes a terrific burden on the actor: not only must his eyeline remain constant, as though he were actually studying an opponent, but Mathews had to stop his sword *cold* whenever it was due to connect with that of the skeleton. And, as all the live-action footage was shot over a single twenty-four-hour period, Mathews found it all rather exhaustive. As he told the fan magazine *FXRH*—which stands for Special Effects created by Ray Harryhausen—"I would stop my sword, which was the most difficult thing because I am not an athlete, obviously, and those swords are *heavy*. And if you've had one in your hand for twenty-four hours and you try to stop it—that was a big problem. My arm began to grow numb." However, at the risk of playing free and easy with Mathews' constitution, the ends fully justified the means.

Inconsiderate of the episode's vivid supernatural qualities—the whole notion of a living skeleton, not to mention Sokurah's grim laboratory and the cold austerity of the cave in which much of the battle occurs—the structure of the confrontation was stunning. Specifically, the fact that the skeleton doesn't just *spring* to life the way the cyclops first came thundering from the head-shaped cave, allows tension to mount. Goaded by Sokurah, the figure drops several feet to the ground and stands there swaying, his head bowed, while he marshals his forces. Then, pulling himself fully erect, the skeleton walks to a wall, selects a sword and shield, and faces Sinbad, crouched and ready for battle. Brewed for mood rather than shock—although the creature's birth always elicits a scream or two from the audience—these opening shots allow the viewer to become accustomed to the uncanny situation before being carried into the heat of the duel. Once the battle is underway, Ray pulls out all the stops. The two antagonists destroy vials and decorations throughout the chamber in their mad struggle, working offensive and defensive maneuvers and *never standing still*. Thus, they go from the laboratory to a hallway to the cave and the spiral staircase in a thrilling and unbroken flood of action. And if one needs proof beyond the precision of the atmosphere, animation, and composite photography that this is the film's *pièce de résistance*, consider that *The Seventh Voyage of Sinbad* sprung from Ray's desire to shoot the scene. "Again, I'm always striving, in my twelve big drawings, for something unusual. In fact, I started with the skeleton, if I remember correctly. Because I thought, what could be more bizarre than a living skeleton? But how do you justify that the thing is alive? Well, there's only one way to deal with it, and that's to have a sorcerer, and the whole story kind of developed from that. So Sokurah and everything else really came out of the skeleton."

The final stop-motion installment of the film is Sinbad's discovery of the dragon and the

Ray Harryhausen and his stop-motion model of the snake-woman.   © Columbia Pictures

monster's clash with the second cyclops. Not as electrifying a character as the other creatures in *The Seventh Voyage of Sinbad*, the lumbering fire-breather nonetheless radiates a sense of sinister omnipotence. Watching the world from beneath devilishly hooded eyes, it lurks in the cave, snorting flames, just *waiting* for some other animal to try to enter its domain. And when it happens, with the arrival of the cyclops, the lizard makes mincemeat of the giant in short order. Indeed, with its fiery breath, the dragon could easily have fried a roc on the side during the altercation.

The battle, which begins inside the cave and carries into the valley, is superlatively conceived and staged. True to its awesome size and nature, the dragon remains on the offensive, making it all the comparatively nimble cyclops can do to keep from those fearsome jaws, let alone inflict any damage of its own. Thus, as we noted earlier, the outcome was predetermined: after raking the cyclops' spine with its claws, the dragon simply uses its weight to pin the one-eyed beast and feast on its jugular.

Harryhausen's mastery of movement, from angry aggression to shocked and fearful withdrawal, is well-showcased in this sequence, along with his uncanny ability to hypothesize how such fanciful animals would act and react if they were alive. The fight also highlights the value of color to the subject such as this: the blue of the dragon and the orange-brown tones of the cyclops underline their incredible nature, particularly when the animals appear in an otherwise natural setting. However, while the selection of appropriate colors was carefully done, Ray didn't always get the effect he wanted in *The Seventh Voyage of Sinbad*. "We try to pick the colors for the reason of making them as realistic as possible. We didn't want to make it *too* normal, because if you're using color you might as well go all the way, I think. There are certain subjects that may demand a muted color. *Golden Voyage of Sinbad* had a much more muted type of color than *The Seventh Voyage of Sinbad*, which was more gaudy and lavish. But you try various things at different times. In any case, the colors in *The Seventh Voyage of Sinbad* are intensified. You see, that was Technicolor, which intensifies the color from your basic model or set. We don't have the time to go through great experiments, making color gradation charts for every shot. They used to do that in the early three-strip process. But you just can't take the time to do that today because you're rushing to the costume company to see if they've got the costumes, and you have to rush here and rush there to get the picture started. Then, some of the colors are intensified by duping. Sometimes we had to make dupe negatives, which would intensify the color. Of course, we always tried to stage a contrast, harmonious colors wherever we can, whenever we have control over it. For instance, shooting in the cave, Wilkie Cooper had the problem of having a minimum number of lights available to him. And the caves were rather monotone, just various shades of white and beige. So he had the problem of picking out on the set—it couldn't be preplanned—gelatins that would bring a relief to the foreground and the background so you'd get some sort of depth

Ray Harryhausen today, with his skeleton from *The Seventh Voyage of Sinbad*. The special "jig" pose of the model is a severe departure from its performance in the film. Photograph by Leslie Rovin.

The models of the cyclops, his cage, and miniature sailors after the completion of *The Seventh Voyage of Sinbad.* Notice that the cyclops' fur is already beginning to loosen.

in the cave. Ted Moore had the same problem in *Golden Voyage of Sinbad*. We went back to the same cave, and although he had more lights to work with, he had the same problem. Only if you build a set can you think about it and control it, because your art director is able to give you a color rendition of the set. But when you're working with live-action backgrounds, as we constantly do—we seldom build a set if we can help it—you're more or less at the mercy of the sun, Eastman Kodak, and your photographer."

Apart from these various glitches with color, did Ray have any general regrets about the result of his work on *The Seventh Voyage of Sinbad*? "Specifically, I was sorry I didn't make a more obvious change between the first and second cyclops. Everybody thought it was the same one. I put a second horn in, and I should have exaggerated it, I suppose, or used a side-horn or gone completely with another type of character. But at the time, we were quite pressed to get the picture finished, and I'm afraid I took the line of least resistance, although it *was* a different model. Generally, there are many shots that I'd have loved to do over, but again, under the pressure of trying to get finished, sometimes you're forced to accept shots that you know you could do better if you had more time."

Happily, when we talk about the acting and scriptural values of *The Seventh Voyage of Sinbad*, there are at least some nuances to discuss. Unlike most of Ray's previous films, where the plots were involving but simple and the roles rigidly played, *The Seventh Voyage of Sinbad* has performances no less colorful than the monsters, and a plot that deftly draws upon the prodigious nature of the subject matter. This is due, in great part, to Ray's very definite ideas about the genre and about storytelling. And, with the importance of *The Seventh Voyage of Sinbad* to both his pride and his career, he made certain that these values were maintained. First, there is his philosophy on the art of spinning a cohesive tale. "There are certain basics I don't think you can stray from, too far, but there's an infinite variety of ways to do it so that it will be different from previous pictures we've made plus other pictures that we know about. One always strives for some sort of originality. However, I don't approve of the so-called modern approach. I mean,

it doesn't satisfy me when I go to films where they just let the story disintegrate and have a series of happenings. I find that quite difficult. I like things resolved in not-too-abstract a manner. There are exceptions, of course; you can't make a flat statement like that, and I realize that. But on the whole, I like things pretty cut-and-dried. I want the writer to work. I want him to tell me, 'Well, this is how we resolved it,' and I'll think that's either clever or not. I don't want to have to work after having paid my three or four dollars admission fee." Not surprisingly, commensurate with this attitude is Ray's view of himself as an entertainer rather than as a preacher. "It's very difficult for a filmmaker, unless you're a crusader, to go out and say, 'I'm going to make a picture that'll change the world.' The medium is not that broad. We set out, essentially, to make something that will make people happy and want to see it. Entertainment. One doesn't set out to make a fantasy film to right the wrongs of the world. You hope that it will have some meaningful message to somebody, even if it's nothing more than black and white: the hero against the villain, which is the basis of any drama. And whether it happens to be the elements, a person, or whatever, you've got to have a negative force. It's always positive against negative. If there's a meaning you can put in it, certainly, I'm delighted to. But we don't go out of our way to say we're going to save the world or make a strong political point, because I rather feel that if you start with that premise, you're starting a form of propaganda, you're trying to tell somebody that this is the way everything should be. Fine, if that's your point of view. But that's not the type of picture we make."

In keeping with these fundamental concepts, the conflict and resolution in *The Seventh Voyage of Sinbad* are overtly classical, with the incorruptible hero—dressed in white—versus every foe from satanic monsters to the hopelessly corrupted villain—dressed in black—all for the sake of the fair princess who, like her lover, is dressed in white. However, there are the exciting and exotic complications to which tales based on myths and epic fantasy are perfectly suited, such as the magic lamp, the mutiny and island of the sirens, the variety of monsters, and the beauty of the locales. These elements, along with Harryhausen's techni-

Ray Harryhausen and his miniature model of Colossa Island. Notice how the sky backdrop ends a few feet above the set. © Columbia Pictures

cal expertise, Kerwin Mathews' sincere and energetic performance, Shakespearean actor Torin Thatcher's finest leers, sneers, and malevolent gestures, as well as appropriately droll dialogue—"You're as tiny as I am!" Parisa tells Barani upon entering the lamp, to which the genie replies, "How else could I live inside a lamp?"—make *The Seventh Voyage of Sinbad* a special brand of entertainment, the witty fulfillment of dreams and nightmares we have all had since childhood. Of course, Ray and his producer knew what kind of product they had in terms of entertainment. Thus, Schneer, with his quick commercial sense, decided

that the wonders of *The Seventh Voyage of Sinbad*—i.e., the story and Ray's newfound ability to work his "reality sandwich" in color—had to be summed up in one word and used to pique the public's curiosity: that word was *Dynamation*. A union of the terms dynamic and animation, it was described in advertisements as "a brilliant new moviemaking process." And that it was. It also capsulized Ray's feelings about the effort that went into *The Seventh Voyage of Sinbad*. "Whenever you make a picture, you always discover new little things, as each picture presents a new set of problems. Each *shot* presents a new set of problems.

So we tried to make people aware of the fact that there was the development of something a little fresh in the picture. And it demanded a different name simply to make it more apparent that this was now a better product. And, apparently, people agreed with us, because *The Seventh Voyage of Sinbad* was a hit, which naturally made us feel very good, very satisfied. But I'm afraid I'm not the celebrating type. I guess I said 'Eureka! They may have confidence enough to make another picture!' Because there's an old saying in Hollywood that you're only as good as your last picture. So our last picture was a hit, and I knew we'd be able to get money for the next picture."

Actually, Ray, with his endearing bent for understatement, was wrong. He and Charles were able to get financing for their next *two* pictures, which went into simultaneous production. They were to have an enormous effect on Harryhausen's life.

In a vignette recounting the labors of Hercules, television's game show *The Price is Right* featured a monster remarkably like Harryhausen's cyclops...right down to its cloven hooves! Photograph by the author.

A matte shot of Gulliver on the Lilliputian beach.

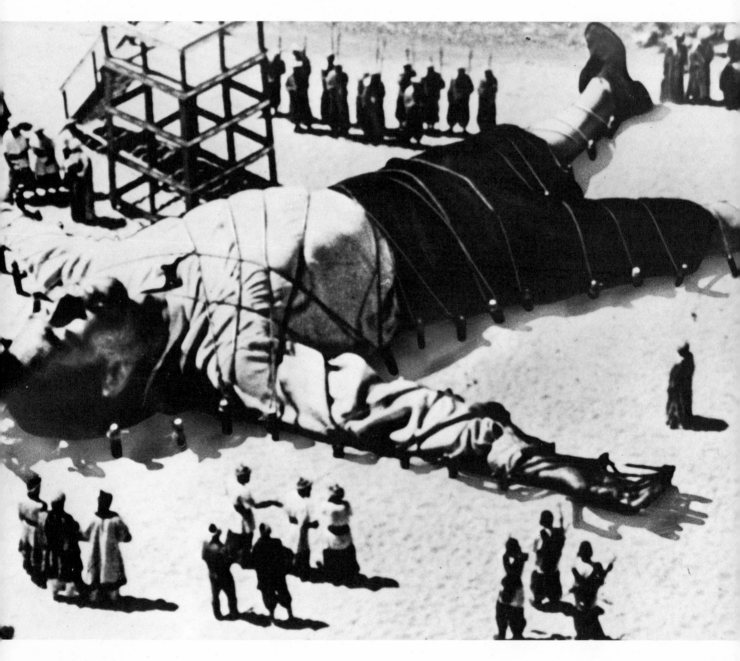

CHAPTER ELEVEN

The Storm-Blown Heroes

In 1959, Ray went to Europe to shoot *The Three Worlds of Gulliver* and *Mysterious Island*—and he has lived there since. However, while the filmmakers went abroad in search of fresh locales, as they had done for *The Seventh Voyage of Sinbad*, Ray relocated in London because of a color special effects process known as *sodium backing* that, at the time, was available only in Great Britain.

The eight traveling-matte shots in *The Seventh Voyage of Sinbad* were accomplished via *blue backing*, which is an extremely involved technique of superimposition. To achieve the matte, an actor is photographed before a blue screen. This action is then printed on a black and white negative that is insensitive to blue, with the result that the background translates as transparent on the new footage. Next, the same color negative is printed on black-and-white film that is sensitive *only* to blue, leaving a transparent silhouette of the performer on a field of black. The two black and white negatives are then printed on high-contrast black-and-white positive film and serve as a matte and a counter-matte for the color footage. When run through an optical printer with the blue-insensitive black-and-white footage and the color positive of the background scene—the setting into which the player is being inserted—a fresh negative records the background with an unexposed hole where the actor had been. This new color negative is then run through the printer a second time, with the blue-sensitive counter-matte and the film of the actor. The counter-matte blocks the blue screen from the fresh negative, thus achieving the composite.

Clearly, blue backing is a long and complex process which, if it's not executed with the utmost precision, will highlight the superimposed foreground element with annoying blue matte lines. The sodium-backing process greatly reduced the intricacy of creating traveling mattes.

In a sodium-backing situation, the players go through their paces before a screen that is lit by a monochromatic yellow light from sodium vapor lamps. The actors, in turn, are exposed to lights coated with didymium, a chemical that nullifies any monochromatic yellow to which they may be exposed. Accordingly, a camera is employed that exposes two rolls of very specialized film simultaneously, a raw stock that will not record monochromatic yellow. Equipped with a prism or *beam splitter* that casts the same image on both spools of film, the camera also contains a pair of filters, one before the aperture of each reel. The first filter, of monochromatic yellow, will create the traveling matte of the actors by allowing only the monochromatic yellow light from the rear screen to reach the film which, because the film is insensitive to that wavelength, leaves the background transparent and the performers in silhouette. A didymium filter is used to record the live action, which will be combined with the background scenes at a later date. A counter-matte is produced from the matte footage and the compositive is achieved, as in the blue-backing process, with an optical printer. The obvious advantage of this matting technique is the elimination of several cumbersome steps, which decrease the likelihood of destroying the hoped-for illusion.

As we mentioned a moment ago, the appeal of Europe was as much its relatively untouched settings as the sodium-backing process. As Ray evaluates the situation in 1959, "Television had used up all the locales around Hollywood, so where do you go for locales? Particularly when you're making a fantasy film." The answer, as he had learned by making the Arabian Nights picture, was in finding new locations overseas. "For example, in *The Seventh Voyage of Sinbad*, we couldn't afford, on our budget, to build the fabulous and exotic Middle Eastern streets. So we decided on Spain, which was the closest country and had relatively operative motion picture units. You could get people who were trained. And we made great use of the places there: the Moorish architecture was ideal for our Sinbad story. It also gave the picture a different and fresh look, other than what audiences had seen in *Kismet* or the Maria Montez films, the typical Hollywood conception of Bagdad. In *The Seventh Voyage of Sinbad*, using real locations also gave us money, in the budget, for other things rather than set construction, which is enormously costly." Thus, organizing the production of *The Three Worlds of Gulliver*, based on Jonathan Swift's satirical adventure classic *Gulliver's Travels*, and *Mysterious Island*, from the novel by Jules Verne, Ray and Charles relocated their operation in London.

The idea to shoot *The Three Worlds of Gulliver* came from an outside source. "Jack Sher and another writer had prepared it for Universal, in a different way than we prepared it. And they had a completed script, which they brought to Mr. Schneer. He liked the idea and we decided to do it, but reworked to incorporate our techniques. We also deliberately kept the animation to a minimum because of the problems of getting it out in less time than a normal animated feature. It was just one of those things where the subject matter required mostly traveling mattes and big people and little people, which would have been difficult to animate. It had already been done: the Russians made *The New Gulliver* in 1935, and they had thousands of little puppets, all speaking. They had about two to three dozen heads for each puppet, and it took them five years to make the picture. We didn't really want to get involved in that. We just wanted to make something a little different from either a cartoon (Ray is referring to Max Fleischer's feature-length, 1939 cartoon *Gulliver's Travels*—JR) or the Russian picture."

Although as originally penned by Sher *The Three Worlds of Gulliver* was quite faithful to Swift's novel, the revised shooting script by Sher and Arthur Ross retains the thematic and narrative essence of the first two of Gulliver's four voyages in the book. Dr. Lemuel Gulliver (Kerwin Mathews), a Wapping, England physician, is tired of being paid in fowl and thank yous alone. Hoping to marry Elizabeth (June Thorburn) and buy a little cottage, he decides to accept a paying position as ship's surgeon for a long ocean voyage. Elizabeth protests, but Gulliver will not accept his poverty and signs aboard. Once underway, the ship runs into a violent storm, but that is not the vessel's only problem. Elizabeth has stowed away to be with her fiancé, and enraged, Gulliver takes her to the rainwashed deck where they argue. Suddenly, a squall-whipped wave carries the physician overboard. Elizabeth screams, but the crewmen arrive too late to rescue her lover. Managing to stay afloat, the dazed Englishman is finally deposited on an island where, just before he loses consciousness, he sees inches-high people....

When Gulliver awakens, he finds himself bound with tiny ropes to the beach of this strange island. A small stand has been erected beside his head: it is mounted, in due course, by the island's minister of finance, Flimnap (Martin Benson), and the minister of the interior, Reldresal (Lee Patterson), the former of whom orders the attendant archers to use their poison arrows and slay the giant. But Reldresal countermands his order and, moments later, Gulliver addresses his benefactor, inquiring as to his whereabouts. The just minister of the interior tells the giant that he is in the kingdom of Lilliput, and that they tied him down for fear of his being a secret weapon of their staunch enemy, the neighboring island-nation of Blefuscu. Just then, the emperor (Basil Sydney) arrives, and Gulliver assures one and all that he is no foe. The king debates about what to do with the man-mountain, as thunderclouds gather overhead; he considers this a bad omen and leans toward having the newcomer shot. However, drawing a hardy breath, Gulliver disburses the storm and, viewing the giant as a maker of miracles, the emperor orders him released.

Time passes, and playing host to a titan is

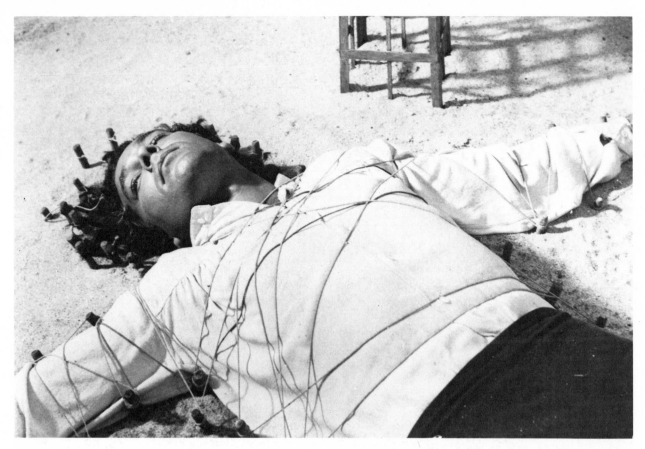

A nonprocess pose of Gulliver's waking moments in Lilliput. Notice the miniature stand for the king by Gulliver's shoulder. © Columbia Pictures

more trouble than the emperor had imagined. Counseled by Flimnap, who frets about what feeding the giant is costing them, the potentate considers poisoning him. However, as Reldresal and Gulliver observe, the Englishman can do the work of several thousand Lilliputians. And to prove the point, Gulliver clears a forest for use as farmland, replants the trees to serve as a windbreak, and scoops up tons of fish in his hat. The king is most pleased. However, before he'll allow Gulliver to build a boat and go searching for Elizabeth, he commands the giant to destroy Blefuscu. The Lilliputians are about to choose between Flimnap and Reldresal as prime minister: after the selection has been made, Gulliver must march against the enemy.

After the dictum is pronounced, the king invites Gulliver to break eggs with them. The physician learns that this ritual is what started the war with Blefuscu, whose king insisted on breaking his eggs at the big end, contrary to the Lilliputian policy of opening eggs at the small end. Shocked, Gulliver suggests the nations compromise by breaking their eggs in the middle. This is dismissed by the emperor as barbaric.

The process of naming a Prime Minister is an unusual one, to say the least. The two contestants are forced to walk a tightrope—a prime minister must always keep his balance—while performing such feats as juggling torches representing the army, the navy, and the budget in a manner as to distract the king from the problems they represent. The more agile man will win the post. And, though Flimnap has his lackeys shake the high wire while

Reldresal is performing, Gulliver pretends to sneeze, blowing them away, and Reldresal is victorious. However, as the emperor prepares to name him prime minister, Flimnap rushes forward to reveal that the minister of the interior has secretly been seeing Gwendolyn (Jo Morrow), daughter of Lord Bermogg (Peter Bull), a traitor who had refused to open his eggs as per the dictates of others. The emperor orders Reldresal to renounce her and, when he refuses, the minister of the interior is imprisoned and Flimnap is named prime minister. Disgusted by this turn of events, Gulliver frees Reldresal and brings him to the beach, so that he can be with Gwendolyn. But the emperor's agents find the renegade minister and a furious swordfight ensues. Full of hatred for these petty tensions, Gulliver has had enough. Storming into the channel that separates the two islands, he seizes the anchors of Blefuscu's mighty armada and ends the war by towing the ships to Lilliput. Needless to say, the emperor is pleased and forgives Gulliver for freeing Reldresal. He even awards the giant the prestigious title of Nar-Dac, but with one catch: Gulliver must return to Blefuscu and slay every one of its citizens. When the man-mountain refuses, the tyrant orders him to *at least* force them to open their eggs at the small end. Gulliver says that he won't degrade any human being by bending them to his will. Flustered, the king departs to a meeting of his council. Several members call for Gulliver's death, but the queen of Lilliput (Mary Ellis) defends him and the king bows to her wishes.

That night, Gulliver attends a royal feast, and even sings for the starry-eyed queen. He may have offended her husband, but Her Majesty is convinced that Gulliver can *never* offend her. Unfortunately,

Gulliver in the miniature set of the emperor's court in Lilliput.

A yellow-backing shot of Gulliver surfacing beside a Blefuscan warship. © Columbia Pictures

when a fire breaks out in a cart filled with straw, and quickly spreads to the palace, Gulliver sees no recourse but to extinguish the blaze with a mouthful of wine. In so doing, he drenches the queen, who is offended and orders his death. Reldresal rushes ahead of the king's archers and informs Gulliver of the edict. Tired of being punished for services rendered to crown and humanity, Gulliver climbs into his boat and rows to the open sea.

By morning, the castaway spots a beach with a normal-sized woman sitting in the sand. Rushing to her side, the Englishman is surprised to find that it is only a mannequin. Moments later, a giant girl spots Gulliver and strides onto the beach. The physician hides in his boat and, seizing the tiny craft, Glumdalclitch (Sherri Alberoni) hurries to the castle of the king. There, His Majesty (Gregoire

Aslan), ruler of the kingdom of Brobdingnag, reunites Gulliver with Elizabeth, who was washed ashore when the ship went down in the storm. He appoints Glumdalclitch their keeper, then marries the couple, who enjoy a pleasant honeymoon in the royal garden—until Gulliver is attacked by a giant squirrel and must be rescued by Glumdalclitch. However, inconsiderate of the ill-fated honeymoon, Gulliver finds Brobdingnag no more a paradise than was Lilliput. When he innocently beats the king in a game of chess, the court alchemist Makovan (Charles Lloyd Pack) ascribes the victory to the fact that Gulliver is a witch. Later, when the Englishman cures the queen of a queasy stomach, the palace wizard is convinced that Gulliver's skills come from the black arts. And he intends to prove it. Bringing the tiny man to his laboratory, he has Gulliver

153

Gulliver and Elizabeth on their honeymoon in the garden of the Emperor of Brobdingnag.   © Columbia Pictures

immerse himself in one fluid and orders him to step into a second vat. A witch, he claims, will turn blue. However, when Makovan is distracted by a fight between his daughter and Glumdalclitch, Gulliver adds a powder to the second liquid and turns red. Certain that only a witch could have tampered with his potion, the alchemist thus informs the king. However, to be unimpeachably sure of Gulliver's guilt, they place him on a tabletop and pit the physician against a huge crocodile. If he is innocent of the charge, he will prevail against the beast. Using an ornamental sword from a jewelry box, Gulliver engages the amphibian and, after a hard-fought battle, pierces the monster's throat. The lizard dies, and the king is satisfied that Gulliver isn't a witch. But Makovan says that it would *take* a witch to defeat the animal, and the monarch is easily persuaded. Thus, acting quickly, Glumdal-

clitch grabs Gulliver and Elizabeth, drops them in her basket, and runs from the castle. Although the royal party gives chase, the girl is able to beat them to a high bluff, from which point she tosses the basket into the sea.

Sometime later, Gulliver and Elizabeth awaken on a beach, a normalsized basket by their side. Whether or not the adventure was real, Gulliver has learned the ills of false pride and greed and promises to amend his thinking. As for Glumdalclitch—she is waiting to be born. Spotting a man in a nearby wood, they ask him if he's ever heard of Wapping or England. "Are ya balmy, guv'nor?" he replies. "This *is* England, and Wapping is just above that rise." Running hand-in-hand, an enlightened Gulliver and his bride head for home.

Even in the telling, one can plainly see that

A matte shot of Gulliver curing the upset stomach of the Queen of Brobdingnag. © Columbia Pictures

The oversized set of Gulliver on the queen's bed, used for close-ups of Kerwin Mathews. © Columbia Pictures

The Three Worlds of Gulliver was a formidable technical undertaking, composed almost entirely of special effects in one form or another. However, it also proved to be a physical ordeal for Ray who, returning to the beach locales of *The Seventh Voyage of Sinbad*, in S'Agaro, Spain, came down with a malaise "called the Tourist Trots, to put it bluntly. And it seemed to get everybody that year. It was some horrible thing that even the native Spanish came down with. I was down to about ninety pounds then (Harryhausen stands six-foot-three—*JR*), and I could hardly get out of my chair to direct the scenes I was supposed to direct." But Ray persevered and, with Jack Sher directing and Kerwin Mathews giving a superb performance as the disgruntled physician, created a largely unrecognized classic of the fantasy genre.

Scholars devoted to the sanctity of Swift have condemned *The Three Worlds of Gulliver* for tampering with the word and structure of the 1726 masterpiece parody. However, in all fairness to Schneer and his staff, few people would have appreciated the fact that, beyond representing France and England, respectively, Blefuscu and Lilliput had substrata that mocked contemporary Britons, ideologies, theologies, and political events. Indeed, one must imagine that the author would have enthusiastically approved of the way in which a popular motion picture was able to retain the bulk of a plot over 230 years old, as well as the gist of its more timeless satire. As Ray points out, "We *could* have told a straight adventure story. But you don't find every form of basic fantasy written by the type of man Swift was, who wanted to tell the type of important message Swift did. Thus, we retained the message phases that were intrinsic to the plot. This is like the question of making message films, which we discussed earlier. It's very difficult to force an issue. You may have little nuances in various sequences that would try to solve the problem of slavery, or something else of that nature. But I don't think one does that consciously. You really have to start with a premise that would accomodate threads of that nature. In fantasy, it so often seems to be

The castaways trying to flip the monster crab on its back in
Mysterious Island. © Columbia Pictures

coming out of left field." Regarding the various changes in plot—in the novel, Gulliver urinates on the fire in Lilliput, and at various points in the narrative Swift discusses cruel punishments as well as Gulliver's sundry problems with sex—Ray discusses it by addressing the entire issue of censorship, both self-inflicted and extraregulatory.

"I think any filmmaker has a moral obligation, in a way, because a great variety of people see a film. That's why I do believe that there must be some form of censorship from somebody. You can't depend on self-censorship, because things that may be simple to one person are often complicated to another. One needs some sort of balance of taste on moral judgment. Of course, that opens a whole can of peas as to who's to perform this judgment. But once the movies get out of hand, I think it causes great chaos. I don't think the ratings systems based on age are sufficient. I feel it's inadequate from the types of pictures I've been seeing in the last few years. I think everybody grows up at a different rate of speed, and they gain their knowledge at a different rate of speed. So it's not right to say that just because you're twelve or thirteen that you should be exposed to this particular phase of life or that particular phase of life. I think each person has to grow up when it suits them. If you're constantly bombarded with the extreme *lack* of censorship, I think you're damaging many more people than you're damaging if you go to the other extreme, and have so much censorship that it becomes a rude awakening when you finally discover the real facts. As for me, I try to make movies in the best taste I know from what I know. Not that I have the final say. Charles and I discuss it, and sometimes the author discusses it, and we see how far we should go: if it's in the best interests of the picture, who is going to see it, and so forth. You can't make a simple judgment in that respect." On matters of taste, as well as plot, Schneer says simply, "Ours is truly a collaborative effort. If Ray disagrees with something, I forget about it, and vice versa. We both have to agree, or convince the other."

Without being vulgar or obscurely topical, *The Three Worlds of Gulliver* retains Swift's general outcry against selfishness and stupidity. An entertaining reminder for adults and a palatable indoctrination to the ways of the world for children,

the picture is exactly the light, moralistic fantasy it should have been. As for the special effects, presented in *Superdynamation*—signifying the improved matting techniques and adding a twist to the by-then familiar Dynamation process—the trade journal *Variety* best described the visual wizardry by acknowledging that "special effects expert Ray Harryhausen . . . rates a low bow for his painstaking, productive efforts." Of course, most of the film was the careful melding of the large and small figures, which Ray executed with awesome precision. To this day, the overall matte work in *The Three Worlds of Gulliver* is unsurpassed. However, there were a few more creative effects in the film, such as Ray's select use of *perspective photography*. A comparatively simple screen effect, it was the end-product of placing the Lilliputian actors off in the distance while Kerwin Mathews stood close to the camera. Using deep-focus lenses, Ray was able to keep both elements in focus. The obvious benefit of perspective photography is that the illusion is created instantaneously and without the use of a matte. Another inventive effect occurred during the fight with the stop-motion crocodile. In one astounding shot, both Gulliver and the serpent wrestle for a piece of jewelry that the Englishman had been using as a shield. One end of the disk is clamped in the monster's jaws; Gulliver holds the other end. Eventually, the crocodile is able to work the shield from his adversary's grip and tosses it away. Like the sequence in *The Seventh Voyage of Sinbad* where the cyclops lifted Sinbad from the treasure vault by his boot, the shot was accomplished through a union of process photography and models. Ray matched his crocodile and its scaled portion of the shield with miniature projected footage of Gulliver, which the camera saw as one image. On the lifesize set, of course, Mathews had been vying for possession of the shield not with the crocodile, but with semiinvisible wires. Still another special effect in *The Three Worlds of Gulliver*—this one an industry staple—was the use of over-sized props to suggest size. These were used principally in Brobdingnag, as during the chess game and Gulliver's garden vacation.

Apart from "eye-filling" and every synonymous adjective one can muster, what remains to be said about the culmination of Ray's efforts in *The*

Three Worlds of Gulliver? Well, summing up the sheer vastness of the undertaking, Charles Schneer observes, "Very few people in our industry today can afford or are stupid enough to spend as much time on one film as we do. And I find it's a very difficult job; because of the various technical processes we have to go through, we're really making a trial-and-error movie. The fellows who invented the camera and lenses and film thought they were creating an exact science. Well, in our pictures we have yet to do that, and I don't know that we ever will. If we shoot a scene and we look at it and don't like it, we have to do it again and hope that nobody finds out how many times we have done it before the money runs out. It's painstaking and its very precise and very nerve racking. Ray's work is so concentrated and so difficult that I have my hair and he's lost his!"

Film may be an essentially visual medium, but sound, too, is important to the impact of a motion picture. And in all of Ray's films, the special sound effects are expertly done. Ray, Schneer, and the sound personnel spend many long hours experimenting with the roars and hisses of their creatures, sometimes finding them in the most unusual places, for example, the whirring of the saucers in *Earth vs. the Flying Saucers* was the humming of motors at a sewage disposal plant. But the sound effects are always fitting and greatly enhance the flavor of each picture. Indeed, the audio was especially critical to *The Three Worlds of Gulliver* as Kerwin Mathews rerecorded all of his dialogue from Lilliput in an echo chamber, which was later dubbed onto the soundtrack to give the giant Gulliver an appropriately pealing and resonant voice.

The music in *The Three Worlds of Gulliver* also contributed enormously to the film. Like the magnificent scores for *The Seventh Voyage of Sinbad, Mysterious Island,* and *Jason and the Argonauts*, it was composed by the late Bernard Herrmann, whose other film scores include *Citizen Kane* (1941), and many of the Hitchcock films, including *Psycho* (1960). Ray remembers Herrmann as, "a man who had his own ideas and was always very candid. If he thought something was not the kind of thing he'd like to do, then he didn't hesitate to tell you. So he apparently liked our movies or he wouldn't have done them. And you

never knew, at first. He was not a man who would come running from the projection room after viewing the rough cut saying, 'I must do this film! I *must* do this film!' He was always reserved. But his way of thinking about music had a gel with our type of picture. Of them all, he seemed to prefer the score for *The Three Worlds of Gulliver*, although I thought his music for *The Seventh Voyage of Sinbad*, personally, was the most versatile, the most unusual and dynamic, rich in orchestration and rich in variety, which is so important. It had vitality. But then, so did all his scores." Herrmann's untimely death in December of 1975—the day after he had finished recording the score for *Taxi Driver* (1976)—left an aching void in the realm of motion picture scoring.

When *The Three Worlds of Gulliver* was in its preproduction stages, it was to have starred Jack Lemmon and then Danny Kaye in the title role. However, both actors backed down, feeling that the picture was insufficiently prestigious. Thus, Kerwin Mathews got the role and did a splendid job, often under terribly adverse conditions. As he told *FXRH*, "The day they tied my hair down was fairly hysterical. It took them so long to tie all my hair down that we cleverly prepared by not giving me anything to drink—so that I wouldn't have to go to the john. I was tied down eight hours that first day. After that, we just had to do it in short pieces, it just wasn't working out. I couldn't move for fear of pulling the ropes out of the sand with my hair, and I started to cramp. Baking eight hours in the Spanish sun was a little much. I began to cook. I remember getting up and not being able to move my neck." Speaking in general terms, Mathews also lamented that in a movie such as this, "You have to do so much character direction yourself, since there really isn't any time to do anything but shoot the picture."

Although Ray points out that *The Three Worlds of Gulliver* "made its profits," the 1959 release wasn't as successful as *The Seventh Voyage of Sinbad*. Thus, greater hopes were pinned on the Schneer-Harryhausen effort *Mysterious Island*, which was a return to the motif of a land filled with unusual stop-motion creations.

Mysterious Island is Jules Verne's sequel to his 1870 novel *Twenty Thousand Leagues Under the Sea*, which Walt Disney had made into a monster

A publicity painting of the phororhacos seen in *Mysterious
Island*... © Columbia Pictures

...and a close-up of Ray's model. With the dissolution of the prehistoric angle, viewers simply assumed that it was an overgrown chicken. © Columbia Pictures

motion picture hit in 1954. Accordingly, in the wake of the Disney success and with *Mysterious Island* in the public domain, Columbia had commissioned a script for a film version of the classic. However, as Ray recalls, "the picture collapsed for some reason or other. So we were handed this script, but decided to start from scratch again because we wanted to adapt the story to make the best use of Dynamation. As you know, the original *Mysterious Island* was basically How to Survive on a Desert Island. So we had to take great liberties. Not that we were trying to out-write Verne, but we felt that as a screenplay, it wouldn't hold an audience. So we had to get the bizarre and the extremes into it, having Capt.

Nemo want to manufacture food for the world, and going to giantism and that sort of thing. But one reason we were anxious to do *Mysterious Island* was that when you're dealing with Sinbad characters, they're so much in the mythical sense that it's difficult to take the time to develop them as you would in a normal screenplay, such as a period piece like *Mysterious Island*. Naturally, when you get involved with rounded characterizations, a lot of times the pace suffers. So depending, again, on the type of story you're telling, one has to be on guard that you don't get too far out of balance by overcharacterizing, which has a tendency to defeat the whole purpose of a fantasy film. But we were

Michael Callan and Beth Rogan are sealed in a huge honeycomb by the giant bee. Both of these photographs are pasted-up publicity shots. Notice how the identical pose of Ray's bee model was used for both stills, even though the players' positions were different. © Columbia Pictures

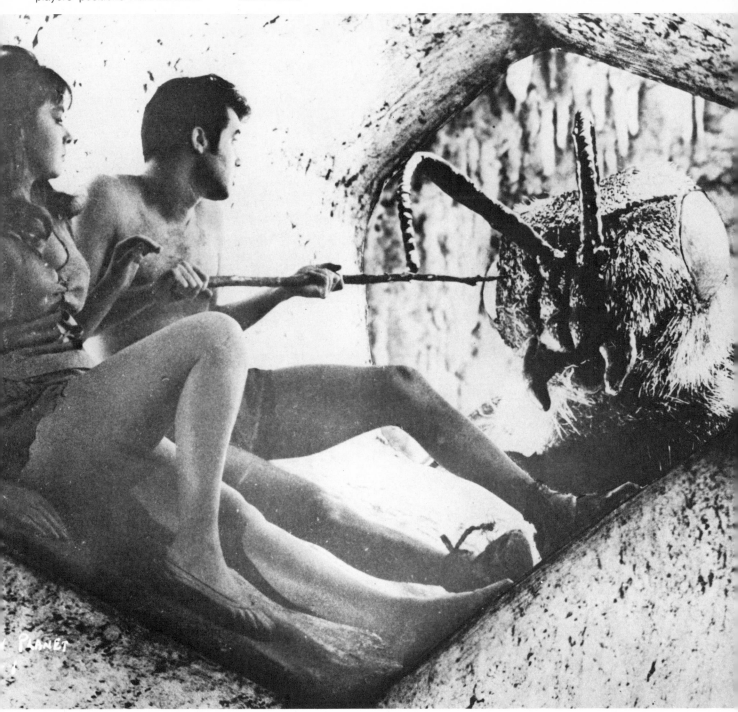

fortunate in *Mysterious Island*: due to the nature of our story, we had the chance to develop strong characterization without distracting from the plot or its pacing."

Almost immediately, we become embroiled in the righteous passions of these characters, specifically Union Captain Cyrus Harding (Michael Craig), former slave Neb (Dan Jackson), soldier Herbert Brown (Michael Callan), and newspaperman Gideon Spilett (Gary Merrill), all of whom are captives in a southern prisoner of war camp during the American Civil War. Loosening the steps that lead to their quarters, the men are able to overpower their guards and head for an observation balloon docked in the square of the compound. A gun battle ensues as Confederate soldiers try to stop the escape—one bold officer, Sgt. Pencroft (Percy Herbert) even jumping at the gondola as the balloon flies into a fearsome hurricane. Dangling from the carriage, he is rescued by the northerners. Sailing beyond rifle range, the soldiers propose to throw the Rebel to his death, but their humanity intercedes. In return, Pencroft reluctantly agrees to obey Capt. Harding's orders, and they apply themselves to the problem of weathering this tempest.

Day after day, the storm carries the balloon west, until the bag begins to tear. Cutting away the gondola to gain flying time, the men drop through the clouds and find themselves over water. Riding the shroud lines for as long as they can, the escapees finally either drop into the sea or are dragged onto a beach, where the deflated sack of the balloon eventually comes to rest.

By dawn, every man is accounted for except Capt. Harding. However, Neb soon sees smoke in the distance, and running along the shore, finds his commander lying unconscious. Capt. Harding comes to quickly, but is puzzled: he informs his companions that when he touched dry land, he was in no condition to start the blaze. It's a mystery, to be sure, but far less pressing than the immediacy of searching the island for food and water. Setting out, the castaways find the island to be little more than a volcanic outcropping in the South Pacific, but at least it is rich in edible fish, fowl, and land animals, with fresh-water streams coursing all about. Thus, returning to the beach assured of sustenance while

they build a boat to return to civilization, the men rejoice. One of them plays a tune on his harmonica while Neb dances, but their joy is short-lived. Erupting from the sand beneath the black man is a monstrous crab; the creature attacks them, snatching Neb in its pincers and threatening to crush the life from him. Grabbing the poles they had used during their hike, the men poke at the creature and prompt it to drop the soldier. Next, they sling a rope about its legs, and pulling the cord while pushing with the shoots, they manage to flip the crustacean to its back. Then, sliding it along an incline in the sand, they shove the monster into a pit of bubbling lava and enjoy a crab dinner.

Erecting a shelter on the beach, the men begin cutting down trees to use for a rowboat. However, their labors are interrupted by the arrival of flotsam to which three people are clinging: one dead sailor and two women. Nursed by the island chef, Mr. Spilett, the women recover from the ordeal of a shipwreck and introduce themselves as Lady Mary Fairchild (Joan Greenwood) and her niece Elena (Beth Rogan). Young Herbert Brown and Elena strike it off quite well, and the routine of survival continues. The group reestablishes residence in a cave fronting the face of a large cliff—once the abode of a man stranded by pirates—and rig a vine-and-wood lift for easy access to these safer, more spacious quarters. They even come into a compass, telescope, sextant, and guns when a chest washes ashore. However, it is not from the ship on which Lady Fairchild had been traveling. Rather, it bears the crest of the *Nautilus*, the submarine of the infamous pacifist Captain Nemo. Before his vessel was sunk, the scientist had used it to sink all armed ships in an effort to eradicate warfare. This parcel is presumed to have come from the legendary submarine.

Work progresses quickly on the boat, and as it nears completion, Spilett takes time out to go fishing for dinner. Sitting by a glistening brook, he is alarmed by the arrival of a huge bird, a prehistoric phororhacos. Chasing the war correspondent to the beach, the flightless bird attacks the ladies, tears down a pen full of livestock, and causes general havoc at the camp until Herbert jumps on the creature's back. Stabbing it with his knife, he is surprised when the beast dies almost immediately, but is thankful nonetheless. That night, feasting on the bird, one of the castaways bites on something hard: a bullet. Since none of them had had time to discharge a weapon, they realize that the shot came from an outside source. The party does not know who is helping them, but the fire they found beside Capt. Harding, the chest, and the felling of the bird all point to a guardian angel. And the mysterious patron is about to strike again.

Working on their boat, the men become jaded when they see a pirate ship on the horizon; they retire to the cave save for Herbert who, with Elena, has gone to the hills searching for the source of honey that is running onto the beach. And they find it: crawling into a cavern, the pair is attacked by huge bees and sealed into a honeycomb. Burning their way through the back of the hive, the couple then stumble upon a dank grotto in which, to their utter surprise, they find the *Nautilus* lying in dry dock. Hastening to inform the others of their discovery, Herbert and Elena swim to the beach, but hide when they see the pirates coming ashore. Feeling completely helpless, Herbert watches as the cutthroats discover the boat, spot the castaways' cave, and open fire from the ship. Their cannon-balls tear gaping holes in the rock until, suddenly, a massive explosion at sea causes the pirate ship to go under. Moments later, a man wearing a water-tight suit and a huge seashell on his back comes wading from the surf. Removing his helmet, he reveals

The men of *Mysterious Island* fight the huge mollusk. The fellow being held aloft is a stop-motion model.

From left to right: Percy Herbert, Joan Greenwood, Beth Rogan, Michael Craig, Herbert Lom, Dan Jackson, Michael Callan, and Gary Merrill. © Columbia Pictures

85/5-M.I-1386

The eruption of the *Mysterious Island* volcano. Everything above the tops of the trees is a miniature model.

Herbert Lom at the organ of the Nautilus.

himself to be Captain Nemo (Herbert Lom). As the group gathers around him, Spilett's reaction is to request the right to pen his life story, but Nemo isn't thinking that far into the future. He points to the island's seething volcano and announces that it will erupt before long. Asking the castaways' help in return for having watched over them, he wants to refloat the pirate ship and use it in lieu of the irreparably crippled *Nautilus* to return to civilization. Nemo's motive: he has found a foolproof means of eliminating war, which involves removing its source, hunger, through his mutated animals, such as the crab and bees. Therefore the scientist must get his notes back to society.

Fitting the men with diving suits, he has them work at patching the carefully blasted hole, while the women build a pipe that will reach from pumps of the *Nautilus* to the sunken ship. However, the volcano is unsympathetic to the scientist's noble

work and begins belching flames and steaming mud long before the restoration is completed. Fortunately, Harding has an alternate plan. He suggests that they place the observation balloon inside the pirate ship, fill it with air, and so expedite the raising. Nemo approves the plan and, stitching up the bag, the men carry it below. Their mission is interrupted by a pause to view the wonders of sunken Atlantis, as well as a fight with a huge mollusk, a squidlike creature which they defeat with electric ray guns invented by Nemo. Eventually, the operation is completed and the ship brought to the surface. Nemo gathers his papers while everyone else boards the vessel: unfortunately, a flash from the volcano causes the *Nautilus'* cavern to collapse, trapping Nemo within his submarine. Thus, as the castaways leave the island, Nemo and his secret of giantism are consumed by the holocaust.

There are actually three *Mysterious Islands*:

the one written by Verne, the one filmed by Schneer and Harryhausen, and the one *almost* filmed by Schneer and Harryhausen. Ray elaborates. "There were a number of different rewrites of the script, and at first, we started to have the island with a prehistoric origin. Hence, the giant shelled octopus, which was a prehistoric type of creature, and the phororhacos. The island itself started out being similar to Atlantis, of Egyptian origin, with undersea temples. We wanted to develop that to a greater degree but, unfortunately, it didn't work out, save for that one brief scene when they were patching up the boat. These things take turns in the script, and sometimes you have a hangover from a previous script. Or sometimes things are dropped entirely. For instance, we had a man-eating plant which was dropped because of length. We had a sequence quite well-planned and ready to shoot, and we found out that we were getting more footage than we'd anticipated. Still, I think it came out an interesting picture."

The *Mysterious Island* that reached the screen suffers slightly for the deletions. By and large, it's a fine film, a tale, as we've indicated, of people and their conflicts with both cruel circumstance and one another. The cynical Spilett is constantly annoying Capt. Harding and for a while, even after they've reached the island, it looks as if the friction between the Union soldiers and Sgt. Pencroft is going to end in violence. When Capt. Nemo appears, he represents yet another source of contention: his single-minded goal of removing the causes and weapons of war creates a pro- and anti-Nemo faction within the camp. In short, there is always some interpersonal strife flavoring what might have been either a simple-minded or overly rhetorical film. Like *The Three Worlds of Gulliver*, *Mysterious Island* says just enough, both thematically and morally. Indeed, the very fact that warfare brought these people into Nemo's midst is, in itself, one of the film's subtle ironies. However, the cuts render the fantasy elements less easy to judge than the film's other values.

Egyptian antiquity and prehistoric life are among Ray's favorite topics and, obviously, he would have preferred to keep these references prominently featured in the film. Unfortunately, as he himself readily admits, "One always has a dream

picture—but then there is the element of having to compromise to form a commercial product. You try to keep a practical approach. I don't want to go off into the clouds too far, though I find dwelling up there quite pleasant. But I think one has to come down to earth and say, 'Can we make this, and are other people going to see this in the same way that I'm fascinated with it?' So you try to reach a happy medium." As a result of these understandable compromises—there is only so much information about plot and character that one can cram into one hundred minutes—the monsters seem to have less relevance than they did in *The Seventh Voyage of Sinbad*. They appear, they fight, and they leave, each within a few minutes. However, there is an advantage to this presentation. Unlike the openly antagonistic cyclops, crocodile, and all of Ray's earlier monsters, each of the *Mysterious Island* animals is going about its own private business when the castaways intrude. The crab is napping in the sand when Neb starts dancing on its back, the bees are building their honeycomb when Herbert and Elena invade the hive, the mollusk is simply minding its own business at the bottom of the sea as food comes traipsing by, and the phororhacos— well, *that one* is actively pursuing a meal. The prehistoric angle *would* have given the picture a more dramatic atmosphere, tying the monsters, the volcano, and the suggested sinking of Atlantis into a solid, semihistorical framework. But the animals' creation by Nemo allows the film to build a mystery about their origin while providing action that doesn't detract from the plot. After all, it's impossible for Ray's overwhelming animals to play a subordinate role in any film. Thus, the beasts come as close to allowing for a balance between narrative, characterization, and adventure as we are likely to find in a Harryhausen picture, although a bit more history would have been welcomed.

Unfortunately, in a technical sense, *Mysterious Island* is somewhat of a letdown from the previous two Dynamation films. The volcano, a six-foot-tall model, erupts with an exaggerated fury common to such miniature stagings, complete with rolling clouds of smoke and colorful fireworks. Even worse are glass paintings of the island which, used in panoramic shots, are flat and unconvincing, while the matting of the cave set into the painted face of the mountain is downright awful. Since such shots are prominently featured at critical junctures in the film, they add a feel of unreality to the goings-on. However, the monsters are all animated with Harryhausen's traditional flair and attention to detail. The crab—a real crustacean into which Ray inserted a metal armature—is the high point of the stop-motion confrontations, an exciting battle with an unusual resolution. The model of Neb in the monster's grip is especially well-animated, although close-ups are executed with Dan Jackson in the grasp of a lifesize mechanical claw. The brightly colored phororhacos is also a showstopper. One of Harryhausen's most spirited creations, it hops about the beach tearing at everyone and everything in sight, even after it has been mounted by the stop-motion Herbert Brown. Close-ups of Brown astride the monster were worked with a full-scale double of the bird's neck. The bees—or bee, as it was actually one bee model duplicated via split screen—were seen only briefly, and the mollusk, like the cephalopod in *It Came from Beneath the Sea*, was moved microscopic increments and photographed through a distortion glass, both of which helped to simulate the look and resistance of water.

The stop-motion work aside, one of *Mysterious Island's* more satisfying effects is the flight in the balloon. "Balloons have always fascinated me," Ray explains, "particularly the idea of escape in a balloon. So I enjoyed designing that whole sequence." Shots of the balloon rising were achieved by interspersing clips of a five-foot-tall miniature with close-ups of a gondola and the actors being lifted by a crane on the life-size outdoor set. Scenes of the balloon flying through the clouds, and of the men abandoning their shattered craft, were worked through yellow backing on a soundstage in London.

Like *The Three Worlds of Gulliver, Mysterious Island* did modest box-office business, both films lacking the promotion, and perhaps, the touch of evil in both the monsters and the antagonist that made *The Seventh Voyage of Sinbad* so popular. If that were the case, then Charles and Ray's next film should have been a blockbuster. It was adequately advertised and features some of Ray's most gripping and satanic work. Yet, *Jason and the Argonauts* was a financial failure. But there were extenuating circumstances—as Harryhausen will explain in defense of his favorite film.

Ray Harryhausen in the grip of the life-size mechanical claw used for close-ups during the attack of the crab. Harryhausen is showing actor Dan Jackson how to play the scene. © Columbia Pictures

CHAPTER TWELVE

Jason and the Argonauts

"I used to get terribly anxious about the future, particularly when I couldn't sell an idea. I found the whole thing rather futile; I'm sure many people go through that. The frustration of thinking that you have a better product than anybody else has ever put on the screen, and nobody else sees it. Of course, I can't afford to worry about it anymore. If it happens, it happens. I learned years ago not to think that far ahead: I take it as it comes. For example, I was particularly upset when I read that RKO was going to make *The Son of Sinbad* (1955) when I had storyboards for *The Seventh Voyage of Sinbad*. And they were going to make it with a strip artist, sort of a burlesque send-up, as cops and robbers in baggy pants with no sense of fantasy. Yet they call it the story of Sinbad. I'm still astounded today when looking back over many of the pictures such as *Jason and the Argonauts* and a few of the others. I've been able to put on the screen some of the most unusual and, I think, dynamic situations, and it seems to be taken for granted! And all of a sudden, a certain picture is made with a man in a gorilla suit and everybody thinks that it's the greatest thing since the invention of the wheel! It's very difficult, in my mind, to rationalize how people think. Charles and I have more in one of our pictures, like *Jason and the Argonauts*, than you see in about six pictures of ordinary calibre. Perhaps that's a mistake. All we can do is try to make our fantasy pictures with all the verve that you would find in a storybook. That's why I really believe that *Jason and the Argonauts* could have and *should* have made as much money as *Jaws*. But there were problems. You see, we had the picture in mind when we first moved to Europe. Naturally, we didn't want to go building Greek Temples in

Hollywood. So we made *Jason and the Argonauts* in Italy. Of course, I'd always wanted to do Greek mythology, and when I think back, it was Charles who prodded me into developing it. However, it's very difficult to calculate what the public is going to buy. A lot of times they say that costume dramas are taboo at the box office, but it really depends upon the *type* of costume drama. But I'd wanted to do Greek mythology for years because I could see all the gods formulating in my mind, and I was delighted when Charles suggested that we actually go ahead and tackle the subject. So we developed it first in twelve big drawings, and then we got the studio interested and we started the script. Unfortunately, the Italians were making all of these so-called spaghetti epics, which is not a nice connotation, since some of them are quite good. But they sort of flooded the market. So, while we knew that they were making these films, we had no idea that they would carry on as long as they did. When *Jason and the Argonauts* was released, people just assumed it was another Italian-made spectacle and didn't bother to go see it."

Jason and the Argonauts is anything but "another italian-made spectacle." It is a labor of love that was over two years in production at an unheard-of cost for a fantasy film of $3,500,000. Nor is it a mindless effort of the sort which followed the excellent Steve Reeves film *Hercules* (1959)—the first movie of this type. There are profound intellectual threads throughout the film that spotlight the way in which ancient peoples regarded themselves and their world. For instance, we are all wont to bandy the term 'fate' rather loosely about. But for the Ancient Greeks—as well as Ray Harryhausen—the notion of Fate and

Hermes, moments before the arrival of Jason and their trip
to Olympus.   © Columbia Pictures

Destiny is a serious matter indeed. And it pervades
Jason and the Argonauts, whose very premise is
rooted in the gods' predestination of Jason as the
ruler of Thessaly.

Preparing to invade the kingdom of Thessaly
and slay King Aristo, the warlord Pelias (Douglas
Wilmer) consults his seer as to the outcome of
battle. The prophet says that Pelias will conquer,
but when Zeus demands it, he shall also surrender
his throne to one of Aristo's children. Such being
the case, Pelias vows that Aristo's two daughters
and son must die with their father. Attacking the
Greek province, Pelias follows a young woman and
a baby into the temple of Hera, Queen of the Gods:
the girl is Briseis, Aristo's eldest daughter, and she
has come to ask the goddess' protection for her
sister and herself. The deity hears her pleas, but
Pelias slays Briseis, thinking that she has brought
Aristo's one son to the temple. Hera (Honor
Blackman) appears before Pelias and tells him that
there is no way to avert the destiny predicted by his
seer: the baby Jason, his fated successor, has already
escaped. Hera also informs the new ruler that to kill
Jason is to kill himself. Parting, she leaves Pelias
with one more thought, the promise that some day,
a one-sandaled man shall come, from whom no one
will protect him.

Retiring to Olympus, Hera asks Zeus (Niall
MacGinnis) for permission to aid Jason, and the
King of the Gods agrees. She may assist the rightful
king on six occasions, the number of times that
Briseis called upon the goddess for sanctuary. And

her first such move occurs twenty years later, when Pelias is out riding. Tossing him from his horse, she pulls him into a river just as Jason (Todd Armstrong) is passing by. Rescuing Pelias—although he does not know him to be the tyrant—Jason loses a sandal. Pelias recalls the prophecy, and invites Jason to his camp. There, the young man informs his host that he has returned to Thessaly to wrest the throne from Pelias. However, before he does this, Jason proposes to secure an icon around which the people can rally, such as the golden fleece that legend says hangs in a tree on the other side of the world. This plan pleases Pelias: Jason's chances of success are slim, which means that the potentate may not have to surrender his kingdom after all. However, to guarantee the failure of Jason's quest, Pelias tells his son Acastus (Gary Raymond) to make certain that he is a member of the crew.

That night, Jason stands on a hillside among the ruins of a temple, and talks with Pelias' seer. Jason admits that he does not believe in the gods, and is criticized by the soothsayer, who tells him that the gods *do* exist. And to substantiate his claim, the old man reveals himself to be Hermes, messenger of the gods. Swathing Jason in a ball of fire, he brings the Thessalian to Olympus. There, Zeus offers the young man a ship and a crew, which Jason refuses. He tells the gods that he will hold games to gather together the boldest men in Greece, and select his crew from among them. As for a vessel, he'll have one built by the finest shipmaker on the Aegean. Zeus commends Jason for his independence, and returns him to earth.

Held on a picturesque Greek shore, the athletic contest draws the best in local brawn—and brain. For when the great Hercules (Nigel Green) is awarded an honorary place on the crew, the lanky Hylas (John Crawford) steps forward. He asks Jason's permission to sail with the crew if he can best the Son of Zeus in any given contest. Jason agrees, and Hercules, scoffing at the lad, selects a discus. Hurling it out to sea, the demigod reaches a distant reef. Selecting a discus, Hylas steps forward: skipping the saucer across the water, he *passes* the rocky outcropping, beating Hercules' throw, and is given a place on the ship. Acastus, too, qualifies for the journey. Thus, when boatbuilder and crewmember Argus (Laurence Naismith) has finished the craft—christened the Argo in his honor—Jason and the Argonauts set sail.

After several days at sea, with no wind of which to speak, Jason addresses the masthead, a figure of Hera. At his request, she stirs up a wind and tells Jason that they will soon light upon land. However, she informs him that when they have reached their destination, they must take food and water and nothing more.

Arriving at the Isle of Bronze, the Argonauts go ashore for supplies, while Hercules and Hylas pursue a herd of goats for milk. The chase carries them to the valley where the legendary Haphaestus forged metallic statues of the gods; in the base of one statue, the Titan Talos, there is a door. Opening it, the two men find a treasure chamber belonging to the gods. Stealing a broach pin to use as a javelin, Hercules and Hylas turn to leave when the heavy stone door slams shut. Edging it open, the two Argonauts step outside as Talos comes creaking to life. The scavengers run as the bronze giant heads for the beach. Spotting the oncoming leviathan, Jason orders the Argo to sea, even while the landing party clamors onboard. However, the Titan has no intention of letting the Thessalians escape. Straddling the peninsulae which form the only exit from the natural harbor, Talos watches as they unsuccessfully try to backwater the craft: stooping, the metal monster seizes and destroys the Argo. However, Jason is able to salvage the figurehead of Hera and asks for her counsel. She tells Jason that Talos will try to kill them all for Hercules' indiscretion, and that he must look to the giant's heel for salvation. That is all she can tell him, and swimming ashore, the Argonauts brace for a second attack. It is not long in coming. Ordering his men to distract the behemoth, Jason runs to its ankle, finds and loosens a massive plug, and allows the monster's ichor, its life blood, to drain onto the golden sands of the beach. In great pain, the giant begins to fragment and the sailors flee. In his hasty retreat, however, Hercules drops the broach pin which Hylas pauses to recover; it is a move that costs the boy his life. Even as the Greek retrieves the golden spear, Talos breaks apart, crushing Hylas as he hits the ground.

The men repair the Argo and make ready to continue their journey. However, Hercules does not believe that Hylas is dead, and elects to stay behind in search of the lad. Stirred by Acastus, the Argonauts refuse to sail without Hercules; thus, Jason is forced to call upon Hera for the final time. She orders the voyage resumed and the men to set a course for the island of Phrygia, where they will seek out the blind seer Phineas. Awestruck, the men leave Hercules on the Isle of Bronze and make for Phrygia.

Phineas' lot, as the Argonauts discover upon their arrival, is not a pleasant one. Years before, the augur had misused his powers and was struck blind by Zeus. But the King of the Gods was not yet assuaged, and sent a pair of huge, batlike harpies to further torment the seer by stealing whatever food is brought to him. Now, however, Phineas has had enough! Zeus has commanded him to assist Jason in his quest for the Golden Fleece, and he will do so, but only if the Argonauts free him from the curse of the harpies. Jason agrees to meet the seer's price. Placing Phineas' table in an ancient pantheon and stationing his men atop the crumbling temple, the Thessalian waits for the harpies to strike. And when they do, he has the Argonauts drop nets from their various positions, which snare the scaly hags. Building a wooden cage for the beasts, he leaves them at the mercy of the sightless prophet. In return for this service, Phineas gives Jason directions to Colchis, the land of the Golden Fleece. However, Phineas warns Jason that he'll never make it through the Clashing Rocks and offers him a charm of the sea god Triton hoping that it may be of some use. Thanking the old man, Jason and his Argonauts depart.

The Clashing Rocks are two peaceful-looking mountains between which one must sail to reach the land of the Fleece. Holding about the perimeter of the inlet, Jason watches as a ship from Colchis enters the narrow channel; in an instant the huge cliffs are alive, heaping boulders at the vessel and sinking it within seconds. Unsettled, but faced with no alternative, Jason cautiously pilots his boat into the strait. And moments later, the mountains are again active. Swearing at the gods for having toyed with him, Jason tosses Phineas' amulet into the sea. Suddenly, Triton, a huge merman, erupts from the water and holds the rocks apart, permitting the Argo to pass unharmed. But what remains of the

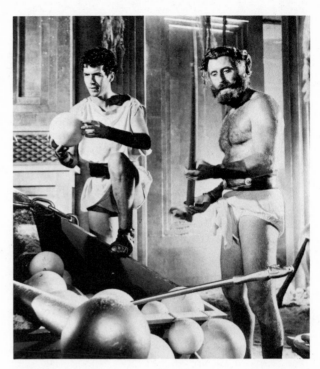

Hercules (right) and Hylas in the treasure-filled pedestal of Talos.   © Columbia Pictures

voyage to Colchis is far from tranquil. First, Jason rescues a woman from the wreckage of the ship destroyed by the Clashing Rocks. Her name is Medea (Nancy Kovack) and she is the high priestess of the powerful goddess Hecate. Next, Jason and Acastus fight over the way in which the son of Pelias has plotted against the mission. Ultimately, Acastus leaps overboard and, swimming to Colchis, alerts King Aeetes (Jack Gwillim) of Jason's plan. When the Argonauts come ashore, the monarch has them arrested.

That night, torn between her loyalty to Hecate and her love for Jason, Medea drugs Aeetes and his men and sets the Argonauts free. Hastening to the cave of the Golden Fleece, Jason touches the ram skin and is attacked by a giant, seven-headed hydra. Crushed in the monster's tail is Acastus, who met his death while trying to reach the Fleece before Jason. Battling the hissing serpent, Jason stabs its underbelly and the monster dies. By this time, however, Aeetes and his soldiers have awakened and head for the cave. They arrive too late to save

174

One of the most chilling moments in film: Talos turns to
stare at Hercules. Actor Nigel Green was composited in the
scene through yellow backing.
© Columbia Pictures

Talos rounds a cliff to slay the Argonauts.
© Columbia Pictures

Todd Armstrong loosens the plug in Talos' heel, a scene filmed with a life-size mock-up of the bronze giant's foot.

© Columbia Pictures

Talos reaching for the life-size Argo. Moments later, just prior to contact, Ray will cut to a shot of a screaming sailor.

© Columbia Pictures

Talos, bridging the only exit from the Isle of Bronze, prepares to seize the Argo. The ship, incidentally, was ninety-two feet long and built over the frame of a fishing barge. © Columbia Pictures

Talos about to drop the miniature Argo back into the sea.
© Columbia Pictures

The harpies nag Phineas at Paestum. © Columbia Pictures

One of the harpies lands on a stop-motion set piece in this otherwise miniature projected scene. Four aerial brace wires can be vaguely discerned shooting from the creature's back. © Columbia Pictures

Triton rises from the deep to save the Argo from the Clashing Rocks.   © Columbia Pictures

Behind the scenes in Colchis with Aeetes (seated on the throne) and Medea (in robe). Courtesy the British Film Institute.   © Columbia Pictures

the Fleece or the hydra, but the king is not yet defeated. Asking Hecate to rain fire from the sky, Aeetes burns the hydra's flesh from its bones and has his men gather the teeth. Pursuing Jason, he confronts the Thessalian, Argus, Medea, and the Argonauts Castor and Polydeuces atop a high hill. Dropping the hydra's teeth to the ground, the king watches with glee as seven human skeletons rise from the earth, each one armed with a sword and shield. Telling Argus and Medea to take the Fleece and join the rest of the crew on the Argo, Jason and his two companions face the army of the dead. The skeletons charge and wage the strangest struggle in history. Unfortunately, the odds favor Aeetes' hell-spawned warriors, and with Polydeuces and Castor fallen, Jason finds himself pinned at the edge of the cliff. Vastly outnumbered, he decides to leap into the sea and, so doing, lures the demons to their second death. Free of his attackers, Jason joins Medea on the deck of the Argo while, in Olympus,

Zeus tells Hera that he will allow the lovers a calm sea and one another, at least until their next adventure.

Alas, the power of the gods is meager when pitted against the punch of the box-office dollar. For Jason, there were no further adventures, as this exquisitely made and ambitious film went widely unplayed. There is talk of it being rereleased, the way Columbia reissued *The Seventh Voyage of Sinbad* to great success in 1975, and one can only hope that this time around the picture will find its well-deserved audience.

As Ray has suggested, there is more excitement in *Jason and the Argonauts* than in most any other half-dozen films one cares to mention. And not only are the thrills *present*, but, like *The Seventh Voyage of Sinbad*, they comprise some of the strangest sights ever recorded on film. However, before we look at these, let's consider how the film benefits from its nonanimation

180

Ray Harryhausen's preproduction sketch of Jason, the hydra, and the slain Acastus.

© Columbia Pictures

The hydra emerges from its cave with a stop-motion Acastus in its grip. Jason and the Golden Fleece are in the foreground.   © Columbia Pictures

values. Filmed primarily around the seaside village of Palinuro, with interiors staged at a small Roman studio, the picture boasts breathtaking locales. Singularly impressive were the 3,000-year-old ruins of Paestum in southern Italy, a site which pleased Ray tremendously. "We got permission to climb upon the ruins and to use them any way we saw fit, just so long as we didn't demolish them. It's a good thing they hadn't seen *Twenty Million Miles to Earth*: I have a reputation for demolishing everything! So we promised not to harm them, and we didn't, of course. But there's nothing quite like real locations as opposed to a set. And when you've got a locale like Paestum, which we used for the harpy sequence, how can you go wrong?" It was an academic question which Ray shouldn't have asked. For, while the picture may have been set in Greece, it was filmed entirely in Italy to keep costly transportation bills to a minimum. Thus, the crew was forced to build exterior sets for such scenes as Pelias' camp and Jason's conversation with the disguised Hermes. And Ray remembers something that *did* go wrong, even in this compromise situation. "We built some sets on a beach and a storm came up and washed them all away. So we had to rebuild them." Perhaps the gods were displeased with the way they were being portrayed! In any case, the various settings proved extremely photogenic and added tremendously to the authenticity of the picture.

Another problem involving the live-action scenes were the ocean-going shots. As Schneer realized early in the planning stages of *Jason and the Argonauts*, there was no way to shoot the adventure without a full-scale Argo. So he built one for $250,000 which, again, led to some remarkable shots as well as a near-trauma for the producer. After losing time and money on several sunless days, with the crew idle and at full pay, Schneer finally had a clear day on which to do some shooting of the Argo at sea. Sailing into a Sicilian bay off "the Isle of Bronze," the producer coordinated the action and began filming. Suddenly, a Spanish galleon from the television series *Sir Francis Drake* came floating about the headland and spoiled an excellent set-up. Jumping from his command jeep on the beach, Schneer grabbed a megaphone and hollered, "Get that out of here, you're in the *wrong century*!"

After a brief talk with the TV program's second unit crew—did he threaten to call upon Talos as an arbiter?—Schneer got the bay *and* his shots. Fortunately, the producer is able to take such disasters in stride: "Well, it's never a piece of cake, and it's never exactly the way you want it. So if you can get it close enough, that's as much as you can hope for."

If things went awry behind the cameras, it didn't show onscreen. Shots of the Argo sailing proudly into sunsets, as well as the seige of Thessaly and the picture's more intimate moments—Briseis' surrender to the care of Hera and Jason's talk with Hermes in the deep blues of early evening for example—are polished and truly inspired. Harryhausen, cinematographer Wilkie Cooper, director Don Chaffey, and Bernard Herrmann made these and other segments very rich and very human. Of course, the handsome production would have been wasted without some superb players. While Todd Armstrong's Jason suffers from the redubbing of his dialogue—the actor's too-American accent did not gel with those of his British costars—what remains of his performance is appealing. His enthusiasm and sincerity make Jason a likable man and a leader of fortitude and courage. Nancy Kovack's Medea successfully communicates the torment she endures loving two opposing forces, while veteran character actor Laurence Naismith makes Argus a tough old salt who fills whatever gaps the inexperienced Jason has in commanding his men and the Argo. Douglas Wilmer is an outwardly wicked but basically frightened Pelias, although Gary Raymond is nothing short of sadistic as his cruel son Acastus. However, of all the players, it is Nigel Green who truly shines as Hercules. Completely unlike the overly muscled, utterly serious character created by Steve Reeves, Green's Hercules is boisterous, cocky, and hedonistic. Harryhausen may be right: "It is difficult to say if one could sustain this type of characterization as a central figure." Because he is a peripheral character, Hercules, as Ray puts it, "could not have bulging biceps. He was supposed to be part of the crew of the Argo, and we didn't want him to look too strange from all the other people; it would have made them look rather insipid. Even though he was the son of a god, he had to fit in with all the other characters.

Argus, Medea, and Jason prior to the skeleton attack. © Columbia Pictures

Jason and his men vs. the Children of the Hydra's Teeth.
© Columbia Pictures

Besides, there are many strong people who don't go down to somebody's gymnasium to get that way. Now, for someone like Maciste of Italian legend, that kind of character may be quite suitable. But we didn't want to simply redo what someone else had already done." Thus, Green was able to create a bravado personality that gives an otherwise very intense film some of its more amusing live action moments, such as the match with Hylas and various exchanges with Jason.

Scripturally, *Jason and the Argonauts* is both literate and fast-paced, written to showcase the adventure of the quest as well as the fantasy generic to the world in which Jason lived. Accordingly, the high quality of the photography, sets, performances, music, and dialogue notwithstanding, the burden of proof—the credibility of the motion picture—fell to Ray Harryhausen. However, to better appreciate Ray's broad contribution to *Jason and the Argonauts*, it is best that we pause to examine the boundaries of his work. After all, he was responsible for the mattes in *The Three Worlds of Gulliver*, built and designed such miniature live action props as the balloon and volcano in *Mysterious Island*, and does the stop-motion work in all his films. In a picture like *Jason and the Argonauts*, where the skeleton sequence alone took five months to animate and, in all, there were eleven stop-motion figures to build and shoot—one with seven heads—is there anything he *doesn't* do? "I'm always involved with all the effects. You see, when you say the word special effects, it can mean a number of different things. Special effects as a heading includes floor effects, from the man who produces fire on the stage and puts gas jets here and there, to the man who creates bullets going across the wall. Those are all called special effects. That's one reason I go under the heading of visual effects: because I design *all* the effects. For example, a traveling matte. Even though it is actually a lab job, putting two pieces of film together, I design the basic idea of using a traveling matte for that shot. Of course, I have my own optical printer and I do certain things in a way that I know how to do them. But I can't do everything, just as I have to farm out a lot of the sculpting of the models. I just don't have the time to do it all myself. But I design the characters right

from scratch. When I have to subcontract, they work strictly from my drawings."

Ray's early illusions in *Jason and the Argonauts* involve the vaporous comings and goings of Hera, the transformation of Hermes from seer to god—which includes his growing hundreds of feet in height—Jason's consumption by flame, and our hero's visit to Olympus. These were all achieved via traveling or static mattes, although several shots of Jason standing on Zeus' chess board of the world were done with oversized props. Ray was also responsible for the stop-motion flight of the disci during the contest between Hylas and Hercules. However, his first opportunity to really stretch his creative legs came during the Isle of Bronze segment, which is the film's longest episode.

Ray has an instinct for movement and personality—Schneer says "It's something you feel; it's something you're born with"—and nowhere are these two qualities more evident than in the battle with Talos. Talos also embodies the elements of grandeur and eminence which appear in a stop-motion character for the first time since King Kong. Initially, what strikes both the characters and the viewer about Talos is his incredible *size*. The bronze giant is nearly 600 feet tall. Thus, he is imposing even at rest, which is how Hercules and Hylas first see him, crouched atop his treasure-chest pedestal looking out across a valley filled with statues, his sword in hand. After the theft, however, as the two Argonauts step outside and gaze anxiously about, trying to see who—or what—locked them in the chamber, there is a grinding of metal as Talos turns his head to glower at Hercules. And, since the camera's point of view is from just behind the Son of Zeus Talos is, in effect, casting his icy stare at the audience. It is one of the cinema's most chilling moments. At this point, Hylas and Hercules run while Talos steps from his perch. Unused to walking, the giant reels slightly and leans against his stand; collecting his wits, he sets out toward the beach.

Talos' stride is great, his step hulking, measured, and suggesting awesome power; his features—especially the empty eye sockets—are immobile and vacant, adding the dimension of soullessness to the monster. Of course, as Ray points out, this is a far cry from the Talos of legend, but there were both dramatic and personal reasons for the change. "Talos comes from the original myth. He wasn't that large, but there are many versions, and it's difficult to dig out the original version. I had the same problem with the fairy tales. In some stories, you find that Talos was a bronze god about eight feet tall that sat in the fire until he got red hot, and then went around hugging the sailors and burning them to death. Well, you could hardly do that for the screen. One has to take dramatic license. So you take the very essence of the fact that there was such a creature in Jason called Talos, and that he did live on this island and tried to prevent the sailors from stealing things. But for theatrical purposes, you have to get the best out of it using the basic premise. As for making him colossal, I did that mainly because I had always wanted to do something with the Colossus of Rhodes. Way back in my childhood, upon first hearing about the Colossus of Rhodes (a huge statue of Apollo on the Greek island of Rhodes, and one of the Seven Ancient Wonders of the World—JR), I thought, 'Oh gosh! If I could only *build* a statue that big!' And that idea stayed with me through the years. So I looked through many Greek statues of various gods, as well as bronzes that were dredged up from the sea. In most of these statues, they had put the eyes in the sockets in white. Well, over the period of time that they were demolished, the eyes had been lost. And what struck me looking at all these bronze figures was this emptiness when you gaze in and see the hollow inside. This grand exterior structure had nothing inside of it! So, apart from the impression of size, that was another thing I wanted very much to capture in Talos."

Although there are many gripping moments in the giant's onslaught—Talos carefully stepping on the Argonauts, or in a frightening close-up, poking his huge hand under a stone arch, slapping it on a group of sailors and dragging them back—the high point of his rampage is the crippling of the Argo. Because of his stiff gait, Talos doesn't actually *step* across the narrow pass: he pivots about one leg, swinging to the other side. And after he has straddled the strait he just stands there, staring ahead, as Jason tries desperately to reverse the course of the Argo. Only when it becomes clear that the ship is doomed does Talos look down. Through

a series of stunning mattes, we see the heartless giant from Jason's perspective, looming over the vessel, while staggered with these awesome scenes are long shots showing both the Titan and the full-scale ship. Finally, in this same long shot, shifting the sword to his left hand when the craft is within range, Talos stoops from the knees and reaches for the Argo. What follows is not only a gripping sequence, but a prime exhibition of Ray's knack for film editing, which he personally executes on all scenes involving his effects. Cutting to a close-up of the bow of the vessel, Ray shows Talos' enormous hand extending toward the prow, but not quite touching it. Following this are shots of panicking sailors, after which Ray returns to his long shot of Talos, as the Titan raises the boat from the water. Shaking it free of bothersome Argonauts, he eventually drops it back into the sea and heads for the beach and a rendezvous with the stranded crewmen. Without resorting to an expensive optical effect, what Ray had done was to simply *suggest* that Talos had grabbed the prow of the ship. The actual taking-hold is never seen; the shots of the sailors consume that footage in which this action would have occurred. Further, these clips allow Ray to return to his master shot of Talos and the harbor, but with a miniature Argo in the monster's grip. Thus, dramatically and technically, this sequence is what class filmmaking is all about.

After Ray began viewing the rushes of his Talos animation, there was some fear that the giant's slow movements would cause the rather lengthy sequence to drag. "There was a great apprehension about that, even as I was designing the sequence. But *Jason and the Argonauts*, like all Greek myths, is much slower paced than Sinbad, for example. So one has to decide what kind of picture you're making. You can't just keep copying *King Kong*, as much as I'd like to. That was a *very* fast-paced picture, and one tries to emulate successes, of course. But it isn't feasible for every type of story to take that approach. We just had to say, 'What is best for this picture and what is most interesting?' Fortunately, it all worked out; Talos' brooding, lumbering presence created suspense in that the audience *knew* something nasty was going to happen, but had to wait upon Talos to tip his hand, as it were. Also, the scene was greatly enhanced by

Bernard Herrmann's Talos theme, which Ray classifies as "a marvelous, savage theme, particularly when the camera panned up to Talos' face. He had an almost *Rites of Spring* savagery to the rhythm."

A perfect contrast to the deliberate, funereal pace of the Talos sequence is Ray's next animated episode, the capture of the harpies. Wicked and semihuman, with two devilish horns, long fangs, reptilian skin, and boned, leathery wings, the airborne demons are the kind of beasts that could easily have crept from Pandora's Box. Like Talos, the harpies occur in classical mythology, albeit as a filthy, ravenous creature having a woman's head and the body of a bird. Indeed, the word has become a part of the English language, used to describe any rapacious individual. However, by their very nature, these monsters create a light, pesky atmosphere that is entirely different from the thundering drama of Talos' attack.

Technically, the sequence is troubled only in the remotest sense by the strobing effect of the wings—a minor quibble against the in toto effectiveness of the segment. For, while the staccato beat of the animals' flight is occasionally distracting, Ray has perfectly captured the *movement* of flight, making the sharp flapping appear to be *stylized*, but never fake. Indeed, Ray's control over the aerial brace maneuvers of his twin demons is astonishing. He has them flit about, light on pillars, and even struggle beneath the weight of the Argonauts' nets, all while supported by thin strands of wire. An especially impressive aerial brace shot is one wherein a harpy grabs Phineas' belt, and spinning the prophet like a top, strips it from his body. This was accomplished by pulling the girdle from Phineas with wires on the Paestum set, and back at the studio, having Ray coordinate his animation of the harpy with this miniature, projected footage. However, the most noticeable achievement in the harpy sequence is the use of Dynamation—referred to as *Dynamation 90* for *Jason and the Argonauts*—to cast the harpies' shadows on the ground. Obviously, there was no way to work this illusion on the life-size set. Of course, one can matte cartooned shadows into a shot, but this process is costly and quite laborious. Thus, Ray found that when taking apart the

background footage to insert his creatures, he could also insert miniature terrain to match that of the ground at Paestum. Although the color of the model and actual turf are not always precisely color balanced, the composite is still quite extraordinary, particularly if you're not watching the film for the twenty-fifth time, expressly *looking* for the effect!

One of the few occasions that has drawn Ray criticism from his fans was the next special-effects sequence in *Jason and the Argonauts*, the appearance of Triton. For the first time in a Dynamation film, Ray chose to represent a creature of fantasy using an actor rather than an articulated model. However, with all due respect to the stop-motion Atticists, the decision was a prudent one. To have animated the giant and the Clashing Rocks, and then matted them into an ocean setting, would have taken months. As it was, shooting the sequence with a miniature Argo in a studio tank took less than two weeks, and the product was most satisfactory.

As Ray is wont to stress over and over again, what many people don't realize about his films is that the budget *is* limited and that the longer a film is in production the more anxious its backers become. Ray would love to have animated the scene, but it just wasn't practical. In fact, Ray notes that several plot twists and technical approaches planned for *Jason and the Argonauts* had to be crossed from the screenplay. "Before the final rewrite of the script, Medea was going to take Jason down into Hell, past an animated Cerberus (the three-headed guardian dog of the Underworld—JR), so he could bathe in a certain liquid in order to make himself invulnerable to the hydra. But again, to do it properly would have taken a great deal of footage, and we just didn't have the time. We also wanted to film the monsters of the Clashing Rocks, Scylla and Charybdis. But we thought about it, realized the animation it would involve and, since we already *had* so much animation in the picture, decided not to do it. Of course, if one had unlimited time, there would probably have been a little more reward by the use of animation. As it was, however, I felt it gave variety to the picture and worked out quite nicely."

Staged in a four-foot-deep tank at the Shepperton Studios in England, the Clashing Rocks

Two discarded sequences from *Jason and the Argonauts*, showing Jason and Medea encountering Cerberus at the entrance to hell... © Columbia Pictures

...and finding the tortures of the damned beyond.

© Columbia Pictures

Ray Harryhausen and one of his harpy models.
© Columbia Pictures

sequence starred a Triton whose body was actually in two different places. The actor playing the sea god was dressed with a beard, crown, and wig, his waist made-up to resemble fish scales, while his false tail was several feet from where he was standing. Mechanically operated, it was made to slap about the water while Triton stood in the tank and kept the mountains apart. Needless to say, beyond being well built, there was only one other prerequisite for the role, as Ray explains: "He was a professional swimmer, and that was one of the necessities of getting the part. He had to be able to handle himself underwater, because it meant submerging, staying under, and not getting panicky. He also had to be treated specially so that water wouldn't disturb his hair, his moustache, or his beard. We went through the whole thing dry at first, and then he examined everything underneath to be sure that he could get out of the crevasse

without coming up at the wrong moment. But it all worked out nicely, and I think he enjoyed the part very much." The entire episode was photographed at high speeds to slow down the action, with select closeups of Jason, Argus, and the prow of the ship added at a later date through yellow backing. However, there was one major disadvantage to shooting the scene in this manner, and that was the problem of water beads.

Whenever a tankful of water is used to represent an ocean, there is the danger that splashed droplets will belie the miniature nature of the setting. There are numerous ways of dealing with this—by lacing the water with powder about which smaller droplets will form, thus creating the illusion of size, or by pouring glycerin into the water to make it heavier—but there wasn't time to experiment with these various techniques. As a result, whenever the plaster and canvas mountains hurl rocks and sand into the water, it beads unnaturally. Although the droplets bothered Ray, he remains pragmatic about the scene: "Yes, it could have been done better if we'd had time to do the various tricks that you have to do to diminish the size of the splashes. But, overall, it gave the effect we wanted, that of a dream world."

No stop-motion creature has ever had as many moving parts as *Jason and the Argonauts'* third featured monster, the hydra. With seven heads and two tails, all moving simultaneously, it presented Ray with numerous tactical challenges, such as remembering in which direction each jaw, tongue, slinking neck, or tail was moving—not to mention the stop motion figure of Acastus with *its* five appendages—and how to position them so as to maintain a balanced screen composition. Ray

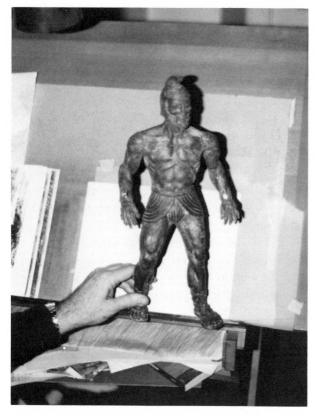

Ray Harryhausen with a visitor to his drawing table. Notice how Talos' wrist joints have eroded in the fifteen years since he was built. Photograph by the author.

outlines yet another very fundamental problem: "Whenever you're devising something as extreme as the hydra, you want to eliminate as much as possible the potentially comic aspects. For instance, the hydra slithered along the ground. But if we had given him little tiny legs, they would have to move so fast in order to get anywhere, that a comic situation could develop. So I arrived at this design to keep it from seeming ludicrous, and because I thought it would be more horrifying to see a slithering snake rather than a semidragon."

The tilt with the hydra occurs in a cave that glistens with the radiance of the Fleece, but is also alive with an eerie mist. Compounded by the monster's seven-tongued hisses, the sequence is quite a contrast from Ray's previous stop-motion lizards, the dragon in *The Seventh Voyage of Sinbad* and the crocodile from *The Three Worlds of Gulliver*. Those monsters moved in colorful, almost gaudy worlds of fantasy; when a creature comes sizzling from a dark abyss *already* carrying a corpse in its tail, it *has* to be more terrifying! Indeed, the inherent melodrama of the tussle is one reason that Ray decided to eliminate planned shots of Jason lopping off the hydra's individual heads and having them grow back, as per the Greek legend.

If this sequence represents extremes in such considerations as light: the Fleece; and dark: the hydra's recess, then it also demonstrates the best and the worst that *Jason and the Argonauts* has to offer in terms of special effects. There is a shot of Jason grappling with a full-size model of the hydra's tail that is static, overacted, and embarrassing; contrarily, the impaling of the creature is impressively done. In a long shot, Ray has Jason duck, lunge at the monster, and withdraw, *his sword still stuck in the hydra's abdomen!* Actually, several frames before the thrust, Todd Armstrong had intentionally dropped his sword which Ray matted from the picture frame-by-frame. Then, while animating his monster before a miniature screen projection of this footage, Harryhausen suspended a prop sword from an aerial brace, positioning it to conform with Armstrong's movements, then sliding it into the model. The realism and continuity of the effect is quite startling. Other impressive shots show a fluidly animated stop-motion Jason coiled in the hydra's tail—the long-shot counterpart of the aforementioned clip showing Armstrong and a life-size reconstruction—and the monster's initial charge, with the wary Jason seen from behind the monster's seven twining heads.

Traditionally, the number seven has a mystical connotation, and Ray has often drawn upon its attraction in his films. To wit, there was *The Seventh Voyage of Sinbad*—in the Arabian Nights, the Prince of Bagdad had six other voyages from which to choose—the seven-headed hydra, the seven castaways on the *Mysterious Island*...and seven skeletons doing battle with three Argonauts in the numbing climax of *Jason and the Argonauts*. Like Ray's skeleton swordfight in *The Seventh Voyage of Sinbad*, and the vitalization of Talos, this confrontation employs the slow build to allow audience tension to mount. One at a time, the skeletons push from the ground, standing rooted to the spot until the full complement of warriors has appeared. Then, at Aeetes' command, they crouch and step slowly forward in unison. Only when the suspense has been fully nurtured do they emit a frightful shriek and charge.

Beyond the animation, Ray used every skill at his command to bring the sequence to the screen. Aerial braces made it possible for one skeleton to lose his head with the swipe of an Argonaut's sword, and permitted others to jump over ruins; a miniature sword, its blade whittled down between frames, was employed for the shot of a skeleton stabbing an Argonaut; the juxtaposition of a model staircase with a real ruin enabled a skeleton to run up and engage its opponent atop the wall; model substitution was used when Jason skewers a skeleton and leaves the sword implanted in its rib cage; and so forth. And, in terms of both menace and special effects, it all worked out so perfectly that Ray looks back on the fight with only one regret: he would have preferred to stage the sequence at night rather than in daylight, to invoke its innately nightmarish qualities. But he was faced with the very real possibility that the already unnerving scene might then have proven *too* horrifying. Hence, he had to compromise. As it was, there were many people in any given audience who laughed during the segment. This worried Harryhausen and his producer—and enraged hordes of Harryhausen fans who were so enthralled with the effort that

they could do naught but sit in the theatre dumb-struck—until it was decided, as Ray puts it, that "they're the type of snickers which you get when the average person sometimes finds extreme visual images so odd and unusual that they laugh purely for relief. That may have been the reason some people laughed at the skeletons. After all, I didn't really see anything basically comical in the situation! There were seven skeletons and they grew out of the ground: I'm sure these were laughs of relief or nervousness. I remember that this was a concern to Bernie Herrmann when he wrote the music. He wanted to write music that wouldn't give the impression of the scene being similar to a cartoon staging. He wrote this strange, sort of low-register rhythm which took a lot of the potential laugh out of the sequence. It is interesting—we never got a laugh out of the single skeleton in *The Seventh Voyage of Sinbad* because it was in a haunted cave with dark lighting. Even so, the situation was different and not as terrorizing as it was in *Jason and the Argonauts*."

If we discount the antics of Hercules, the only intentionally light-hearted scenes in the film are

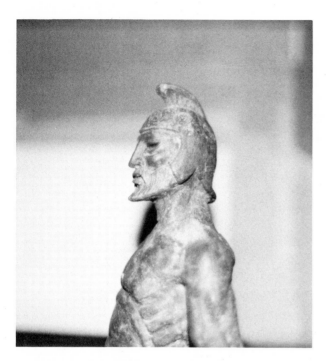

Talos today. Photographs by the author.

those set on Mt. Olympus, where the timbre is whimsical, not unlike the mood of the immortals in the "Pastoral Symphony" segment of Walt Disney's *Fantasia* (1940). This is splendidly illustrated at one point in the film as, manipulating mortal lives on the chessboard of the gods, Hera impulsively shifts a warship—not the Argo—into shallow waters. Though hundreds of people most certainly died on the board's terrestrial counterpart, Zeus simply chides his wife saying that she must learn how to play the game without cheating. The sad values of omnipotence! And Jason's plight is treated with like levity, the only difference being that while the Thessalian, too, is only a pawn in the game of Destiny, he often defies the gods, admirably preferring dignity to the guarantee of survival. Yet, this playful tempo on Olympus carries more dire implications than the clean-cut matter of Fate vs.

free will, as Zeus makes a shambles of earthly law. He sanctions murder by decreeing that Aristo fall before Pelias, and in fating Jason's recovery of the throne condones piracy, having the Argonaut steal the Golden Fleece from its rightful owners, to whose land it has brought peace and prosperity. Why not have simply left Aristo on the throne in the first place? The answer, of course, is that there is no sport in peaceful constancy. For, as Ray views the gods, "When you think of them, you always say 'at the whim of the gods.' It's a standard expression. So, one would assume that they're rather blasé about who they're shuffling around down below. Thus, it was natural that we present the gods in this fashion. Besides, I think that if we had approached them too seriously, it could have gotten ludicrous." Thanks to the entertaining counterpoint between the glib deities and the very grim Jason, as well as the brilliantly subtle performance of Niall MacGinnis as Zeus, the two worlds were ideally melded.

Until its release, *Jason and the Argonauts* was called *Jason and the Golden Fleece*. "But we had to change our title," Ray recalls, "because we discovered that there was already an Italian film called *Jason and the Golden Fleece* (1960) (released in the United States as *The Giants of Thessaly—JR*). However, a film by any name is still the sum of its parts, and *Jason and the Argonauts* was composed of flawless and majestic elements, from its stirring musical themes and title paintings to its simplest sound effects to its incredible stop-motion and live-action performances. Truly a supreme motion picture production, and an extraordinary fantasy adventure.

In case anyone is interested, *Cleopatra* won that year's special effects Oscar, no doubt for supporting Elizabeth Taylor's bosom in a variety of low-cut gowns. An admirable enough achievement—but better than Talos? Sorry, Ray. As you've known since your youth, it is inevitable that beauty shall kill the beast!

191

Inside the moon, Selenites begin dismantling the sphere.

CHAPTER THIRTEEN

First Men in the Moon

During the production of *Jason and the Argonauts*, Ray returned from Italy and married the former Diana Bruce, a direct descendant of Dr. Livingstone, of Stanley and Livingstone fame. Did Ray's marriage to the charming Englishwoman have any effect on his work? Well, his next film *was* the very British production of Englishman H.G. Wells' *First Men in the Moon*. However, it was a project that had long been considered as a potential Dynamation production.

"I've always wanted to do an H.G. Wells story, and I had approached Charles several times on *First Men in the Moon*. We discussed it very thoroughly, but felt that inasmuch as people were planning to go to the moon in a very short space of time, it would no longer be as shocking a thing as it was in the Victorian period. So we set it aside. There really weren't enough contents in the basic story to make a feature film. Then we began preparing *Food of the Gods*—until we met Nigel Kneale, who is a Wells expert, and dug out *First Men in the Moon* again. Kneale knew all of Wells' works, and he took a very enthusiastic view of the story, trying to solve the problem of making it a period piece as well as bringing it up to date, which I think he did. The introduction gave you the modern, and then went back into the Victorian time to a Wellsian type of story."

Set in the late nineteenth century, Wells' tale was framed by the occasion of mankind's first lunar landing, a modern-day achievement with an international crew. Disembarking from *United Nations One*, the astronauts begin their exploration of the moon, only to find, tacked on a boulder, a Union Jack and a summons credited to one Katharine Calendar. Radioing a photograph of the artifacts to earth, the spacemen's British liaisons trace the name and learn that Katharine Calendar has recently died, but was married to an Arnold Bedford, who lives in a nursing home. Visiting the aged Bedford (Edward Judd), who has long claimed to have once traveled to the moon, they listen as he tells his strange story.

In 1899, Bedford, a writer, fled his debts by going to visit fiancée Katharine (Martha Hyer) at Cherry Cottage, her country home. There, he meets Cavor (Lionel Jeffries), a maverick scientist who has invented a marvelous paint that nullifies the force of gravity. And, having built a huge sphere in his greenhouse, Cavor intends to use the substance, called Cavorite, to fly to the moon. Coating shutters on the sphere's windows with the remarkable paint, he plans to open and close them and thus use the gravity of the earth, the sun, and the moon, to control his trajectory. Sensing a fortune to be made in Cavorite, the mercenary Bedford agrees to accompany the scientist on his voyage. However, Kate is none too pleased with what she views as her lover's death wish, and is even more incensed when, while the men are preparing to launch, she receives a summons that holds her responsible for Bedford's lagging finances. Storming over to Cavor's residence, she pounds on the sphere moments before it is due to take off. With no choice but to open the hatch and pull her inside, Bedford holds Kate as the spaceship rumbles and explodes through the roof of the greenhouse. Mesh supports and a cushioned interior preserve the trio from the buffeting they receive, and a few days later, they reach the moon, the sphere's huge bumpers absorbing the harsh impact of landing. Slipping Kate into the transport's storage compartment, Cavor and Bedford

The original advertising art for *First Men in the Moon*.

don diving suits and step out to the rocky lunar terrain. When the customized diving bell has been repressurized, Kate climbs back into the living quarters.

Jumping about in the moon's one-sixth gravity, the explorers plant their flag, leave Kate's summons behind as a legal document, and crashing through a strange, crystalline crater, find that the moon's interior has a breathable atmosphere. They also learn, much to Bedford's terror and Cavor's utter delight, that these inner caverns are *inhabited*! Approached by four-foot-tall bipedal insects known as Selenites, Bedford reacts with aggression, kicking masses of the creatures from a high ridge. Cavor condemns his partner's vicious instincts, but the die has been cast; fleeing, the men return to the landing site and find that the sphere is gone. It has been dragged through a large hexagonal doorway cut in the side of a mountain. Forcing the two stone slabs apart, the explorers slip inside and follow the tracks

left by their craft. However, the intruders' progress is slowed by the attack of a huge lunar centipede. Rescued by blasts from electric guns belonging to the Selenites (who breed the giants for food) Bedford and Cavor now have no choice but to accompany the lunarians to their colony.

Nestled between huge vats of liquid, where oxygen is torn from water to make the inner world habitable, the Selenite settlement has a caste system composed of workers and thinkers. And just now, Kate is enclosed in a glass-and-stalactite chamber where she is being studied by a handful of thinkers. Livid with indignation, she is not a willing subject, although Cavor is thrilled with this opportunity to converse with beings of an alien race. As for Bedford, distressed with Kate's lot, he no longer wants any part of this scientific undertaking. Stealing to the sphere, which has been partially dismantled by the Selenites, the writer pulls an elephant gun from the storage compartment and

194

liberates Kate. Meanwhile, Cavor has been brought before the Grand Lunar, the ruler of the moon, who asks the scientist to tell him of earth. Cavor is pleased to oblige, and eventually, happens to mention war to the Selenite leader, a quality unknown on the moon. The notion of violence raises the apprehension of the Grand Lunar, who fears that other terrestrials may one day reach the moon, bringing warfare with them. Cavor assures the lunarian that there needn't *be* any others, since he is the only one who knows the formula for Cavorite; overhearing this, Bedford panics. He realizes that the Selenites now have no recourse but to keep them on the moon, and shoots the Grand Lunar to create a diversion for their escape. But Cavor doesn't want to leave, and pleads with his associate to stop this rampage. Bedford apologizes, but says that he and Kate intend to go home, something they cannot do unless the scientist helps them to reassemble the sphere. Astonished that Bedford would dare ask a favor after the damage he's done, Cavor nonetheless realizes that he has no right to detain the couple on the moon. With the chemist's aid they repair the craft, and for the final time ask him to join them: Cavor insists that he *must* remain behind, and securing the bulk head, the lovers send the sphere flying toward earth. They crash land in water and their craft sinks, leaving the pair with no proof that the journey had ever been undertaken.

At the conclusion of Bedford's narrative, the Space Agency representatives turn on a television to show the old man live pictures from the moon. The astronauts have just entered the pit into which Bedford first fell upon his arrival. Oddly, the caves as well as the great diaphanous structures of the Selenite civilization are all rotted and crumbling. There is no sign of life and, as Bedford and the scientists suddenly realize, the 1899 lunar mission had introduced terrestrial bacteria to the satellite, germs against which the aliens had no natural immunity. The entire race of beings has thus been annihilated, destroyed, ironically, by a man of peace.

To date, *First Men in the Moon* has been Ray's only motion picture in *Panavision*, the wide-screen process that squeezes a sweeping image onto 35-mm film. When projected with an anamorphic lens, the picture is stretched to its full and original horizontal ratio. Schneer felt that the epic proportions of Panavision would give the film a dimension of audience participation and thus increase its box office revenue. Unfortunately, as Ray told his producer, he couldn't adapt his reality sandwich techniques to the Anamorphic system without spending time and money to perform experiments. And since Schneer didn't *have* those commodities in excess, Ray was forced to make do using mattes without miniature screen projection. Considering this handicap, the film's visual effects came out enormously well.

The opening sequence, showing the separation and descent of a lunar lander from its mother craft—with models based on up-to-the-minute NASA designs—was shot using aerial-brace stop-motion spaceships and traveling mattes. It was so convincing that television newscasters used it to simulate the maneuvers of *Apollo Eleven* four years later. As for the astronauts' hike across the craggy *mare* of the airless world, it was staged on full-scale, highly detailed sets built at Shepperton Studios. The Cavorite launch and flight to the moon were similarly executed, the design of the sphere—both a

United Nations-One astronauts discover a Union Jack on the moon.   © Columbia Pictures

life-size and miniature model in the film—being Harryhausen's based on Wells. "I felt very obligated to try to stick with the Wellsian concept, rather than go off on my own and make some sleek, modern design. It wouldn't have fit in that particular situation. So I read the novel several times again and tried to visualize what this thing would be. Wells thought things like this out very carefully, and I expanded upon what he had written. Like his other marvelous descriptions of how to become invisible or travel through time, they may not have worked, but they certainly read as though they were feasible." However, if the quaint sphere of Harryhausen and Wells was in contrast to the very robotlike craft of the twentieth-century astronauts, so were the way in which the Victorian and contemporary crew approached lunar exploration! As opposed to the steady tread of the men of the *United Nations One*, Bedford and Cavor went jumping about the surface of the moon. Of course, they were aided in this by thin wires which, at one point, were called upon to lift Cavor into the air and lodge him squarely between two closely-spaced crags. A touch of slapstick? Yes. But after the suspense of the flight, during which the untimely raising of a shutter sent the sphere tumbling toward the sun, it was a welcome bit of comic relief!

If the surface sets are superb, then the vistas within the moon are even more exciting. The life-size sets are most unusual, and as Ray observes, rather costly: "That's one of the problems of doing a picture where you're creating an alien civilization. You have to create everything from scratch. But we had no choice, we *had* to build them because real caves were just too familiar, too normal. We felt we could create something a little more unusual in those crystalline forms, with our buildings based on the design of a honeycomb." To create the more expansive panoramas, such as the spectacle of huge rock formations, of massive energy-producing gems and huge pillars of bubbling liquids, of criss-crossing beams of light and energy, Ray used miniature models, often composited with the actors and sets in up to four matte exposures-per-single shot. This kind of matching between models and studio sets was not new to Ray, but he had never before attempted it on so grand a scale as in *First*

Men in the Moon. That it all worked out is further proof of his phenomenal talent.

Another visual effect realized on a rather lavish scale was the creation of the beings who populated these colorful catacombs. All the laborer Selenites were, of necessity, youngsters wearing costumes built by Harryhausen. Only the Selenite scholars and the Grand Lunar were stop motion models, for reasons outlined by Ray. "To save me from an eternity of animating Selenites in the mass effects, we had to use little children dressed in suits. After all, we didn't want the moon to be populated with just one or two stop-motion moon people. But we also felt that there could be a civilization of two or three different types of ant creatures. As Wells described it—from his Socialist point of view—the creatures who did the work with their hands had enormous hands, whereas in early illustrations from the book the Grand Lunar was shown with an enormous brain under which there was a little tiny head. Wells' description was so grotesque that we had to be very careful not to go to *that* extreme or it would have bordered on the comical. Of course

Bedford examines photographs of the artifacts found on the moon by modern-day astronauts. © Columbia Pictures

Bedford's chair flies to the ceiling after it has been coated with Cavorite.   © Columbia Pictures

Wells, as well as the other nonworker Selenites, were animated because it gave them a stranger appearance. You were always aware of the separation between them and the little people in the suits. And the way the story is structured, you dwell on the stop-motion characters much more than you do the crowds hovering over the sphere. You can get a stranger atmosphere out of the animated figures; sort of soulless, without too much feeling. If you'd used a man in a suit, you could never get such thin, emaciated arms in the close-ups. It gave it an eerier quality." Fortunately, there were seldom any close-ups of the live-action Selenites, and the low-keyed lighting of the milling masses allowed Ray to pull off the illusion most satisfactorily.

Depending upon how literally the book has been illustrated, the giant centipede—or, more accurately, the moon calf—has been portrayed as everything from a huge cow to a spotted bronto-saur. However, as Ray observes, Wells is quite specific in his presentation of the monster: "The moon cow was supposed to be something like a slug, so we made it a variation of a garden worm or caterpillar, in keeping with the insect evolution of the moon. Of course, we did it on an enormous scale." And with its grinding mandibles and waves of shuffling little feet—"There weren't that many, actually; it gave you that impression because they were all moving in separate synchronization"—the creature was indeed a sensible breed of foe that both complemented its environment and dramatically razed a great many vitreous landmarks in its pursuit of Cavor and Bedford! The monster was also briefly portrayed in skeletal form later in the film, when Bedford passed through the cavern and found that the Selenites had stripped the beast of its meat, remains which were, in reality, a one-foot-long model. Yet another skeleton in *First Men in the Moon* was that of Kate, seen when a glass wall of

197

Cavor and Bedford on the excellent lunar surface set
constructed at Shepperton Studios.   © Columbia Pictures

Katherine Calendar in the X-ray chamber of
the Selenites.   ©Columbia Pictures

The huge centipede.

Cavor (left) and Bedford chase down their stolen-space
sphere amidst the strange foliage of the inner moon.

Cavor and Kate discover that at certain times, the Selenites
spin webs under which they hibernate. © Columbia Pictures

Lionel Jeffries and Martha Hyer between takes at
Shepperton Studio. © Columbia Pictures

Cavor pleads with Bedford not to attack the Grand Lunar, but Bedford prevails. © Columbia Pictures

Director Nathan Juran instructs Edward Judd how to go leaping about the moon. © Columbia Pictures

Ray Harryhausen and his model of the Grand Lunar. Photograph by Leslie Rovin.

Kneale's first script, we had to incorporate a woman for female identification, to try to get more people to come into the cinema. And it *is* a boy's picture, rather than something for a universal audience which, I suppose, is one reason for their insistence that you have some sort of love interest. Robert Armstrong expressed it very clearly in the original *King Kong*: 'Everybody likes a pretty face to look at.' So he was more profound than we gave him credit for! But what does one do? Jump on their hat and say, 'No, I will not make the picture unless we leave the woman out!' People in the film business who control the money obviously have some sensitivity about who will go to see what type of film."

Despite its many strengths, including the special effects, the action in Panavision, an

An in-theatre promotional gimmick: a newspaper that announced, in the most eye-catching fashion, the coming of *First Men in the Moon.* © Columbia Pictures

her prison is used as a fluoroscope. The skeleton is shown raving at the Selenites, threatening to hit them with its shoe. And, while Ray is a craftsman of unquestionable integrity, did he actually create a costly model for this short clip? "Dare I say it?" he laughs. "Already having seven skeletons in my closet, I could hardly build another one!"

Although Ray tried to make *First Men in the Moon* as true to Wells as possible, the script took several liberties with the original novel. Principal among the changes was the addition of a woman to the all-male crew of the sphere. Like the use of Panavision it was one of those things that Schneer and Columbia thought would be best for the film. Ray explains that "the front office feels it's important that you have love interest for identity. In *First Men in the Moon*, Wells never wrote about taking a woman to the moon. But after Nigel

absorbing storyline, and fine characterizations, particularly by Lionel Jeffries, whom Ray describes as, "a marvelous actor and a very wonderful man. He's got such vitality and he's able to play a villain or a comical character with great skill. He's very versatile," *First Men in the Moon* lost money for Columbia. Schneer analyzed its failure as the result of "a tongue-in-cheek presentation on the advent of the actual landing on the moon. And the world quite rightly took that as a very serious scientific step forward. Not knowing whether the Russians or the Americans would be setting foot first, we put them both up there in the prologue. But the story Wells told, and which we told, was that the *British* got there before anybody else. And as we know, they'd probably be the *last* ever to get there. So the whole humor of the situation was quite obvious in Britain, certainly. But America didn't have that humor about it, and because the picture *was* a satire really, it was not as successful as our straight fantasies." Because of the movie's sluggish box office performance, Schneer went searching for more down-to-earth pictures to produce, and the result was the musical film *Half a Sixpence* (1966). Ray, meanwhile, stuck with fantasy. And ironically, *Half a Sixpence* posted poor receipts while Ray's next film proved to be one of his top-grossing efforts!

Victor Mature and Carole Landis vs. a lizard in the original
One Million B.C.   © United Artists

CHAPTER FOURTEEN

Bring on the Dinosaurs!

As much as the work of Ray Harryhausen adds class to any film, it was not completely the animator's contribution to *One Million Years B.C.* that won the picture its wide following. The British remake of the 1940 D. W. Griffith film *One Million B.C.,* was a hit primarily because it starred cinema newcomer Raquel Welch in the role that Carole Landis had made famous. John Richardson co-starred as Tumak, the part originally played by Victor Mature.

Life is not easy for Tumak and members of the dark-haired, warfaring Rock Tribe. They live by capturing and eating dangerous animals, and when they're not out hunting, they're usually fighting against each other. One such struggle is rougher than most, as Tumak takes on tribal leader Akhoba (Robert Brown) over a portion of roast boar. Tumak puts up a fair and noble fight, but he is no match for the brutal chieftain; pushed from the cliffside cave into a clump of foliage, the vital young Neanderthal is rendered unconscious. When he awakens, Tumak elects to face the world alone rather than live under the cruel reign of Akhoba, and sets out across the desert. Several days of wearying travel ensue, during which the caveman is menaced by a huge iguana lizard and a monstrous tarantula. Surviving these prehistoric beasts and enduring a harsh baking by the sun, Tumak finally collapses near a beach, the residence of the fair-haired, peace-loving Shell People.

The first person to spot Tumak is the nubile Loana (Raquel Welch), who runs to the parched and blistered caveman and ministers to his wounds. Unfortunately, her work is interrupted by the arrival of an archelon, an enormous turtle that is making its way to the sea. Although the amphibian apparently means no one any harm, Loana uses a shell horn to alert the men of the settlement. Hurling spears at the snapper, they dispel whatever notions it might have entertained about feasting on a human or two. When the beast has vanished beneath the waves, Loana helps Tumak to the tribe's cave. There, the outcast is nursed to health.

When he has recovered, Tumak tours the camp and is greatly impressed by the culture of the Shell People. They paint, they weave, they make weapons, skills unknown to the Rock Tribe. They also fish, which is something that Tumak has never tried. Loana is only too happy to coach the rugged stranger. Standing in a stream, she shows Tumak how to spear a fish, then hands him the lance. But try as he might, the newcomer can't seem to master the art of anticipating the fish, and becomes terribly frustrated. Fortunately, Tumak excels at fighting dinosaurs, and it is a talent he brings to bear when a hungry allosaur invades the village. Stalking a young girl who has climbed a tree, the monster is engaged by Tumak, who uses the fishing spear to force the carnivore from its intended meal. Made bold by Tumak's example, several of the Shell People join the fierce battle. One of them dies, crushed by the dinosaur's massive jaws, and others scatter when the allosaur tears down a hut. Cornered and alone, Tumak appears to be a certain casualty as the animal closes in. However, acting quickly, the caveman grabs a sharpened strut from the devastated lean-to and impales the approaching creature. So frenzied was its charge that the dinosaur is carried aloft by inertia, and as Tumak rolls to one side, the meat eater slides painfully down the stake.

With the allosaur dead, Tumak reasons that he

Raquel Welch (third from right) and ladies of the Shell Tribe watch the arrival of Tumak.   © Hammer Films

has earned the right to keep Loana's spear, but Ahot (Jean Waldon), Loana's betrothed, disagrees. The weapon belongs to him and he wants it back. This leads to quite a row, and Tumak is exiled from the realm of the Shell People. Realizing that she is in love with the brash young man, Loana joins him to face whatever lies ahead. Together, they push toward the harsh domain of the Rock Tribe, encountering a race of strange apelike beings, barely escaping death amidst the turmoil of a triceratops battling an aggressive ceratosaur. Eventually, however, they reach the cave of Akhoba, only to learn that the tyrant has been deposed by Tumak's sadistic brother Sakana (Percy Herbert). Thus, Tumak must fight the young upstart for the privilege of staying; defeating him, it is then Loana's turn to fight Nupondi (Martine Beswick) for the privilege of keeping Tumak.

Alas, our hero's triumph is short-lived. The next morning, while fishing by a river, Loana is kidnapped by a pteranodon. Flying the buxom morsel to its mountaintop nest, the winged dinosaur prepares to feed her to its offspring.

However, the girl's abductor is suddenly attacked by a second airborne monster, a rhamphorhynchus. Carrying their quarrel over the ocean, the leathery giants beat and peck at one another, the pteranodon ultimately dropping its captive. Striking the water, Loana recognizes the sea as that which borders the settlement of the Shell People. Swimming to shore, she is rescued and cared for by her native tribe. Meanwhile, Sakana leads a revolt against his brother, Loana mounts an expedition of Shell People to the land of the Rock Tribe, and a lusty conflict follows the confluence of the various primitives. However, the outcome of the clash is not determined by strength or wile: an earthquake rips the continent asunder, causing fissures and landslides and terminating not only the war, but most of the local population. When the eruption finally subsides, partisan affiliations have become meaningless: under the leadership of Tumak and Loana, what is left of mankind unites to face the future.

Told in pantomime and spiced with an occasional grunt—but featuring *no spoken*

The archelon passes the camp of the Shell Tribe on its way
to the sea.   © Hammer Films

dialogue—the one hundred minutes of *One Million Years B.C.* is thoroughly mesmerizing. More so than most period pictures, this Hammer Films production successfully evokes an alien time, recreating the heat, the barbarity, and the constant danger of our primeval world. But there are anachronisms. One can be fairly certain that few cave people were as attractive as Raquel Welch, Martine Beswick, and John Richardson, or that they wore makeup as subtly sensual as that of Miss Welch. Too, there is a sparkle of intelligence in the players' eyes that the earliest people would not have had. However, as with the original picture, the greatest charge leveled against the film is that Homo sapiens did not yet exist when dinosaurs ruled the earth. This may be true, and people who are conversant about the era have every right to complain. But as Ray is quick to point out, "they're

Tumak saves a young girl from the allosaur. The portion of the spear just beyond Tumak's left hand is an aerial brace supported miniature matched with background footage. This enabled the dinosaur to actually touch the weapon.

© Hammer Films

A miniature spear has been substituted entirely for the live action prop in Tumak's battle with the allosaur.

pushing humans back further and further, and may even find that they *did* live in the days of the dinosaurs. And I will have the last laugh! But everybody says, 'How can you bear to put these things on the screen, human beings living in the age of the dinosaur?' Well, that, obviously, was done for dramatic license. What drama is there in just a bunch of animals running around?"

Known for its stylish updates of films featuring such classic monsters as Dracula, Frankenstein, and the Mummy, Hammer Films lavished time and money on *One Million Years B.C.* For authenticity, they sent the cast and crew to the rocky and barren Canary Island of Lanzarate, which gave the picture what Harryhausen calls, "a nice mood, a vacuity of eternity, with nothing but these dreary-looking rocks and volcanic cones. It certainly had a different mood than the original film. Two or three

of the islands in the Canaries are pure volcanic rock. And they lent themselves to this type of forgotten prehistoric world." Indeed, watching *One Million Years B.C.*, one feels that the filmmakers must have lived a life as Spartan as that of Tumak, working on this uninviting terrain. Not so, relates Harryhausen. "Actually, we lived in a hotel, we didn't bivouac on the peaks of the lava flows. We had very pleasant quarters in a Spanish Parador hotel. But still, it *is* a bleak island, there's no doubt about it. Now, I think, it's been made into a tourist attraction because of its unusual structure."

Beyond the scenery, Hammer producer Michael Carreras also felt that Harryhausen's presence well justified the longer production schedule and greater cost than if live lizards had been used to impersonate their prehistoric forebears, as they had in the original film. As a matter of

Raquel Welch and John Richardson prepare to leave the Shell Tribe. Their trek across the desert was greatly aided by a bleak and evocative Mario Nascimbene musical score.   © Hammer Films

fact, Harryhausen says that Carreras' enlightened attitude was the only reason he agreed to make the film. "I did it because I had the opportunity to utilize an animated process for dinosaurs. I mean, I wouldn't have wanted to go back and do an alligator and an iguana locked in mortal combat. And Hammer didn't feel that that would be suitable for this period. After all, they're not really dinosaurs. You may glue a fin on an alligator's back, but that would never fool the smallest child into believing that it's a dinosaur. It's a *lizard*!"

Although the technical processes used in *One Million Years B.C.* were Harryhausen stand-bys, the animator's contract with Schneer and Columbia precluded any use of the Dynamation label for the film. However, Carreras wasn't counting on

Dynamation, per se, to sell his film: both during and after production he headed massive media campaigns to promote Raquel Welch. As a result, the picture made a great deal of money, while Raquel and her furry bikini became one of the mid-sixties' foremost icons. Fortunately, Carreras cared as much about the *virtue* of his product as its marketability, so that the tens of thousands of people who went to see *One Million Years B.C.* predominantly for the visual effects were not disappointed, save for one uncharacteristic lapse in quality.

Many Harryhausen fans have expressed dissatisfaction over the first two monsters in the film, the iguana and the spider, both of which were live rather than stop motion creatures. Aesthetically, the criticism is well justified: although the beasts

A triceratops attacks Loana and Tumak...

...only to encounter a ravenous ceratosaur.

Loana examines the decorations in the cave of the Rock
Tribe.

are superimposed with Harryhausen's typical expertise, their presence cheapens the product. But it was decided that a transient menace of some sort would make Tumak's long trek through the wilderness just a little more exciting. And to have animated two additional dinosaurs would have pushed the film way over budget. Hence, the admittedly unpleasant substitutions. As it was, when the stop-motion budget began to climb, a planned brontosaur attack on Tumak's tribe late in the film had to be replaced by Sakana's rebellion against his brother. However, since the brontosaur model *had* been built, Ray used it for color, having it lumber briefly across the horizon during Tumak's crossing of the desert.

The appearance of the archelon was an altogether more satisfying effect than the scenes using live animals. Ironically, reading newspaper critiques of the film, spawned by woefully ignorant reviewers, one was led to believe that Harryhausen had simply magnified a box turtle for the sequence. "Well, in a way it's a compliment," Harryhausen reflects, "because they assumed it was a real tortoise." However, negative comments *do* invariably gall Harryhausen, try though he might to maintain a balanced perspective. "Often, I feel that the criticism is unjust, when it's done in a superficial way. Many critics are *anti* this type of picture to begin with; perhaps it's just too simple for them. I don't know. We've even found critics sleeping through our pictures, and then we learn that they're writing a review, and you wonder how!? Then you read the review and you realize that because they were asleep, or have chosen to be condescending about the film, they didn't see any of the values that were placed in the picture, which the *audience* enjoyed the most!" Happily, it's popular taste and not the miserably elite critics that makes or breaks a film.

Of the archelon, Harryhausen says, "He didn't want to hurt anybody: all he wanted to do was to head for the sea, and these people got in his way. But we didn't want him to be a terror, or a frightful thing." Thus, its demeanor was intentionally calm, used to create spectacle while saving the real thrills for later in the film. And thrills there were, Harryhausen's next character being among the most vicious he has ever created! However, the raid

of the allosaur is outstanding not only for its action, but for an unparalleled use of model substitution. Harryhausen's previous work in this area—Kerwin Mathews' boot for *The Seventh Voyage of Sinbad* or the shield from *The Three Worlds of Gulliver*, for example—has always been impressive, but the spearing of the allosaur is the kind of movie magic that causes an audience to miss a breath or two. Like the props in the aforementioned effects, the bulk of the pole was a full-scale set piece, while the portion imbedded in the stop-motion dinosaur was a complementary miniature. Thus, to have Tumak fall back with the allosaur thrashing wildly at the end of the spike, Ray raised the monster with an aerial brace, always keeping the miniature section of the stake in careful juxtaposition with its life-size counterpart. The product was a perfect and dynamic visual effect! Another clever matching of the real and imaginary in this sequence was the use of pulleys to lift a caveman from the stream where Tumak and Loana had been fishing. When Ray added his animal, it appeared as though the Shell tribesman was caught in the allosaur's teeth. Mercifully, Ray replaced the actor with a stop-motion double when it came time for the dinosaur to eat its hapless victim. This latter technique was also utilized when the pteranodon swoops down and picks up Raquel Welch. The real Miss Welch fell below a ridge of sand where she hid while the cameras continued to roll. Back in his workshop, Ray had the aerial braced dinosaur pick up the duplicate Loana before this miniature projected footage. Only in a close-up showing the pteranodon about to feed the cave girl to its offspring was a different technique employed: Ms. Welch, in the grip of large prop talons, screamed and struggled before a blue screen, with the stop-motion baby dinosaurs being added several months later.

The two animated battles in the film are excellently staged, as is the eerie encounter with the ape people. Seen only from afar as Tumak and Loana hide in a tree, these missing links were all actors in costumes. Unfortunately, just as the visual effects in *One Million Years B.C.* got off to a stumbling start, so do they end on a slightly sour key: the climactic earthquake, created on an extremely small budget, lacked the punch of Harryhausen's earlier mass disasters. Shots of

Nupondi has Tumak all to herself, now that Loana has been kidnapped by a pteranodon. © Hammer Films

A pteranodon drops from the sky to make a withdrawal—Loana—from the river bank. © Hammer Films

people falling into the earth or being buried beneath tons of rock were traveling matte unions of actors and miniature sets. Atypical of the visual-effects director's work, these composites seemed hastily slapped together, with less than the usual care taken to match the lighting of disparate elements. Then there were were troubles beyond the resources or money allotted the holocaust. Harryhausen recalls, "We were doing a shot with a treadmill and it wouldn't work. So we were stuck. You can't call everybody back some other time just because the treadmill doesn't work. So we told the actors to try to simulate it, to run in position, which was very difficult for them. We put the scene together and there may be a brief shot from it in the finished film. But situations like that are the sort of compromises one is sometimes forced to make. We just couldn't spend the type of money that Cecil B. DeMille would have spent on it, so whatever people may think, it did take a lot of ingenuity to design the scene so it could be made within our budget." In short, the heart was there but after nine months of animation, finances were understandably restricted. This, then, just wasn't a purging that befit the harsh and otherwise expertly crafted world of *One Million Years B.C.*

Tempered by his unsuccessful leave of absence from the fantasy genre, Charles Schneer reunited with Ray Harryhausen in 1967 to revive an old Willis O'Brien project. As Schneer recently told me, he was glad to be home. "I have always been a great advocate of putting on the screen something that the mind's eye has visualized but has never really seen. That's a fascination which dates back from Aesop's Fables to the Arabian Nights to the more latter-day H.G. Wells and Jules Verne. And few have been able to do these stories successfully in the motion picture medium. So I feel that if we can always build a better mousetrap, people will always demand it. And for the last twenty-five years that's proven to be the case. Our pictures have never depended upon the whims of the public with respect to their likes or dislikes for film stars, some of whom come and go very rapidly, and some of whom are more enduring than others. But long after the Marlon Brandos and Steve McQueens have come and gone, the Jules Vernes, the H.G. Wells, the Jonathan Swifts, and the great legends of all time will still be with us. The film medium is essentially an escapist medium, and that's why we're survivors. Not because of the color of our eyes, or the complexion of our faces, but because our pictures do outstandingly well. I don't expect the screen, powerful medium that it is, will overturn the world like *The Communist Manifesto* or the advent of Christianity. It's an entertainment medium; a dreams medium. That's what it's all about, and that's what we're all about."

Back in 1950, Ray had worked with Willis O'Brien during the preproduction stages of *The Valley of Mist*. The film, of course, was never made. However, as Ray tells it, "O'Bie had given me a copy of the script some years before, and I had filed it away. I came across it again while searching for something in my garage. Charles and I happened to be looking for a subject, and felt that the script certainly had a lot of excitement in it—the western coupled with the dinosaurs—and also saw that it had a great many possibilities for showmanship." After spending several months tracking down the owners of the property, the filmmakers bought it. Warner Brothers approved production, and the renamed *Valley Where Time Stood Still* was launched as a Dynamation project. In 1969 the film was released as *The Valley of Gwangi*.

The year is 1912, and the setting is a small town in Mexico. One night, just beyond the village, gypsy Carlos Dos Orsos (Gustavo Royo) finds his brother's corpse ouside the Forbidden Valley, a mysterious land from which no one ever returns alive. Beside the dead man is a canvas bag containing a small, struggling animal. Carlos takes the sack and heads for the village, ignoring the gypsy witch Tia Zorina (Freda Jackson), who predicts that the animal's theft will be avenged by Gwangi. Meanwhile, the touring T.J. Breckenridge Wild West Show has just opened in a local arena, and an interested first-day observer is Tuck Kirby (James Franciscus), who was at one time engaged to marry the show's lovely owner and star Teresa Juanita Breckenridge (Gila Golan). Tuck has come with an offer to help the struggling show by purchasing T.J.'s stunt horse Omar for Bill Cody's outfit. The girl refuses to sell. In fact, she wants nothing whatsoever to do with this man, who jilted her when he realized that he didn't want to be tied

The live-action elements were filmed, the model was built, and Ray shot this publicity still of a brontosaur attack on the Rock Tribe—but the sequence never reached the full-animation stage due to budgetary restrictions.

down. T.J.'s manager and self-appointed guardian, the rough Champ Connors (Richard Carlson), does his best to remain calm when Tuck comes calling.

Attendance is poor for the second-rate show, even the daring leap by Omar and T.J. from a high platform into a tank of water failing to draw an audience. However, Carlos brings T.J. an attraction which he is certain will pull in the crowds. The animal whose capture in the Forbidden Valley led to his brother's death. Elsewhere, Tuck and his young guide Lope (Curtis Arden) have wandered into the desert where they find the British paleontologist Prof. Horace Bromley (Laurence Naismith) scouting for fossils. The scientist shows Tuck one of his prize finds: the perfectly preserved imprint of an eohippus, a long-extinct, foot-tall horse. Tuck returns to the village musing about what a great sideshow attraction a prehistoric horse would be when suddenly, Lope crawls into the Wild West

arena and is attacked by a bull. Tuck rescues the boy and T.J.'s concern for her ex-beau's safety convinces him that she still loves him. And indeed she does, so much so that she gives Tuck a preview of their newest attraction: Carlos' find, the eohippus El Diablo. Tuck is astounded, and summons Prof. Bromley to confirm the animal's identity. The scientist arrives and is amazed by its authenticity. However, showing the dawn horse to Prof. Bromley was a mistake, as he *must* know where it was found. Asking Tia Zorina, he is turned away, and so tries a different tack. Aware of the blind witch's desire to have the eohippus returned to its home, he tells her where it is kept. And that night, when she has the animal stolen, the scientist follows its abductors to the Forbidden Valley. Carlos tries to stop the theft and is clubbed from behind; Tuck arrives moments later and rides off in pursuit of Prof. Bromley. Naturally, when T.J. and

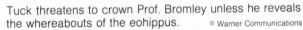

Tuck threatens to crown Prof. Bromley unless he reveals the whereabouts of the eohippus.

The pteranodon flies off with a stop-motion Lope in the *Valley of Gwangi*. © Warner Communications

Champ find Carlos, they assume that Tuck had clubbed Carlos and stolen the eohippus for his own greedy purposes.

Early the next morning, Tuck catches up with the professor, and shortly thereafter, T.J., Champ, Carlos, and their hands Rowdy (Dennis Kilbane) and Bean (Mario De Barros) find Tuck. The facts in the theft are set aright, but the group has arrived too late to prevent Tia Zorina from releasing El Diablo at the entrance of the Forbidden Valley. Pushing through a mountainside rift that leads to the land of the legendary demon Gwangi, the party tries to rope the small horse but to no avail. Pressing on, they are stunned when a pteranodon dives at Lope, plucks him from his horse, and flies away. Fortunately, they are able to coax the beast to earth, and jumping on its back, Carlos breaks the

creature's neck. Moments later, they spot an ornithomimus, a fleet, human-sized dinosaur which they chase ever-deeper into the valley. But the bizarre round-up ends when, springing from behind a cliff, the giant allosaur Gwangi kills the ornithomimus and proceeds to hunt down the intruders. Racing to a cavern atop a narrow ridge, they settle down for the night.

The next day, the group is attacked by Gwangi, and instead of fleeing, they try to lasso the giant. Successfully dogging and finally spilling the allosaur, they prepare to bind him more securely when the prehistoric quadruped styracosaur charges from the bush. Letting Gwangi loose, the cowboys retire while the monsters do battle, reappearing only to spear Gwangi's sluggish adversary. Eventually, the allosaur defeats the

219

The battle between Gwangi and the styracosaur.

Gwangi goes to church...

...and is met by James Franciscus. The monster is destroyed, although in his next film, *Beneath the Planet of the Apes* (1970), it is Franciscus who dies in a cathedral.

styracosaur and turns on its tormentors. Riding hard toward the sole exit from the Forbidden Valley, the team slips through the narrow opening to the outside world; trying to reach them, Gwangi causes a cave-in and is dazed by falling rocks. Realizing that the dinosaur would be an awesome exhibit for their wild west show, the small-time entrepreneurs build a cage and transport the monster to the stadium. However, Tia Zorina has promised to punish those who have desecrated the Forbidden Valley, and on the day of Gwangi's debut, her dwarfish aide unlocks the monster's cage. After thousands of patrons have filed into the arena, the curtain is raised and Gwangi goes free. Prof. Bromley tries to prevent the creature's escape and is crushed to death for his efforts. Slaughtering an elephant, the allosaur smashes through to the street where it is greeted by the shotgun-toting Tuck. Looking to be rid of the pest, Gwangi follows him into a large cathedral. Thinking quickly, the American shuts all the doors, and after a hair-raising game of cat and mouse, Tuck grabs an ornamental spear and jabs it into the dinosaur's skull. Scratching the lance free, the beast vents its fury by roaring and switching its tail, overturning a brazier of live coals in the process. Exposed to the smouldering embers, a wall of drapery catches fire and the monster is quickly trapped in a ring of flame. Within moments, the cathedral is a raging inferno, and running to the street, Tuck watches with T.J. and a crowd of villagers as the house of worship collapses, killing the age-old reptile.

For the first time since *Twenty Million Miles to Earth*, Ray made a picture with one central stop-motion character. And if Gwangi doesn't lend itself to audience empathy as readily as Ymir—"The only way you can really work sympathy into an animal is if it's a mammal or if it has a humanoid structure," Ray maintains—the allosaur is nonetheless an arresting focal point for the film. Dramatically, it is cold-blooded, ferocious, and in each of its *over three hundred separate shots*, representing nearly 60,000 frames of film, is always involved in some manner of eye-filling activity. Technically, the matte work and Dynamation effects are as impressive as ever, and Gwangi is animated in such a way as to make it the most sinister Harryhausen creation to date—something which Ray attributes to the character's cold-blooded nature and the model's necessary versatility. "It had more things to do than an ordinary animated character, so I had to make it much more detailed, keeping in mind what activities are going to be utilized so it can perform them all. You have to give a central figure a great deal more variety." The only scene in which Gwangi is a disappointment occurs during the cave-in, when Ray buried a stiff, plaster model of his dinosaur beneath the avalanche. "Of course," Ray admits, "we could have rigged it to move, and, naturally, I'd rather have *had* the model move. But it was a question of time. It's not that you don't want to do your best, but you have to have a practical point of view." Again, these pictures are made to be seen one time, and by the casual theatergoer, not by animation fans who scrutinize each frame of film to better appreciate the art of Ray Harryhausen.

As ever, Ray tried to surround his star with an interesting variety of animated characters, in this case the eohippus, the pteranodon, the ornithomimus, the styracosaur, and an elephant. Harryhausen explains the choice of dinosaurs: "We had to use animals that would fit the situations which developed. For instance, an iguanadon, though unusual, was a vegetarian and wouldn't have been as menacing as an allosaur. So we tried to use creatures that hadn't been seen on the screen before, as long as they suited the story." The first stop-motion figure was the eohippus, which was in the original O'Brien script. "I think O'Bie once said that they were going to use small horses that had been discovered recently, small ponies. But we decided we would make it even smaller. Besides, it would be very difficult to make a real animal act and react, so we decided to animate it. It was appropriate to the scene. The actors were discussing what the eohippus' figure would be, and we wanted to get some sort of reaction out of the moment and the circumstance. So we had the eohippus play along with the role rather than just stand there and twitch its tail. We tried to give it a cuteness and coyness. But I just dreaded doing that sequence because it was so simple. And if you make something too simple, you're always criticized for actions that people are familiar with. It's easier when you're animating a dinosaur rather than an elephant or a horse, since very few people have ever seen a dinosaur and therefore aren't as critical."

Since Ray doesn't like to repeat himself, either plotwise or visually, he staged the pteranodon's seizure of Lope not with a stop-motion model of the actor—as he did in *One Million Years B.C.*—but with the actual performer. Cantering along on horseback, actor Curtis Arden was wired with cables and lifted from his saddle by a crane. Then, during Dynamation photography, Ray had his aerial-braced dinosaur model wing down and, at the proper moment, "fly off" with the miniature projected Lope. In subsequent cuts, Arden was relieved by a stop-motion Lope. An even more exacting piece of special-effects wizardry can be seen later in this sequence when Carlos is wrestling with the grounded pteranodon. For close-ups, a full-scale pteranodon prop was used while in the long-shots, actor Gustavo Rojo tangled with an imaginary nemesis which Ray eventually added via Dynamation. However, to insure absolute realism in these latter clips, Harryhausen modeled small stop-motion hands, which he positioned so that they issued from Rojo's miniature projected wrists and allowed him to make clear physical contact with the animated monster.

The roping of Gwangi and the stabbing of the styracosaur were both executed with the cowboys attacking a jeep, which Ray hid behind the dinosaur models during animation. Once again, the life-size lariats and spears were duplicated in miniature and carefully juxtaposed with their counterparts on the background footage. In all, Ray spent nearly a year

Ray Harryhausen's sketch of the roping of Gwangi.

and a half creating the special effects for *The Valley of Gwangi*, which also included his supervision of the glass paintings used to create many of the primeval rock formations seen in the Forbidden Valley; the burning of the miniature cathedral for exterior shots, and its matting into a real location; the superimposition of fire over both Gwangi and the interior of the Cuenca Cathedral; and so on.

The live-action scenes in *The Valley of Gwangi* were all filmed in Spain, with a cast composed of Spaniards, an American (James Franciscus), a Briton (Laurence Naismith), and an Israeli (Gila Golan). All performed admirably, though they were struggling with somewhat hackneyed human drama. In *One Million Years B.C., First Men in the Moon*, and so on back through *The Seventh Voyage of Sinbad*, the audience was present when interpersonal conflicts were developing. But the strife between T.J. and Tuck is conveniently and tritely explained through dialogue during lulls in the action. The script could have been more carefully conceived to flesh-out these problems as well as the people they involve. However, at least the story was written to give Ray the slow build that he so much admired in *King Kong*. Of course, as this *had* been Willis O'Brien's project, it's not surprising to find many similiarities between the two films.

In all but Gwangi's melodramatic dying moments—which, like the death of *The Beast from Twenty Thousand Fathoms*, gave the allosaur a moment of pathos—the creature was simply a heartless villain. Nor does Ray feel that the picture would have been improved had he made Gwangi a sympathetic character like Ymir. It just wouldn't have worked with a dinosaur because, as Ray explains, "there are very few people in the world that would call a dinosaur *cuddly*!" However, one of those rare individuals just *happens* to be Ray's daughter Vanessa. As Diana Harryhausen tells it, when the fourteen year old was considerably younger, the two of them went shopping in a fashionable metropolitan store, Vanessa innocently pushing her doll carriage. A pair of elderly women thought that the young girl looked so sweet, and while Diana was making a purchase, they went over to Vanessa. Commenting about how nice she looked, one of the women playfully took a peek into the carriage. Suddenly, she shrieked and withdrew. Bundled beneath the blankets was Ray's stop-motion model of Gwangi, which inspired the women to chastise Diana. How *could* she let her daughter play with such a horrid toy?! They stormed away before Diana could respond. Clearly, there is a moral in this tale, which we'll save for a book on *The Hazards of Living with a Stop Motion Artist*. Until then, as Ray said in commenting upon the lamentable encounter, "Ah—it's all part of the vicissitudes of life!"

CHAPTER FIFTEEN

The Golden Voyage of Sinbad

Jason and the Argonauts, First Men in the Moon...and now *The Valley of Gwangi*. In their last three collaborations, Charles and Ray had suffered three box office failures. Ray attributes the inability of *The Valley of Gwangi* to attract an audience as the result of the suddenly permissive, generally nihilistic era in which it was released. Not to pass judgment on their individual merits, the vogue was toward deeply troubled works such as *The Killing of Sister George, Midnight Cowboy*, and *If*. Even in the realm of science fiction and fantasy, the emphasis was on obscure or heavily allegorical films like *2001: A Space Odyssey* and *Planet of the Apes*. There was simply no market for a well-made, untaxing tale of adventure. Or, as Ray has said on numerous occasions, "A naked dinosaur just wasn't outrageous enough."

Schneer, as a producer, had now endured four consecutive flops. And for a person whose job is to raise money for subsequent productions, he was in an unenviable state. "You are picked and chosen by your last effort," he recently explained. "They look at the producer whose track record shows good results, and they decide whether they're going to take a gamble on his next effort. And if they do, in our case they say, 'Go ahead. We'll see you in three years.'" Fortunately, in 1970, the aggressive industry veteran was able to raise the money for an effort that *had* to succeed if he were to retain his credibility. Accordingly, it was decided to return to the scene of their greatest triumph, the Arabian Nights, for another adventure with the indomitable Sinbad. The picture was *The Golden Voyage of Sinbad* and, happily, it was a huge success. And, unlike *The Seventh Voyage of Sinbad*, which drew

upon the cyclops, roc, and serpents of the original legend, the stop-motion characters and situations in *The Golden Voyage of Sinbad* were based on less-familiar branches of Middle Eastern lore.

Sailing from an unspecified destination, Sinbad (John Phillip Law) and his crew are horrified to see a small, batlike being hovering over their ship. Acting rashly, one of the men, Omar (Aldo Sambrell), looses an arrow at the creature, grazing it and causing it to drop a golden amulet to the deck. Retrieving the gridlike talisman, Sinbad pauses as he is assaulted by strange visions of storms, weird figures, and a girl with a single eye tatooed on her palm. The sailors urge Sinbad to toss the charm overboard, but the captain elects to wear it around his neck. That night, Sinbad's sleep is troubled by more devilish images, a nightmare which is interrupted when his ship sails into a frightful storm. Hurricane winds carry the vessel far off course, and by morning they are just outside the port of Marabia. Strangely, Sinbad recognizes the city from his dream. Hoping to solve the puzzle of recent events, Sinbad swims ashore and is greeted by a black-cloaked figure on horseback, the sorceror Koura (Tom Baker). Koura demands that the Prince of Bagdad turn over the golden trinket and when he refuses, the magician's aide Achmed (Takis Emmanuel) attacks. Beating him back, Sinbad steals the lackey's steed and rides into Marabia proper. There, he meets a man wearing a golden mask, the principality's Grand Vizier (Douglas Wilmer), whose men set out after Koura. Causing a huge iron gate to block the entrance to the city, the magician escapes and returns to his castle. Unused to and disdainful of failure, he gathers up

The masthead has just come to life in *The Golden Voyage of Sinbad.* © Columbia Pictures

the devilish homonculus that was responsible for losing the amulet and sends the creature to spy on Sinbad.

At the Vizier's palace, Sinbad is made welcome by the potenate and led through a stone corridor to a somber lower level. There, the Vizier reveals the story behind his mask and the golden charm. When the Sultan of Marabia died without a son, he left the Vizier two parts of the riddle, that when fully realized, would lead him to the crown and make him the rightful successor to the throne. The first part of the bequest was an amulet, like that which Sinbad wears about his neck. There are three such tokens in all. The second was a huge disk surrounded by unintelligible characters. Within these figures was a painting that described the dangerous path to the crown. Unfortunately, no sooner had the Sultan died and the Vizier gone to study his legacy than Koura sent a huge fireball to engulf the room and destroy the painting, a tempest which cost the Vizier his face. Intent on subjugating Marabia, Koura wanted the road to the crown obliterated, lest the Vizier beat him to it. Therefore, the only surviving clues to the throne are the three golden amulets scattered about the globe. The Vizier has one, Koura found the second which is now in Sinbad's possession, and the third remains hidden. But their meaning is still a secret, until Sinbad latches the two latticed artifacts together and allows their shadow to fall on the barely discernable markings about the perimeter of the scorched disk. Their design outlines the markings in such a way as to form a nautical chart. Hence, even without the central painting, Sinbad and the Grand Vizier have a map to the third amulet which, in turn, will lead them to the crown and assorted treasures. They make plans to set sail the following morning. However, as the men prepare their strategy, they spot the homonculus hiding in the corner of the chamber. Sinbad chases and captures the creature, but no sooner has he taken hold of it than Koura turns his spy to ash. The quest has suddenly taken on a new dimension: through the creature's eyes, the magician has literally seen and heard everything that his rivals have discussed. The search will now be a race, with the throne of Marabia as the prize!

While his ship is being provisioned, Sinbad decides to take a walk through the streets of Marabia. After a time, he becomes aware of someone following him. Turning to face the predator, Sinbad learns that it is the merchant Hakim (Gregoire Aslan), who has a boon to beg of the captain. Leading the sailor to his abode, he pleads with Sinbad to take his good-for-nothing son Haroun (Kurt Christian) on his next voyage. The merchant is convinced that a post at sea on a perilous journey will make a man of the wastrel. Hakim offers to pay the prince handsomely, but Sinbad refuses. Suddenly, Hakim's servant girl Margiana (Caroline Munro) enters the room, and Sinbad recognizes her as the marked woman who had appeared in his dream. Sensing that their meeting was fated, Sinbad agrees to take Haroun as long as he can also have the girl. Hakim willingly agrees to the price.

Once Sinbad is underway, the ship hired by Koura sets out, clandestinely tailing the Prince's lateen-rigger. However, Sinbad's mate Rachid (Martin Shaw) spots the enemy vessel and the Captain pilots his ship into the Sea of Mists. With a chart to navigate these treacherous waters, Sinbad easily loses his nemesis. Recognizing their predicament, the Captain of Koura's craft gives the word to drop anchor; the magician countermands the order. Retiring to his cabin, Koura casts a spell bringing the masthead of Sinbad's ship to life. Thus, the forlorn Haroun, bemoaning his lot to the figurine, is shocked when it turns, looks at him, and rips itself from the prow of the ship. The unwilling seaman cries for help, and within moments, Sinbad and his men are on deck. The sailors try to stop the creature with fire, but she beats them back using a heavy, metal harpoon, and smashing through the wall of Sinbad's cabin, snatches up his charts. Leaping overboard, the masthead remains underwater until Koura's ship passes overhead, at which time she surfaces. Although the Prince of Bagdad carries the course in his head, the sorcerer now knows the route to Sinbad's destination, the legendary island of Lemuria, and the race has suddenly become more urgent. This is especially true for Koura: every time the wizard uses his dark powers, he ages. And he is forced once again to delve into the black arts when he creates a new homonculus for future use; accordingly, if the magician does not reach Lemuria before too long, he will have wasted away in vain.

Ray does a great deal of his historical research in the British Museum, and this ancient figurine bears a striking resemblance to the masthead. © Columbia Pictures

Both ships arrive at the ancient land in close proximity, but Sinbad, Margiana, the Vizier, and their small band are the first to reach the subterranean cave which houses the Oracle of All Knowledge. The disembodied head appears in a pillar of flame and tells Sinbad to search underground for the charm and treasure he seeks. Unfortunately, Koura has been eavesdropping, and when he has the necessary information, seals the entrance to the cave and heads for the caverns of which the Oracle spoke. However, Sinbad is not easily defeated. Using his bow to shoot an iron rod through a ventilation hole above the Oracle's fiery pit, he climbs the attached rope of sashes and clothing. Although Koura's second homonculus arrives to try and dislodge Sinbad, an arrow fired through the creature's small body ends that threat.

Climbing from the cave of the Oracle, Sinbad and his game party head for the lair of a race of green-skinned natives. There, they hope to uncover the third amulet. Instead, the sailors find Koura, who is rummaging for the charm in the treasure chests of the temple of the six-armed goddess Kali. Unable to find it, but sensing victory within his grasp, the magician brings a giant idol of Kali to life, throwing her a sword which multiplies into six. At Koura's instructions, she attacks the newcomers, slashing away with her half-dozen metal arms. Eventually, the besieged sailors carry the battle up a flight of stone stairs, from which they nudge the statue; she shatters, and in her hollow body is the third amulet. Unfortunately, Koura is the first to reach it when the green-skinned Lemurians, in awe of the magician's power, take Sinbad's crew prisoner. Preparing to decapitate the Prince, the natives halt only when they spot Margiana's tatooed hand. A single eye is the symbol of their powerful god of darkness; Margiana is thus viewed as a fated sacrifice for the diety. Lowering her into a mysterious labyrinth, the Lemurians return to the job of slaying those who defiled the temple of Kali. Thinking quickly, Sinbad tells the Vizier to remove his mask and his hideously scarred face causes a lapse in the natives' attention. Using this distraction to break their grip, Sinbad and his men leap into the pit after Margiana. However, their descent comes too late, as the Lemurians' demon-god, a huge, one-eyed centaur, has just carried the girl away. Pursuing the monster, Sinbad waits until it has released Margiana, then hurries to her side. Together, they flee the beast's purlieu.

Pressing through the underground caverns, Sinbad finally reaches his long-sought goal: the Fountain of Destiny, where the fortunes of Marabia lie. But Sinbad finds that Koura has already arrived and been rewarded with youth and an awesome embellishing of his mystic strength. Employing his new-found skills to summon the centaur, Koura watches gleefully as the monster prepares to slaughter Sinbad and his men. Yet, Evil will not triumph without a responsive battle from Good: no sooner has the centaur appeared than it is engaged in mortal combat by a golden gryphon, a beast that is half-eagle, half-lion. Unfortunately, Koura is able to slice one of the gryphon's hindlegs and the crippled animal is handily bested by the centaur. Emerging from the heat of battle, the one-eyed beast attacks the Vizier's seconds. Several of Sinbad's crewmembers fall before the monster until the Prince is able to mount the man-horse; plunging a dagger into its back, he brings the deity to its knees, and moments later, the centaur is dead. But Koura has yet to be reckoned with, and making himself invisible, the magician hides in the waters of the Fountain of Destiny, waiting for an opportune moment to strike at his foe. Fortunately, Sinbad is able to see the wizard's outline in the churning waters and drives his sword home. Koura falls, and the fountain turns red, then golden. Gazing into the pool, Sinbad sees the crown of Marabia. Although the throne is rightfully his, the Prince does not wish to be tied down to a kingdom. And so, placing the crown on the Vizier's head, he watches with satisfaction as the ruler's mask vanishes and his facial features are restored. Returning to the ship, the crew weighs anchor and charts a course to Marabia.

Harryhausen had a singular pleasure in *The Golden Voyage of Sinbad* that all but exceeded the challenge of the special effects. Charles Schneer summarizes it thus: "Ray and I have our artistic differences, and one of them is that Ray is very much taken with Fate and Destiny. I think you *make* your own Fate and Destiny. But he doesn't believe that." What Ray *does* believe is the mythos highlighted by *The Golden Voyage of Sinbad.* As he

The homonculus in the Cave of the Oracle.

Achmed (left) watches as Koura creates a second homonculus.

From left to right: The Grand Vizier, Omar, Rachid, Haroun, and Sinbad, with Margiana and several sailors in the background.   © Columbia Pictures

puts it, "The movie was based on the Middle Eastern point of view of Destiny: that everything is the will of Allah. You're not your own free-will agent; there's some sort of pattern. The whole of life is plotted out ahead of time. Although we didn't use the visual device in this picture, the way we did in *Jason and the Argonauts*, of showing the actual gods manipulating people on a chessboard, this film was *steeped* in Destiny. For example, Margiana was meant to meet Sinbad. She had that eye tatooed on her when she was a girl; arranging their meeting

probably went on way back to infinity. It probably created cause and effect in her parents' world. So we had Destiny, and we also tried to capture a feeling of the occult in the picture. We had magic at every turn. I personally find the whole of the occult world very fascinating, and I would like to put much more of it on the screen. I think it aided the box office of *The Golden Voyage of Sinbad* because most people are interested in Fate and the occult; they always have been."

The Golden Voyage of Sinbad was backed by a

234

substantial media blitz from Columbia Pictures, which emphasized not only the wonder of the tale, but the brilliance of the "new" special effects process *Dynarama*. Yes, gone was *Dynamation*, but only in name. Dynarama was simply a fresher, snappier designation for Harryhausen's reality sandwich technique. But the Dynarama hard sell worked as did Melies' early efforts, O'Brien's *The Lost World* or *King Kong* or, more recently, *2001: A Space Odyssey*, *Earthquake*, and the new *King Kong*; the public will traditionally respond to the promise of extraordinary special effects. Fortunately, the studio was able to apply itself to the marketing of *The Golden Voyage of Sinbad* because, Ray feels, "there was a scarcity of theatrical product, and since there are not too many films being made today, the advertising department can give attention to the films they do have." However, Schneer—who does careful market research to understand why people go to the movies—believes that the popularity of *The Golden Voyage of Sinbad* was due to something more personal than the quality and thrust of the advertising. "The groups that came to see the film were, interestingly enough, the young people—the teenagers and those people in their late twenties—and what the industry calls the ethnic groups. Because when you have in your advertising a man with a turban on, even if he is John Phillip Law, they feel kin to him. So it's obvious that those groups were inclined to see this kind of picture." Indeed, Schneer says that the only thing which prevented *The Golden Voyage of Sinbad* from having an even wider audience was that, at the time, "there were people who would rather have seen violence for violence's sake and contemporary dramas for the foul language that's in them. I presume that by now the thrill is beginning to wear off." As Ray notes, neither he nor Schneer will ever make that kind of film. "I don't think *The Golden Voyage of Sinbad* would have been any more successful if we'd had gushes of blood coming out of the gryphon, or dyed the feathers red. We went to that extreme more or less only when we had Koura stabbed in the stomach and had this great gush of red water come out of the Fountain of Destiny. But it was more symbolic than literal, and not as nasty as if you had seen his guts pour out all over the floor. So we put blood where it's necessary,

but there's no point in overdoing it. I think there's an extreme where some people do it just for the sake of shock, but I think we have more to our films. We want to reach the widest audience we can without making some people sick."

Because *The Golden Voyage of Sinbad* is so dependent upon the occult—the breaking down of barriers between the real and the mystic, and between Good and Evil—its mood and color are much more sombre than in any of Ray's previous films. Like *The Seventh Voyage of Sinbad*, a host of Lemurian backdrops was supplied by Spain's gloomy Caves of Arta, while the Temple of Kali, the rooms beneath the Vizier's palace, Koura's castle, and many of the scenes on shipboard—including the storm and the entire Sea of Mists episode— were staged on sets built and photographed in dreary, threatening tones. As a result, the stop-motion characters and special effects had to complement this low-keyed atmosphere. Unlike the previous Sinbad picture, there couldn't be an orange cyclops or a blue dragon!

The first monster, the homonculus was a tiny creature that tenaciously clung to the shadows for protection. Indeed, venturing from dark recesses, it thrice met with doom: passing over Sinbad's ship in daylight, creeping from a dim corner of the Vizier's underground chamber, and attacking Sinbad in the well-lighted opening atop the Cave of the Oracle. Its scaly, humanoid appearance and large, spiny bat wings made it a fittingly devilish extension of the wicked Koura. Of course, until science began toying with DNA in brightly lighted laboratories, the work of fostering artificial life went on only in the tenebrous world of the alchemist, as though its practitioners were hiding from the sight of God! Even Dr. Frankenstein performed his sorcery in graveyards and in a cold, stone tower under stormy skies. Needless to say, since manufacturing life is the job of Ray Harryhausen, he has a creative if not a moral affinity for such dark experimentation. "The idea that you could fashion a living being has always fascinated me, and I was rather taken with the idea that a magician could build a synthetic being to do his bidding. So we played it from that point of view. Originally, since the homonculus was so appropriate to the mood of the picture, it had an expanded role: at one stage in the structuring of the

235

Ray Harryhausen's preproduction sketch showing the birth
and dance of Kali.   © Columbia Pictures

The gryphon and centaur square off.   © Columbia Pictures

Kali and Sinbad duel. Miklos Rozsa's strange and atmospheric music was a tremendous asset to this and other conflicts in the film. Notice how Ray has modified his design of Kali since the preproduction phase.

The centaur approaches Margiana.   © Columbia Pictures

An atmospheric shot of the battling monsters and the Stonehenge-like Fountain of Destiny set.

© Columbia Pictures

The centaur strangles the gryphon before the Fountain of
Destiny.　© Columbia Pictures

Sinbad challenges the centaur. In the frames that follow, the man-horse will throw his club, which flies through the air via aerial brace. © Columbia Pictures

John Phillip Law in a relaxed moment behind-the-scenes.

script, we had a scene devised, which took too long to tell, where the amulet was dredged from the sea. Then we latched onto the homonculus and felt that we wanted to incorporate it into the story line. So we had it discover the amulet on an island, and it was bringing it back to Koura when Sinbad's crew shot at it. This was logical enough: the seaman shot at it as the average person gets gun-happy if they see any living thing moving in the bush. If they happen to have a gun, they shoot at it. Remotely, of course, in the back of my mind, I may have been thinking about the Ancient Mariner. But scripts pass through so many states, and we never did elaborate on that. We even had one phase in the script where Koura impersonated the man in the golden mask, the Grand Vizier, to attract Sinbad to the island. But that had to be discarded."

Technically, Ray performed some very intricate visual effects with his homonculus which, beyond the already difficult aerial brace techniques, included an ambitious traveling matte of the beast taking wing from Koura's arm. Shots of the sorcerer tailoring the monster were executed with a rubber model cast from the mold Harryhausen had used to build the stop-motion figurine. In fact, in an otherwise perfectly conceived and executed set of animated scenes, the only complaint which has been leveled against the homonculus is that it looks too much like Ymir. Ray answers the charge by simply stating that "it may have had a tail and crouching legs like an allosaur, but I certainly didn't consciously try to design him like the Ymir."

The film's second and third stop-motion characters, the masthead and Kali, have a great deal in common. First, they are both women. Second, like Talos, neither figure has eyes, which gives them a vacant appearance that accents their coldhearted nature. Third, they are inanimate statues which Koura brings to life to work his evil deeds. And finally, the models are each a deep shade of brown-green, something that is consistent with the subdued look of the film. Yet, each character is distinct.

The creaking birth of the masthead is slightly reminiscent of Talos' initial head-turning in *Jason and the Argonauts*. I asked Ray if he had intentionally repeated this move for the masses of people who hadn't seen the earlier film; Ray claims that, no, he was just performing an action that seemed suitable for the scene. As for the idea of bringing the masthead to life in the first place, that stemmed from an old film. "After all the years that Ray Bradbury and I have known one another, we finally, over dinner, had the same remembrance of a silent film that we both must have seen at a very early age, about a sculptor and a great statue. He was modeling this vast statue by a big window, and vaguely, we both remember that it fell over on top of the sculptor. That's about all I can recall of it. And it's interesting that Ray has the same remembrance. He runs a cinema club and they've been trying to find out what this picture was. But of everyone I've asked who has a memory of these old films, no one seems to be able to answer the question of what film it was, whether it was a French or German gothic film. It may even have been part of *The Golem* or another version of *The Golem*. So that haunted me when I was very young, and I think that has been a constant inspiration for making statues come to life. I'm also fascinated with the idea that through a very strong mental will, you could make objects move by telekinesis, the willpower of the human mind. So it was a combination of those ideas that brought the sequence about."

Unlike the creeping manner of the reptilian homonculus, the masthead glides trancelike about the deck of the ship. Her movements are stiff, and coupled with her blank expression, make the nocturnal encounter both ethereal and frightening. On the other hand, the fight with Kali was constructed without the edge of terror that characterizes the battle with the masthead. As Ray observes, "Kali comes from Indian mythology and symbolizes the destructive aspect of nature. Actually, she has a belt of skulls, but we wanted to tone it down slightly, and used only the motif that she was out to destroy." An awesome piece of action, it was enough to subject a viewer to the six death-dealing arms, let alone a nightmarish mass of perambulating skulls!

The scene is mounted so that as Koura searches Kali's temple for the amulet, during which time Sinbad arrives to thwart his scheme of conquest, the statue of the goddess is visible in the background, posed atop her altar within a huge vertical ring. Her inanimate presence is thereby established, and the viewer quickly takes the statue for granted. Thus, when Koura brings her to life, the impact is greater than if he had simply called her from some netherworld. Marching down the steps, her limbs shifting and grating in unison, Kali pauses at the foot of the altar to await her master's bidding. But Koura is not ready to send her after the sailors. Hence, the magician has her perform a writhing, symmetrical dance as an exhibition of his control over the monster. The sequence also illustrates Harryhausen's mastery of his foot-tall models: Kali's show is one of those rare movie moments that, in itself, is well worth the price of admission. Ray admits to having pampered himself with the segment: "Well, I've got to get some joy out of making these things!" he quips, going on to say that, "I'm very fond of East Indian music and East Indian lore, as well as that of Egypt and the Middle East. I like the exotic and have a great admiration for the strange and wonderful. So I felt that this was a chance to get in a dance. Of course, we tried to write it in such a way that it wouldn't be too obvious. But we didn't want to just start another slam-bang fight or you'd have just a series of fights all through the picture. So Koura called upon her to dance simply to demonstrate his powers." In all, it's the kind of self-indulgence that Ray's fans would love to see more frequently!

Full-scale models were used when Kali fell from the steps and the masthead was fished from the sea. This is the only time in each sequence that nonanimated figures are seen. However, there is one brief segment in *The Golden Voyage of Sinbad* where a supernatural character is played by an actor: the Oracle is actually a man in a mask. Like the Grand Vizier's golden headpiece, the face of the Oracle was designed by Harryhausen, and he feels that it is one of the largely unrecognized assets of the film. "I'd been trying to get an oracle into a picture for a long time, and I think it was one of the more exciting sequences." With the head of a goat and the features of a man, its voice rasping from amidst a well-spawned column of flame and phosphoresence, the sage of the adytum is indeed an imposing personality! And his wont to speak only in riddles added significantly to the mystery and supernatural flavor of the scene. Only his abrupt appearance and hazy visage kept him from

being a more widely-lauded character.

Given the trio of unfeeling fiends that has gone before, the centaur is comparatively a clement beast. Feral when aroused, it is calm and almost compassionate in its natural state. As Harryhausen understands his monster, "I don't see him as Bette Davis' character in *Beyond the Forest*, for example, where she was really diabolically evil, with very few, if any, redeeming features. The centaur was often barbaric, but that was his job as part of Destiny." From the first, the man-horse is rather different than the animator's other creations. Its entrance is subdued, one of the few times that Harryhausen has opted for this approach. The camera lingers on the mouth of the monster's subterranean cave as the hollow beating of hooves echoes from within. Then, slowly and regally, the monarch of this underground domain steps forth. The beast looks at Margiana, gently reaches out to her—his placid features assuring both the girl and the audience that he means her no harm—cradles the sacrifice in his arms, and walks off. The last time a Harryhausen monster was compassionate toward anyone was in *Mighty Joe Young*! Unfortunately, the honeymoon ends when Sinbad rescues Margiana and the centaur finds them by the Fountain of Destiny. With club in hand, the mythological hybrid charges the Prince and his crew, to preserve both his offering and the cause of Koura, his companion-in-darkness. However, the gryphon arrives to champion our heroes and personify, in the words of the Oracle, the eternal struggle between Good and Evil.

The Golden Voyage of Sinbad has been criticized, and rightly so, for pulling the gryphon from a proverbial hat. As Harryhausen observes, the scenario was not always so threadbare. "The gryphon was stronger in one version of the script than it ended up in the final picture. All the strange and wonderful animals that you find in mythology have rather profound origins. And I think the origin of the gryphon, as much as we were able to discover, was to guard a treasure. So there was a version of the script where we were going to have a stone statue of the gryphon in the vault where there was the discussion about the necessity of gaining the three tablets in order to find the Fountain of Destiny. That made the gryphon a more integral part of the script than it ended up appeared in the

Caroline Munro. © Columbia Pictures

final film. I can't remember why we changed certain parts, but we found it necessary to keep the story moving. Of course, we'd liked to have played it up a little stronger at the end, because the gryphon just simply came out from the cave."

Obviously, Ray doesn't have the opportunity to endow his gryphon with much in the way of personality. However, the centaur is one of the animator's more graphic and emotive figures. Thus, while the contest between the two quadrupeds lacks the dynamism inherent in the pairing of such utterly dissimilar creatures as the cyclops and dragon, its aftermath allows the centaur to exhibit a broad range of expressions. Particularly effective are the creature's stumbling last gasps after Sinbad's assault with a knife. During these scenes, the Prince was, of course, a stop-motion likeness of John Phillip Law.

While many Harryhausen observers have condemned the centaur's single eye as being an attempt to exploit the continuing popularity of the cyclops from *The Seventh Voyage of Sinbad*, Ray denies that one had anything to do with the other. "I did it because it's unusual! I mean, we've seen *normal* centaurs, but you haven't seen a cyclopean centaur, have you? Too, the one-eyed thing has always fascinated me. It can be interpreted as a symbolic concept: we find the single eye in the middle of the forehead in Indian religion; the Third Eye. There's the whole concept of mental telepathy as the Third Eye, of seeing into the future, and, of course, the single eye was prominent in the original Sinbad stories." Besides, even if Ray had *wanted* to reheat yesterday's soup, as it were, his producer was on hand to prevent it. Schneer maintains that one of his foremost goals in filmmaking is always to approach his subject in the most original way possible. "Ray and I have made quite a few films, and I would never permit us to repeat ourselves. When you're making a picture about the Arabian Nights, there are certain things that you're going to have that are repetitious, like a sword and a turban. But as far as incidents, plot structure, characterizations, and monsters are concerned, we hope that they are widely divergent. And we think we've succeeded there."

On par with *One Million Years B.C.* as a recreation of hostile times and alien sensibilities,

Ray Harryhausen by his drawing board with the centaur model. Photograph by the author.

with an icy streak of deviltry that is missing from Ray's more genial fantasies, *The Golden Voyage of Sinbad* is one of his most satisfying efforts. It is also Harryhausen's most adult picture, as there is nothing particularly gay about. the journey, the history of the Grand Vizier, or the slow withering of Koura. And the timbre of the plot is ably complemented by the players. John Phillip Law, affecting a Middle Eastern accent, creates a confident but cocky Sinbad, giving some otherwise melodramatic moments a dash of spice, while Tom Baker is an introspective villain beyond whose piercing stare is an aura of great tragedy. These characterizations are certainly a far cry from the earnest Kerwin Mathews and the flamboyant Torin Thatcher of *The Seventh Voyage of Sinbad*! Both were appropriate for their particular film, but Law and Baker approach their roles on a less black-and-white level. Indeed, Ray coined the term "antivillain" to describe Koura, as the erosion of his body and stamina makes the viewer wish that the sorcerer might just achieve his goal! As for the other actors, Douglas Wilmer, the wicked Pelias of *Jason and the Argonauts*, makes for a kindly and distinguished Vizier, while Sinbad's crewmembers,

The centaur. Photograph by the author.

especially Kurt Christian, all perform with above-average sincerity. As for Caroline Munro, well, she shows more of her anatomy than Kathryn Grant ever did, and performs capably within the rather restricted confines of her role.

When *The Golden Voyage of Sinbad* proved to be the surprise hit of 1973, Columbia reissued *The Seventh Voyage of Sinbad* in Dynarama—although the opening credits still carried the Dynamation title—and immediately funded the production of a new Sinbad picture. Developed as *Sinbad at the End of the World*, the third Harryhausen Arabian Nights adventure was released in the Spring of 1977 as *Sinbad and the Eye of the Tiger*.

Talos and the centaur looking deceptively calm on the desk of their creator. Photograph by the author.

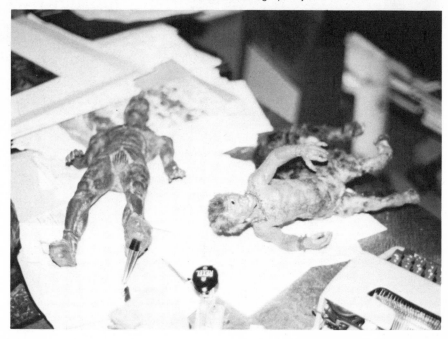

Holding the *One Million Years B. C.* brontosaur, Ray Harryhausen asks the author's wife if she would like to take the photograph in *Dynarama*, while the author toys with the skeleton from *The Seventh Voyage of Sinbad*.

CHAPTER SIXTEEN

Sinbad and the Eye of the Tiger

As of this writing, Columbia has just begun distributing *Sinbad and the Eye of the Tiger* for select previews, and the completed film has yet to be screened. However, what the author has seen of the picture indicates that Schneer and Harryhausen have another hit on their hands.

Arriving at the city of Charak to wed Princess Farah (Jane Seymour), Sinbad (Patrick Wayne) learns that her brother, the Caliph, has been placed under a spell by the sorceress Zenobia (Margaret Whiting). With the aid of the mystic hermit Melanthius of Casgar, the party sails for the Land Beyond the North Wind, which is the Valley at World's End. There, they confront and defeat Zenobia.

Harryhausen is at his best when animating a humanoid figure, something into which he can inject mannerisms and personality. And there are two very realistic characters in *Sinbad and the Eye of the Tiger* which, from what the author saw of the film, one could easily mistake for living beings: the huge Troglodyte and his companion, the baboon. In fact, watching the rushes of one particularly fluid scene, I commented to Ray on how far he's come since the days of the Cave Bear. A pained expression twisted the animator's features and he moaned, "Oh gosh, I hope it's not *too* realistic. People will think it's a man in a costume!"

Oddly, with a rather lengthy animation schedule—which ran from October of 1975 through March of 1977—one would have thought that a real baboon could have been employed, thus allowing Ray to concentrate on the eight other animated creatures in the film. But, he assured me, "Baboons are very difficult to train. I can't even say that I've *ever* seen a trained baboon. They're apparently very

intelligent in their own way, but they're also very vicious. You couldn't get them to do what you'd want them to do. I doubt that we could have trained a baboon to play chess, which is a very important sequence in our picture." Contrarily, the Troglodyte is also a nearhuman figure which, for a while, was *supposed* to have been played by an actor rather than by a stop-motion model. "There were moments when we had decided, possibly, to use a big man madeup. But I think that what we have gives it a much stranger quality, which works for our type of story. That's what we're striving for: that fantasy effect that the first *King Kong* had, that wonderful never-never land of fantasy." Not-so-coincidentally, many Kong-like gestures are evident in the giant Neanderthal, as Ray sketched a memorable and very sympathetic personality onscreen. His death at the claws of a saber-toothed tiger is all the more moving because Ray took the time to develop the Troglodyte's personality.

Discounting the six- to eight-inch-tall figures of featured players which Ray occasionally uses, the Troglodyte is the closest thing to a human being that he has ever animated. To make it just a bit less familiar, Ray has an ivory horn jutting from the character's head. Once again, it suggested the cyclops. But, Ray says, "We were certainly not trying to imitate the cyclops. The fact that he does have a horn I know will cause many people to say that we're back to the cyclops again. But that did not even pass through our minds when we decided to do it. We felt that it gave him the appearance of being something other than just a big man, and it also became functional in his fight with the tiger." Horn or no horn, the Troglodyte is an innocent and oddly ingratiating character that allowed Ray to create the kind of pathos that has gone unseen since *Mighty Joe Young*.

On the opposite end of the emotive spectrum, a pair of appropriately stolid and purely destructive creatures are the giant wasp and a monstrous walrus, which Sinbad and his crew discover in the Arctic. Ray also staged a nocturnal raid on Sinbad's camp by a trio of ghouls which, the animator assures us, "don't go around eating bodies. You find, in the Arabian Nights, that the term ghoul does not mean what it does in the Western world. The original ghoul and genie were sort of one and the same, in a sense. They have different functions, but in Turkish mythology you find the term ghoul is certainly not used to connote a grave robber. That was something that developed later. So they do not chew on the sailors' bones, as one might anticipate that they would." However, inconsiderate of these and the more human models, the characters that will probably emerge from *Sinbad and the Eye of the Tiger* as the most popular are the Minotan and the titular tiger.

The Minotan is a golden minotaur which, in the script, is a mechanical slave of the featured sorceress Zenobia. Sporting the same vacant, immobile face as Talos, the masthead, and Kali, the brooding half-man, half-bull looks to be the film's most dynamic and memorable figure. That is, if he survives the flak from fans when they discover that, in several shots of Minotan rowing his mistress' boat, Ray used a man in a minotaur costume. However, it was the most expeditious way to achieve the camera angles that best suited the story, and does not detract from the character's overall impact. As for the tiger, it will no doubt be mistaken for a trained and disguised feline, so natural are its movements. But if the ignorant masses of film critics bother to *watch* the picture, they'll realize that the cat is unlike any they have ever seen in the zoo. As Ray enlightens us, "The saber-toothed tiger, of course, was entirely different from the tiger as we know it, an Indian or Malayan tiger. They did not have stripes. Scientists have found pieces of fur in the La Brea tar pits, so the restorations are quite accurate. They were more like a great puma or a great lion rather than a tiger. But for some reason, they were called saber-toothed tigers." The fanged mammal is involved in a monumental brawl with the Troglodyte, a fight which is far superior to the centaur-gryphon match. Particularly striking is one aerial-braced maneuver wherein the Neanderthal flips the great cat over his back, rolls with the beast in a somersault, and then pushes the tiger along the ground, goring it with his horn. Once again, as is so often the case with Ray Harryhausen, it is a prime example of inspired filmmaking.

The wonders and specifics of *Sinbad and the Eye of the Tiger* and Ray's other films aside, the question of inspiration is a vital one to Ray. It more or less dictates the course that each picture and, indeed, the remainder of the animator's career will take. "Inspiration is very important because it shows in the end product. One does an enormous amount of research, so you have to be fascinated with the subject matter. As for the initial creative process, I get inspiration by listening to a concert or a record, or just from glancing through books. That sometimes stimulates ideas. Sometimes I sit and spend hours looking at a blank page. But one has to stimulate himself in order to start forming the continuity of action. That's all formulated before you ever decide to do a particular sequence. You have to see whether you can make a beginning and middle and end."

Right now, of course, Schneer and Harryhausen are riding high on the success of their recent efforts. But dedication and inspiration are only one part of the overall process of motion-picture making. There is also the question of finances. And as time goes on, this type of picture becomes more and more expensive to make. Might there come a day when stop-motion photography is no longer viable as a means of creating visual effects? "It depends," Ray admits. "How does one know? These types of pictures are rare; every studio doesn't make them. And, as we have discovered in recent years, there are still people who believe that a man in a gorilla suit is functional. I thought that went out with *White Pongo*, but unfortunately it hasn't. So there are many different ways of doing things. It depends on how you go about it. Of course, it's difficult to predict about stop motion. It depends on the subjects that come up and the money that's available. It could die out tomorrow, if a stop-motion picture doesn't make its money back."

However, as Schneer optimistically observes, "There have been some very poor fantasy films through the years, and they've depreciated the market for the films of those who really exercise the skill and talent and time that it takes to make them. But quality survives, and we're still here to talk about it." And to be certain that he and Ray remain in business, Schneer devotes his energies to both the creative and business end of his productions. "The creativity and business go hand-in-hand, in that one without the other would never succeed. You must combine both efforts. Anything else is untenable."

If this sounds like a gutsy way of making a living, it is. But Schneer long ago learned that to deal with the transient, insecure nature of the industry, you must be a hustler and you must have absolute confidence in your product. "When we were younger," he recalls, "Ray and I used to worry about tomorrow. But the business today is quite different than when we came into it. There was a continuity then; now it's a wildcat industry. And very often, from the time they give us the go-ahead to the time when the picture is finished and delivered, the person who approved it is no longer there. That's a very unsettling circumstance, and it's one reason that we never sign multipicture deals. You never know what company is going to be in business by the time we're ready for the next picture, or what the intentions of the management are. So we have to pick and choose at the time we're ready. Very often some companies have better years than others, and their money is less restricted; you have to go with a company that can afford you."

The matter of funding a movie is, of course, common to all filmmakers. However, compounding the problem of creating an animated picture is the fact that its success or failure rests squarely on the shoulders of one individual. In any film, directors can and have been replaced. Temperamental stars are invariably appeased or dismissed. But in a Schneer-Harryhausen production, the film cannot be begun, shot, or completed without Ray Harryhausen. And needless to say, this kind of very necessary control occasionally causes problems on the set. As Ray explains, some directors resent his hold on a picture. "They feel that I'm taking their power away from them, which I dislike to do. I certainly don't do it purposefully. Unfortunately, we're out to make a picture, a product, and we have to work this way. Because you can use up enormous sums of money by having a director say, 'I *insist* that this camera be placed here,' whereas if he moved it and changed his concept a little bit—which wouldn't sell another ticket, if I may say so—it could make the difference between being able to do the sequence for a reasonable amount of money or a vast amount of money. Perhaps that's too practical a point of view, which might upset people who have more aesthetic points of view about making motion pictures. But this is one reason I draw continuity sketches, which we try to put in all the scripts. Since you haven't the time to go into this type of discussion on the set, the director and actors can see, ahead of time, what we're aiming for." Schneer draws an equally hard line when it comes to supporting his animator. "Ray designs the picture in a method which makes it proper for him to shoot it. That locks a director into many set-ups that he otherwise would not choose. But if we're going to live with our system, such as we do, then the director has to understand that there are certain ground rules that he has to comply with. And he buckles under to that, knowing that any other suggestion which he might make, more often than not, would technically not be possible for us to do. But all of these strong come-ons occur before the camera ever turns. We understand exactly what we're doing before we get before the cameras. There's no reason, then, for any departure because it's all very carefully laid out."

Although one doesn't like to dwell upon it, with so much riding on Ray, Schneer always takes the precaution of insuring him against some unforseen occurrence. "Fortunately," Schneer muses, "at Ray's tender age, he's still insurable. I don't think you'll find anyone else in the world who can do what he can, or can develop the skill that he has." All of which leads one to wonder about the fate of Dynarama should Ray ever decide to retire. There are aspects of the process in which only he is versed, and about which he is very secretive. As Schneer reveals, "That's my one jibe at Ray. I tell him, 'Ray, don't you think it's fair to the younger generation to bring in a younger man who is enthusiastic and interested, and to teach him what you know? I mean, after all, Michelangelo had a school.' But Ray feels that it's not a matter of telling the public his secrets. It's a matter of doing on your own, and by doing learning. So Ray invariably tells me two things whenever I bring this up. 'First,' he says, 'in the time it would take me to teach someone else to do what I do, and think the way I do, I could do it myself.' Well, this, to me, is a self-defeating argument. The second thing he tells me is that 'this is my skill and it's going to die with me. Someone else can develop his skill his way.' Well, that is a seflish attitude, and he and I have never agreed about that. But he is the king is his own realm, and that is only one of the small or large differences that we've ever had.''

With so much autonomy in the creative process, one would assume that Harryhausen has an enormous ego. But this is far from the case. He is the kind of good-natured man that anyone would want for their uncle. In fact, in his Introduction to *Film Fantasy Scrapbook*, Ray Bradbury summarized Harryhausen's status as an international citizen by saying, "He is 'Uncle' Ray at our house. Damned if he isn't Uncle to a whole new generation of film lovers and fanatics." Schneer characterizes Ray as "tremendous, not only as an artist but as a human being," and the author, who has known the animator for four years, would embellish that sentiment by describing Ray as gracious, articulate, and a true gentleman. Thus, when all is said and done, if this text manifests even a small measure of the admiration that I and fans the world over feel for Ray Harryhausen and his work, or if the reader is driven to *see* these remarkable films, then I shall consider this study of his career to have been a success.

CHAPTER SEVENTEEN

Tsuburaya, Danforth, and Others

Although the emphasis in our look at special effects has been on the towering figures of Melies, O'Brien, and Harryhausen, there are several other craftspeople whose work merits our attention. They, along with our featured artists, represent the foremost purveyors of motion-picture fantasy.

Without question, the most popular filmmaker of all time is Walt Disney, whose animated cartoons won him an international following. Beginning with the combination live-action/animation *Alice's Wonderland* short subjects in 1923, he moved to ever more ambitious projects, creating Mickey Mouse in 1928 and releasing the world's first feature-length cartoon, *Snow White and the Seven Dwarfs* in 1937. *Treasure Island*, his first live-action production, premiered in 1949, while his initial nonanimated epic fantasy was *Twenty Thousand Leagues Under the Sea* (1954). In this latter film, Walt had his technicians build a large mechanical model for the sequence in which a monster squid attacks Captain Nemo's *Nautilus*.

Walt Disney was personally committed to both fantasy and technology, interests which were well-represented in most everything he did. He had undertaken cartoon animation because it allowed him to spin fairy tales while experimenting with sophisticated forms of motion picture equipment. This latter fascination led to Disney's being the first animator to employ sound and then color in his cartoons, not to mention experimenting with 3-D and *Cinemascope* as well. However, cartoons, like stop-motion photography, could only work through the camera: looking ahead to automated cities, household robots, and such, Disney used his motion pictures as a means of nurturing various forms of

technology. The *Twenty Thousand Leagues Under the Sea* squid, the talking umbrella and singing bird in *Mary Poppins* (1964), the enchanted Volkswagen in *The Love Bug* (1968), and other live-action oddities, were created with electronics, pneumatics, and such since the basic technology could be made to work both on and off the screen. And the first practical results of this on-the-job research were the audio-animatronics figures of Abraham Lincoln and various dinosaurs at the 1963-64 New York World's Fair. Currently, the computer-run, fully mobile characters can be seen in *The Pirates of the Caribbean* and related attractions at *Disneyland* and *Disney World*. Unfortunately, while these various endeavors are undeniably valuable in an engineering sense, they are aesthetically inferior to cartoons and stop-motion. Unless it is very carefully designed and edited, a filmed mechanical effect *looks* like a filmed mechanical effect. To wit: Bob Mattey, whose mechanical skills sparked the aforementioned film creations, was more recently responsible for the hydraulic sharks seen in *Jaws* (1975). Scenes featuring the robot fish, with its limited repertoire of movements, were far less effective than shots of its real-life counterpart.

George Pal is a filmmaker with less grandiose plans for the world-at-large, although his twelve feature-length fantasy and science-fiction films are no less appealing than those of Walt Disney. Immigrating from war-troubled Europe to the United States in 1939, the stop-motion novelty film producer began making his famous *Puppetoons* for Paramount. When these were discontinued eight years later, he went into the production of full-length motion pictures. Pal's first film, *The Great Rupert* (1949), was about a trained squirrel and

The fight with the squid from *Twenty Thousand Leagues
Under the Sea*, filmed full-scale in a studio tank.

The multiplane camera. A variation of Willis O'Brien's use of horizontal glass paintings to simulate depth, this Ub Iwerks invention allows animators to place the foreground, midground, and background drawings, as well as the characters, on different levels, and thus cause the illusion of dimension by panning in and out of the action.

The destruction of George Pal's miniature set for *Atlantis, the Lost Continent.* The special effects were supervised by industry veteran A. Arnold Gillespie.

starred a stop-motion figure in the title role. His subsequent productions, *Destination Moon (1950)*, *When Worlds Collide* (1952), and *War of the Worlds* (1953) all won Oscars for their special effects; *Conquest of Space* (1955), *Tom Thumb* (1958), and *The Time Machine* (1960) followed, the latter two features both using stop-motion for select scenes and winning Academy Awards for their screen wizardry. *Tom Thumb* had Tom (Russ Tamblyn) performing a dance with a roomful of toys, all of which were animated by Gene Warren and Wah Chang; stop-motion was used to make plants grow and a slain mutant decay during the travels of star Rod Taylor in *The Time Machine*. Cartoon animation was seen in conjunction with a death ray in *Atlantis, the Lost Continent* (1961), but it was Pal's next production, *The Wonderful World of the Brothers Grimm* (1962), that made extensive use of the process. A romanticized biography of the fairy-tale anthologists, the picture wove their popular fantasies *The Dancing Princess*, *The Singing Bone*, and *The Cobbler and the Elves* into its narrative tapestry. The last two segments rely heavily on animation: in *The Singing Bone*, the cowardly knight Sir Ludwig (Terry-Thomas) and his servant Hans (Buddy Hackett) go dragon hunting, while *The Cobbler and the Elves* was the famous story of dolls which come to life to help a kindly shoemaker (Laurence Harvey) fill an excessive order for the local gentry. The picture's stop-motion chores were handled by Warren, Chang, Jim Danforth, the late Tim Barr, and Pal's son Dave. Danforth was Oscar-nominated for his work on Pal's next picture, *The Seven Faces of Dr. Lao*—a film which we'll discuss in context with Danforth's career—and an animated skeleton was briefly seen in Pal's science-fiction classic *The Power* (1967). Cartoon snakes were on-hand in the producer's last effort to date, the camp adventure film *Doc Savage* (1975).

Pal recently told me that, "If somebody says to me, 'Here is something impossible,' then I'm already interested." Like Harryhausen, the Hungarian-born filmmaker thrives on creating incredible visions for the screen. But Pal's grab-bag of cinemagic is not limited to stop-motion photography. His *War of the Worlds* Martian was a man in a costume; the snakes in Medusa's hair for *The Seven Faces of Dr. Lao* were magnetically controlled; his *Atlantis, The Lost Continent* was a miniature island in a studio tank; the rocket used by forty people to flee our doomed earth in *When Worlds Collide* was a wire-operated, live-action miniature; and so forth. As a result of this versatility, Pal has been able to produce films abundant in scientific hardware, like the semidocumentary *Destination Moon* or *Conquest of Space*, as well as such untaxing larks as *The Great Rupert* or *Doc Savage*. Of course, having a different technical staff on each picture, and constantly moving from studio to studio has made it difficult for Pal to retain a continuity of design in his films—something that gives the works of Harryhausen and Disney their popular appeal and extraordinary character. However, Pal's devotion to the fantastic and its credible realization through special effects marks him as one of the most important filmmakers in the history of the genre.

To date, young Jim Danforth has shown great promise, but it remains to be seen whether he shall ever become an animator of the O'Brien-Harryhausen calibre. Like Harryhausen, Danforth was inspired by the works of Willis O'Brien to become a model animator, and after graduating from high school, went to work for Clokey Productions, Art Clokey's animation firm responsible for such characters as *Gumby* and *Davy and Goliath*. During this period, Danforth had the opportunity to visit Ray Harryhausen during the stop-motion phase of *The Seventh Voyage of Sinbad* and set his heart on the making of featurelength films. Pursuant to this, he joined the Chang-Warren organization *Projects Unlimited*, where his earliest assignment was building several live-action miniatures for *Master of the World* (1961). *Wonderful World of the Brothers Grimm* was next, followed by a film with a bizarre genesis, *Jack the Giant Killer* (1962).

When Ray Harryhausen first showed his sketches for *The Seventh Voyage of Sinbad* to various producers, one of the men he saw was the late Edward Small. Small turned the project down, and naturally, when the Charles Schneer film made a great deal of money, he regretted not having undertaken the picture. Small, therefore, resolved to copy Harryhausen's film as closely as possible,

Eiji Tsuburaya instructs his Godzilla (right) and Ghidrah actors what to do when the cameras roll. On the set of *Monster Zero* (1965).   © Toho International

featuring Kerwin Mathews and Torin Thatcher as the hero Jack and the villainous sorcerer Pendragon, respectively, hiring Nathan Juran, the director of *The Seventh Voyage of Sinbad*, and signing Jim Danforth to create the stop-motion special effects. Thus, Jack's quest to save the lovely Princess Elaine (Judi Meredith) was far from a chance repetition of Sinbad's Colossa Island adventure. However, the imitation—which one must suspect was hardly flattering to Harryhausen—did not stop with the cast and concept. A great deal of hoopla was accorded the special effects process *Fantascope*, which was allegedly developed in secret over a two-year period. In fact, it was the reality sandwich technique which Danforth admits he stole from

Harryhausen. Mr. Small, of course, acted as though Fantascope were a remarkable innovation, commenting in a press release that, "at long last, film-process shots are treated in color." Obviously, the special effects in *The Seventh Voyage of Sinbad* and *The Three Worlds of Gulliver* had been accidental. If so, then they were rather extraordinary accidents, for Small had Danforth and his associates study *The Seventh Voyage of Sinbad*, examining every frame of stop-motion to make certain that the monsters in *Jack the Giant Killer* walked, flew, and slithered in exactly the same number of frames—known as a *cycle*—as Ray's beasts.

Paradoxically, *Jack the Giant Killer* is not a bad film, although it's difficult to drum up any amount

Godzilla vs. the Smog Monster (1972): Men in costumes as giant monsters.   © Toho International

of sympathy for Small, whose efforts resulted in a formidable box office flop. It embraces a great deal of fantasy and spectacle, and the monsters are not without some impact in spite of themselves. There is Cormoran, a horned giant with the shaggy, hooved legs of a goat—sound familiar?—and there is a two-headed version of the same creature known as Galligantua. Galligantua ultimately battles a cephalopod-like sea serpent, while Jack fights an enormous gargoyle over the open sea. Yet, fluid though most of the animation is, it is technique without heart. Harryhausen's creatures live; Danforth's simply move. Compounding this problem is the creatures' lack of skin detail which, coupled with some gross anatomical inaccuracies, detracts from their overall realism. The Fantascope

work is adequate, but it is a far cry from the precision of Dynamation-Dynarama.

Danforth managed to survive this debacle, after which he did the animation for *It's A Mad, Mad, Mad, Mad World* and worked with *Projects Unlimited* on several segments of television's *The Outer Limits*, building monster costumes and animating an occasional creature. It was during this TV period that he landed the assignment to animate the climax of *The Seven Faces of Dr. Lao*. Based on Charles Finney's classic 1935 novel *The Circus of Dr. Lao*, the film exposes the residents of a small, turn-of-the-century Southwestern town for the heels they really are, using bizarre circus sideshows to invoke each individual's true colors. In the end, everyone is purged and reformed—save

An aerial-braced live-action model of Rodan swoops across a miniature set.

Sea Monster Answers the Imp's Call

A preproduction sketch of the sea serpent from *Jack the Giant Killer*. This design was eventually rejected by producer Edward Small, and another creature conceived.

Kerwin Mathews slashes at an imaginary monster in *Jack the Giant Killer*. The gargoyle will be added during special-effects photography.

Cormoran. © United Artists

The two-headed giant. © United Artists

Marcel Delgado's miniatures from *Dinosaurus*.

The huge mechanical model of a djinn's foot gives Sabu a scare in Alexander Korda's *Thief of Bagdad* (1940). Until the advent of *Dynamation*, Korda's film remained the epitome of the spectacular fantasy film.

A sea-going funeral pyre is disturbed by the appearance of
an elasmosaur in *When Dinosaurs Ruled the Earth*.

A glass painted foreground, a stop motion monster,
animated cave people (left), matted cave people (holding
ropes and by the stone), and miniature projected cave
people (by hill) in an admirable and complex shot from
When Dinosaurs Ruled the Earth.

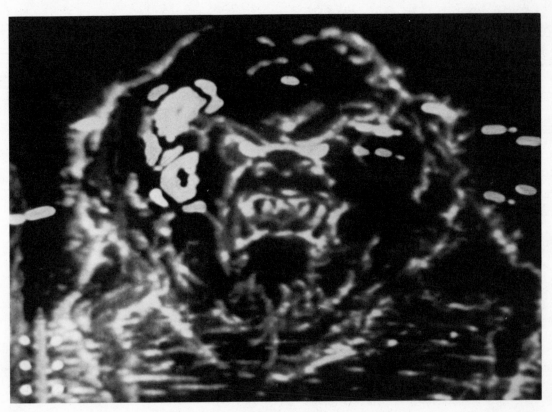

Joshua Meador's Monster from the Id as it appears in *Forbidden Planet*. The creature was a cartoon animation composited with a live-action background.

A huge ant—a mechanical model—menaces Joan Weldon and James Arness in *Them!* (1954). The picture won an Oscar for special effects.

A man in costume plays *Gorgo* in the 1959 film. The special effects by Tom Howard were equal to those of Eiji Tsuburaya. © Metro-Goldwyn-Mayer

for a pair of rowdy ranch hands who return to the circus to destroy it. There, they find Dr. Lao's pet slug, a submarine animal which when exposed to air will allegedly become the Loch Ness Monster. The cowboys don't believe the legend and shatter the bowl: the tiny creature begins to grow, and within moments, is a huge flippered serpent. After tearing down the circus and chasing the two men through the desert, the monster is returned to its innocuous natural state by a rain storm. The animal's metamorphosis, *seen in an astounding single take*, was accomplished by edging the creature toward the camera between exposures, and at the appropriate moment, substituting progressively developed models to represent its successive stages of maturation. The ruffians, also visible in this shot, were rear-projected, while the circus foreground was added via static matte.

Danforth lost that year's special effects Oscar to Walt Disney's undeserving *Mary Poppins*, but was nominated again in 1970 for *When Dinosaurs Ruled the Earth*, his first animation feature since *The Seven Faces of Dr. Lao*. Danforth's sole interim assignment has been *Around the World Under the Sea* (1965), which used live action rather than stop-motion creatures to represent the imagined monsters of the deep.

When Dinosaurs Ruled the Earth was Hammer Films' sequel to *One Million Years B.C.*, recounting the tribulations of Sanna (Victoria Vetri) who flees the tribe that would have sacrificed her to restless gods, experiences a variety of adventures, and with her mate Tara (Robin Hawdon), is one of the few survivors of the upheaval that results when a chunk of the earth goes flying into space to become our moon. Originally planned for Ray

267

Marcel Delgado's stop-motion models animated by Tim Barr, Wah Chang, and Gene Warren in *Dinosaurus* (1960).

The special-effects set-up for the 1959 Canadian documentary *Universe*. This is a well-dressed studio.

The *Puppetoon*-like figures for Michael Myerberg's 1954 production of *Hansel and Gretel*.

Harryhausen, *When Dinosaurs Ruled the Earth* went to Danforth because of Harryhausen's simultaneous involvement with *Valley of Gwangi*. And, much to Hammer's distress, Danforth required over sixteen months to complete the special effects, causing the budget to go over that of *One Million Years B.C.* As a result, Hammer's subsequent prehistoric film, *Creatures the World Forgot* (1970), was filmed without any dinosaurs whatsoever.

Like the monsters in *Jack the Giant Killer*, the animals of *When Dinosaurs Ruled the Earth* lack the dynamism that one finds in a Harryhausen creation. The models are not as realistically crafted as they might have been and, with the exception of what appears to be a mother and baby of the protosuchus family, the monsters are rather bland. The plesiosaur attack on a seaside village, the cave people's fight with a chasmasaur, Tara's battle with a rhamphorhynchus—a scene in which Danforth effectively eliminated strobe by backwinding the film to reexpose each frame with the wing in a

different position, thus blurring the flapping action—and a raid by a horde of monstrous crabs all lack the distinctive motion and presence of Harryhausen characters. Yet, however lackluster, the animation *is* smooth, the composite work is generally excellent, and Danforth's glass paintings—which he creates himself, as opposed to Harryhausen who farms the work out—are breathtaking. Overall, *When Dinosaurs Ruled the Earth* is a commendable effort that certainly deserved the Oscar over yet another technically mediocre Disney film, *Bedknobs and Broomsticks*.

Danforth's most recent theatrical effort has been *Flesh Gordon* (1973), a low-budget, pornographic film that featured his sword-swinging cricket creature, the one-eyed penisaurus, and a giant of the Cormoran school. A popular film with some interesting animation and miniature props, *Flesh Gordon* nonetheless shines dim in the Danforth log. Considering the fantasies of which the animator is apparently capable, his development will depend largely on whether or not he can find a Charles H. Schneer, a patron who will fight for the value and integrity of the stop-motion art form.

Models, both stop-motion and mechanical, are not the only form of monster making. And when *The Beast From Twenty Thousand Fathoms* proved that atom-spawned leviathans could be potent box-office commodities, the wily Japanese dressed an actor in a rubber costume and loosed a saurian terror of their own, the legendary Godzilla. Raised from eons of subsea hibernation by nuclear tests in the Pacific, the four-hundred-foot-tall, fire-breathing dinosaur has appeared in over a dozen films, and inspired his home studio of Toho to shoot numerous spin-off pictures featuring Rodan, Mothra, and various other creatures. Huge city-razing behemoths all, they were the issue of the late Eiji Tsuburaya, the only special-effects artist who has been able to work a credible illusion with a man in a monster suit.

Although Tsuburaya's characters have since become semicomedic heroes, appealing to a juvenile audience by protecting the earth from such invaders as Ghidrah, Megalon, and Gigan, the earliest efforts, particularly *Godzilla* (1954), *Rodan* (1957), *The Mysterians* (1959), and *Mothra* (1961), were excellent. A self-educated cinematographer,

269

Al Whitlock and one of his remarkable glass paintings from
Earthquake (1974). Whitlock won an Oscar for his forty-odd
glass paintings used in the film.　© Universal Pictures

A closeup of an Al Whitlock glass painting from *Earthquake.*
The blackened area is for the insertion of a live action
element in an optical printer.　© Universal Pictures

Tsuburaya supervised the building of sets on a 1:80 scale. These sprawling miniature replicas of the Japanese countryside, Western and Eastern cities, the surface of alien planets, primitive islands, waterfront locales, and spaceships in earth orbit, were carefully detailed and assembled to crumble, quake, or explode beneath the monster's tread or by the efforts of off-camera technicians. Yet, important though these floor effects were, Tsuburaya's job was more than just ravaging the landscape. One particularly critical aspect of his work was the way in which he shot his monsters and minatures at high speeds to give them the proper mass. In addition, he was very meticulous about camera placement. The illusion of size was invariably best served by placing the camera as low to the ground as possible.

The clear benefit of Tsuburaya's method over all other special effects processes is that it is fast and economical. The obvious disadvantage is that an actor within the stiff monster suit can stomp, roar, and destroy, but not emote. However, as these giants are supposed to be nothing more than mindless engines of destruction, the viewer accepts their limitations. Thus, while Tsuburaya was not an artist in the same creative breath as O'Brien and Harryhausen, he surely knew how to make the most of what he had!

More than once, people who create or enjoy fantasy films have been asked, "Why bother with something as frivolous as wizards and monsters?" And the answer, strange as it may seem, is that fantasy happens to be a very germane medium.

Putting fantasy on the screen is more than simple technique. It is a state of mind, an affection

The collapse of the Hollywood Dam for *Earthquake* is filmed in miniature on the Universal Studios backlot. © Universal Pictures

for the genre and a feel for its nuances. Increasingly, the move in cinema has been toward the negative, with cynicism replacing optimism, and the losers held in higher esteem than the winners. The result of finanical and social brutalization, it is a dangerous trend, and an acknowledgment of defeat which bodes ill for civilization.

Beyond their visual splendor and merit as escapist fare, the worth of the films we've been discussing is multifaceted. First, they allow justice to triumph, something that has become terribly unfashionable. But what a vicarious thrill to see Sinbad, Jason, Joe Young, or even Godzilla overcome the forces of evil! Also, these movies create pathos for the underdog, something which fosters a charity and camaraderie that the viewer is likely to carry outside the theatre. Finally, as we've just seen, there's the dedication of the people who make these movies, the Melies, the O'Briens, and the Harryhausens. Theirs is an example of excellence that is well-worth emulating.

In any society, it's more difficult to build than to destroy, and the ideals of fantasy, of the hero vs. the villain, of idealism and poetry, are most constructive. If *that's* frivolous entertainment, then we had better reexamine our collective values or prepare for a most dismal future.

As this book was going to press, we received word that long-time Harryhausen collaborator Charlott Knight had died at the age of eighty-three.

In addition to working with Ray on his fairy tales and on *Twenty Million Miles to Earth*, the actress-author appeared in, among other films, Liberace's *Sincerely Yours* (1955) and Sophia Loren's *Desire Under the Elms* (1958). In recent years she had been working on the stage and in television.

Ray Harryhausen, on tour to promote *Sinbad and the Eye of the Tiger*, and commuting between the United States and England in preparation for his next film, *Perseus and the Gorgon's Head*, could not be reached for comment.

Young professional stop-motion artist Ernie Farino works on the clay design of a dragon model. His is a name to watch among the up-and-coming ranks of animators.

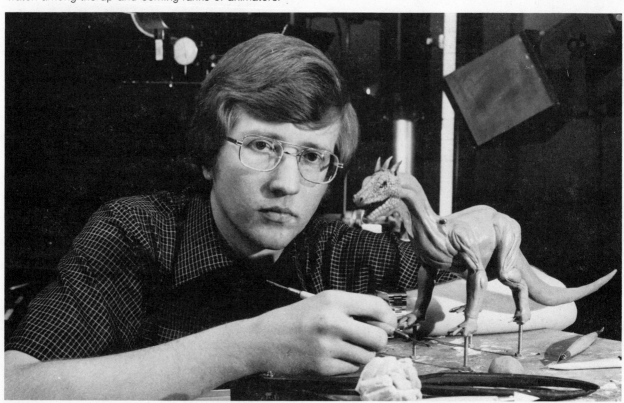

Sinbad and the Eye of the Tiger

These photographs from *Sinbad and the Eye of the Tiger* were *just* released by Columbia Pictures. Used by permission.

The Minoton, Harryhausen's striking half-man half-bull.

Jane Seymour as Princess Farah plays chess with her brother, who has been transformed into a baboon.

The troglodyte battles the sorceress, who has transformed
herself into a sabre-toothed tiger.

Sinbad and his men battle a huge walrus.

Index